NEW DIRECTIONS
IN LOCAL HISTORY
SINCE HOSKINS

NEW DIRECTIONS
IN LOCAL HISTORY
SINCE HOSKINS

Edited by Christopher Dyer, Andrew Hopper,
Evelyn Lord and Nigel Tringham

University of Hertfordshire Press

First published in Great Britain in 2011 by
University of Hertfordshire Press
College Lane
Hatfield
Hertfordshire
AL10 9AB

British Library Cataloguing in Publication Data
A catalogue record for this book is available from the British Library

ISBN 978-1-907396-12-0

Design by Mathew Lyons
Printed in Great Britain by Henry Ling Ltd, Dorchester

Contents

Figures

Plates

Tables

Contributors

Stephen Caunce is Senior Lecturer in History at the University of Central Lancashire in Preston, having begun his career in museums. His research takes the form of a multi-stranded investigation of the development of northern England between 1550 and the present.

Malcolm Chase is Professor of Social History at the University of Leeds. A former honorary editor of the Cleveland and Teesside Local History Society, his most recent book is *Chartism: a new history* (Manchester, 2007).

Claire Cross is Emeritus Professor of History at the University of York. Her chief interests lie in late medieval and early modern English religious, social and political history. Her latest book, co-edited with P.S. Barnwell and Ann Rycraft, is *Mass and parish in late medieval England: the use of York* (Reading, 2005).

Malcolm Dick is Director of the Centre for West Midlands History at the University of Birmingham. His research and publications focus on the Enlightenment in the English Midlands during the late eighteenth and early nineteenth centuries and the history of minority ethnic communities in Britain.

Christopher Dyer was Director of the Centre for English Local History at the University of Leicester, and is now Emeritus Professor in that University. His research is mainly concerned with the agrarian, economic, social and landscape history of England in the later Middle Ages.

David Dymond was formerly Director of Studies in Local and Regional History at the Institute of Continuing Education, University of Cambridge. His main research interests are in the social and religious history of rural communities in the later Middle Ages and sixteenth century.

Paul Ell is founding Executive Director of the Centre for Data Digitisation and Analysis at Queen's University Belfast. He has published seven books, two with Cambridge University Press. His current research interests focus on religious geographies in Ireland, British and Irish censuses, grid technologies and Web 2.0 applications.

David Hey is Emeritus Professor of Local and Family History at the University of Sheffield and President of the British Association for Local History. He is a former postgraduate student of William Hoskins.

Andrew Hopper is Lecturer in English Local History at the University of Leicester. His research is focused upon local allegiances during the English civil wars and he is currently writing a cultural history of side-changing and treachery during that conflict.

Jane Howells is editor of *Local History News*. She is co-author of *Salisbury Past* (Chichester, 2001) and is co-editing *Cherished memories and associations of William Small* for the Wiltshire Record Society (forthcoming 2011), both with Ruth Newman. Her research interests focus on the economic and social roles of nineteenth-century women.

C.P. Lewis worked for the Victoria History of the Counties of England (*VCH*) from 1982 to 2009, and edited with C.R.J. Currie *English county histories: a guide: a tribute to C.R. Elrington* (Stroud, 1994). He is currently Research Fellow at King's College, London, working on a project on English landed society in 1066.

Evelyn Lord is an Emeritus Fellow of Wolfson College, Cambridge, and review editor of *The Local Historian*. Before retirement she was course director for the Masters in Local and Regional History at the University of Cambridge. At present she is working on a micro-study of the 1665–6 plague in Cambridge for Yale University Press.

Edgar Miller is an Honorary Visiting Fellow of the Centre for English Local History at the University of Leicester. His current research explores how the problem of insanity was dealt with under the old poor law.

Ruth Paley is a Section Editor at the History of Parliament, working on a study of the House of Lords 1660–1832. Her personal research interests are in the social history of the law with particular reference to the administration of criminal justice in eighteenth-century London.

Edward Royle is Emeritus Professor of History at the University of York. His principal interests lie in the social history of modern Britain, with special reference to religion in Yorkshire since the Evangelical Revival.

Mark Smith is University Lecturer in Local and Social History at the University of Oxford. His principal interest is in the history of religion in England since 1700.

Sheila Sweetinburgh is a Research Fellow at the University of Huddersfield and an Associate Lecturer at the University of Kent. Her research interests include Lady Anne Clifford and late medieval urban history, and she is the editor of *Later medieval Kent, 1220–1540* (Woodbridge, 2010).

Nigel Tringham is a Senior Lecturer in the Department of History at Keele University and County Editor of the *Victoria County History* for Staffordshire.

Emma Watson was recently a Research Assistant at the Borthwick Institute for Archives at the University of York, working on a project on the cause papers of the diocesan court of York. In addition to her work on church courts, her research is mainly concerned with popular responses to the Reformation and post-Reformation Catholicism.

Preface

This book is based on the papers given at a conference held at the University of Leicester on 9–12 July 2009. The conference was the result of collaboration between the Centre for English Local History at the University of Leicester and the British Association for Local History (BALH). The original idea came from Professor Claire Cross of the University of York (and of BALH), who had attended an earlier conference at Leicester on landscape history and recommended that a similar gathering be devoted to commemorating the fiftieth anniversary of the publication of *Local history in England* by W.G. Hoskins in 1959. Together, the Centre and the Association set up a committee representing both bodies, whose members were the four editors of this book and Claire Cross, Alan Crosby, Gillian Draper and Danielle Jackson. This committee then arranged the conference, which was attended by over 180 delegates, with over 50 speakers, including plenary lecturers John Beckett, David Dymond and Sarah Pearson. The conference was not intended to be a commemoration of Hoskins nor even of local history's past, but more a review of its current preoccupations, with an eye to future developments. The 15 papers published in this book were selected with great difficulty and are intended to reflect the range of subjects and approaches presented in the conference.

Acknowledgements

Danielle Jackson administered the conference. It was helped by sponsorship from Carnegie Publishing, the journal *Midland History* and Phillimore publishing. The University of Leicester provided a reception, opened by Councillor Roger Blackmore, Lord Mayor of Leicester, himself a local historian, Leicester graduate and long-time admirer of the work of W.G. Hoskins. We are grateful to Oxbow Books and Maney Publishing for having provided bookstalls and information stands. We would also like to thank Richard Buckley, Dr Richard Jones and Professor Charles Phythian-Adams for leading the conference excursions to the city of Leicester, the villages of east Leicestershire and the Welland valley respectively. We are also grateful to Martin Marix Evans and Peter Burton of the Naseby Battlefield Project for hosting the tour of Naseby. The conference rooms were enlivened by poster presentations by eight postgraduate local history students from the Universities of Leicester and the West of England, while Leicester postgraduates James Bowen and Tom Kimber ably aided and directed delegates throughout the conference weekend. We would also like to thank the staff of the University of Leicester's conference services for ensuring the event went smoothly. Lastly, we are particularly thankful to Jane Housham and Sarah Elvins of the University of Hertfordshire Press for their patience, expertise and encouragement.

Permissions for Illustrations

Fig. 6.1 is reproduced by permission of © Hythe Town Council. Figs 9.2, 9.4 and 9.5 are reproduced by permission of Salisbury and South Wiltshire Museum, while Fig. 9.3 is reproduced by permission of the *Salisbury and Winchester Journal*. Figs 12.1, 12.2, 12.4–12.19, 12.23 and 12.25 are © Edward Royle; Fig. 12.3, is taken by permission of the University of York from W. Ellerby and J.P. Pritchett, *A history of the Nonconformist churches of York*, ed. E. Royle, Borthwick Texts and Calendars, 18 (York, 1993), p. 157; Figs. 12.20 and 12.21 are © Kirklees Image Archive: www.kirkleesimages.org.uk and are reproduced by permission. Fig. 13.1 is reproduced by permission of © Oxfordshire County Council Photographic Archive, while Figs 14.1–14.3 are by permission of the National Archives. Plates 1–8 are © David Hey. The base map for Plates 9–12 is taken from Ordnance Survey County Series 1:10560, 1st Revision 1900.

Abbreviations

AHDS	Arts and Humanities Data Service
AHRC	Arts and Humanities Research Council
BALH	British Association for Local History
BHO	British History Online
BI	Borthwick Institute for Archives
BIHR	*Bulletin of the Institute of Historical Research*
CDDA	Centre for Data Digitisation and Analysis
CERC	Church of England Record Centre
CRSP	Catholic Record Society Publications
CKS	Centre for Kentish Studies
ECAI	Electronic Cultural Atlas Initiative
EcHR	*Economic History Review*
EHR	*English Historical Review*
EKA	East Kent Archives
EPNS	English Place-Names Society
ESRC	Economic and Social Research Council
GBHGIS	Great Britain Historical Geographical Information System
HA	The Historical Association
ICT	information communications technology
IHR	Institute of Historical Research
JCO	St John's College, Oxford Archives
JISC	Joint Information Systems Committee
JSTOR	Journal Storage

KB	Records of the court of kings bench
LP Hen VIII	*Letters and papers of Henry VIII*
MLT	MacDonald Lands Trust
ODNB	*Oxford Dictionary of National Biography* (online)
ORO	Oxfordshire Record Office
P&J	*SS. Philip and James, Oxford, Parish Magazine*
PRO	Public Record Office
SAC	*Sussex Archaeological Collections*
SDF	Social Democratic Federation
SSRC	Social Science Research Council
SWJ	*Salisbury & Winchester Journal*
THAS	*Transactions of the Halifax Antiquarian Society*
TNA	The National Archives
Transactions	*Transactions and Papers of the Institute of British Geographers*
TRHS	*Transactions of the Royal Historical Society*
VCH	*Victoria County History*
WAM	*Wiltshire Archaeological and Natural History Magazine*
WEA	Workers' Educational Association
WSHC	Wiltshire and Swindon History Centre

Introduction: local history in the twenty-first century

Christopher Dyer, Andrew Hopper, Evelyn Lord and Nigel Tringham

No branch of history thinks and writes about itself as much as does local history. Political history, social history, economic history, cultural history and the rest have their introspective moments, but local historians, in books and in the pages of such journals as *The Local Historian*, constantly engage in discussion of their subject. They debate its roots, seek to justify its existence, worry about its content and methods and wonder about its future. Tens of thousands of people throughout the country belong to local history societies, attend lectures and read books and articles on local history topics. Thousands of these take their activities a stage further by engaging in research and writing their own local history. This activity is not new, as is shown by Hoskins's correct assumption that there would be a large readership for his handbook on how to write local history. Changes in printing technology have provided new outlets for these enthusiasts. Alongside the established journals and publication series there now exist numerous small-scale newsletters and ephemeral journals, together with short-run editions of pamphlets and books. The Internet has opened up another range of opportunities for the distribution of written material and illustrations. All these forms of publication are catering for a numerous public who would not regard themselves as committed in any specialised way to local history, but have some curiosity about the places in which they live. An even larger audience read the 'Our past' column in local newspapers, or hear and see the various versions of local history to be found on radio and television.

Local history is found throughout the world, and attracts much public interest in very old and stable countries such as Norway, as well as in relatively new post-colonial societies. A recent international symposium on the subject showed that local history seems to thrive when the past is insecure and debatable. In countries where large numbers of migrants came from the Old World, such as Australia, there is much anguished concern for the indigenous peoples who have been displaced or downgraded by the waves of new settlers, while among the various groups of migrants there is a necessity to establish and celebrate their identity in a new setting, which has given rise to histories of the Italian communities in various parts of Australia, for example. Problems of ethnicity and belonging are encountered in acute forms in eastern and central Europe, where minorities assert their own language and culture. Hungarians in modern Romania write about places which they inhabit and value, but for which there is another history in the view of the Romanian majority. Norway did not attain its full national independence until 1905, and lost it again in 1940–45, which may help to explain the enthusiasm of its people to have their roots in their farms and landscapes researched and published. There are obvious parallels in different parts of Britain. The resurgence of historical interest in Scotland and Wales has been stimulated by a growing consciousness of nationality which bears some resemblance to the commitment to history among the various minorities and relatively newly independent countries in parts of continental Europe. In England the awareness of regional differences, most obviously in the north or in Cornwall, has not yet been a great spur to political activity, as Caunce demonstrates in his contribution to this book, which implies that regional loyalties now have a limited influence on the writing of local history.

However, the national and regional 'questions', and anxieties about ethnicity and ownership, are not the main reasons for the discussions and disagreements about the role of local history in Britain. One obvious cause for concern, to which Dymond refers in his essay, is the co-existence among those practising the subject of both academics employed in university history departments and those who do not earn their living from their work in the subject. The parallel activities of these two types of historian are obviously liable to lead to resentments and misunderstandings. In depicting these two strands of practitioners the present editors prefer to avoid the words 'professional' and 'amateur', as these imply a value judgement about the quality of the work done. Many of those who pursue the subject in their spare time are 'professionals' in their full-time employment and are capable of higher levels of thought and skill than some of those who are qualified historians. One of the contributors to this book, for example, is a retired professor of psychology, though he falls between the two camps as he has acquired a postgraduate degree in local history. Perhaps there is no need for disquiet about the division into camps, as they seem to learn from each other and have developed a degree of interdependence. The two organisations which came together to plan the 2009 conference from which this book grew are both dependent on the participation of academics and those who are not specialist local historians. The Centre for English Local History at Leicester is staffed by academics, but many of its adult students who work for part-time postgraduate degrees are enthusiasts, many of whom have no first degree in history. The same is true of other graduate local history courses offered in a number of universities. The British Association for Local History brings together members of many voluntary local history societies as well as academics, and encourages best practice through its activities and publications.

The conference of 2009 celebrated the fiftieth anniversary of the publication of *Local history in England* by W.G. Hoskins, and he epitomises the fusion of those who work inside and outside academic institutions. In the 1930s he was employed at Leicester in the social science faculty, where he gave lectures in economics, but he taught classes in local history to adult students in his spare time and published much of his early work in the pages of the journal of the local society: the *Transactions of the Leicestershire Archaeological Society*. His 1959 book was intended to provide advice, guidance and encouragement for local historians scattered all over England. Herbert Finberg, Hoskins's successor as Head of the Department of English Local History at Leicester, had been a printer and had taught himself historical methods. While at Leicester one of his missions was to foster the groups of adult students who researched their locality with the guidance of an extra-mural or adult education tutor. 'Group work in local history' was a way of pooling the efforts of busy people who had limited time for research, and also made use of the varied talents and expertise available in such a class. A recent example of the successful development of this approach has been that organised by the *Victoria County History* in forming volunteer groups to contribute to the research for the England's Past for Everyone paperback series, which is funded by a grant from the Heritage Lottery Fund. Now volunteers are being drawn into all parts of the *VCH*'s activities, including work towards the famous 'red volumes'.

With such examples before us, the local history community might be tempted to say that there is no problem, and that the division across the subject is not as profound as is imagined. There are difficulties, however, partly because university history is becoming more specialised and is under new pressures. Hoskins's successor today would be criticised for publishing as he did in a county journal, as the aspiration now is for articles to appear in 'international peer-reviewed journals'. Academics are being encouraged to develop the skills needed to mechanise their research and increase their output by using online sources, as

Ell urges in his contribution. Scholars used to pride themselves on writing with clarity, and even with wit and elegance, but now some branches of history use a specialised language and do not give high priority to communication with outsiders. Perhaps the folly of this lapse into obscurity has been recognised, as academics are now being urged to make the results of research available to a wider public, and to collaborate with organisations outside the academic institutions. The normal practice of university local historians in previous generations of publishing in local journals and giving lectures to local history societies has become acceptable again. Unfortunately the educational administrators who urge academics to communicate with the general public to increase the 'impact' of academic research imagine on the one hand a superior professional provider of knowledge and on the other a receptive audience of amateurs. They do not realise that in the local history world the potential audience is sophisticated and skilled. The local journals, for example, which are often edited by well-qualified professionals, keep one step ahead of the bureaucrats by refereeing articles systematically. County journals have for many decades had a subscription list covering libraries in all parts of the world which give them a much larger potential international readership than many 'professional' journals. Ironically, an important channel of communication has been lost because of the action of governments driven by a utilitarian agenda: the adult education movement which made local history and archaeology a major dimension of its work has diminished and even died in many regions.

Meanwhile the local historians working in their communities, meeting in village halls and printing their newsletters and more substantial publications have become more confident of their own ability to conduct research. They find that their sources are more readily accessible on the Internet and they learn methods from magazines and television programmes as well as the historical literature. The enormous growth of family history has created an appetite for research and an acquaintance with sources and record offices. Their output of materials, glossy and well-illustrated, looks attractive, and the best work that is done is very successful not only in appealing to a local readership but also in drawing the interest of those with a more academic agenda. Yet sometimes these writings can be embarrassingly ill-informed. They often lack a long-term or comparative perspective, misunderstand sources and provide inadequate interpretations or no interpretation at all. Poor-quality local history writing has always existed, but printing costs once held back the number of substandard publications. Now they flow without inhibition thanks to desktop publishing and small print shops.

The other major reason for self-doubt among local historians, especially those who are employed in educational institutions, is their awareness of the patronising disdain with which they are regarded by other historians. For scholars wrestling with twentieth-century international relations, or philosophical debates in the eighteenth century, or the Nazi holocaust, local history looks small-scale and low key. They ask, 'Are regional marriage patterns or town drainage schemes really important enough to justify much time or money to be spent on research?' This is a long-standing condescension issuing from a misguided association of all local history with an unquestioning antiquarianism devoid of academic purpose. 'Proper' historians pioneer new methods using IT and sophisticated statistics, while those with more advanced outlooks display fashionable sensitivity to the language of texts and are aware of post-modernism. Local historians may know about these modernities, but their approach to the subject can be positivist and empirical. Local history has been slow to embrace modern concerns with gender, though we have just heard that a county record office has recently hosted a seminar on the relevance of local sources for work in 'queer studies'.

Local historians should, of course, take note of these criticisms, but they ought not to feel excessively defensive about their subject. The researcher is often focused on a restricted geographical area, but that provides the opportunity to extend the time frame to explore long-term changes and continuities: local historians can take the long view. If they understand a single village or town very well they are able to connect political, social, economic, religious and cultural history in a way which takes full account of the physical and social environment. In other words, local history, far from being narrow and restricted, can hope to write 'total history'. To take two contributions to this volume which make connections between different fields of inquiry: Hey shows how, in villages on the edge of the Derbyshire moorland in the seventeenth century, a particular type of entrepreneur could be linked with a distinctive form of house; while Royle links the various branches of nonconformity, mainly in the nineteenth century, to the style and structure of chapel appropriate to their needs and cultural preferences. These two examples also show how local history practises interdisciplinary methods, in these cases connecting social and religious history with the study of architecture. Indeed, much recently successful local history combines specialist fields such as landscape studies, place names, oral history, industrial archaeology and material culture. A third positive quality of local history is its aim to be accessible to a wide readership, which means that academic jargon and excessively technical language is avoided in order to maintain effective communication with a wider public through speech, websites and publications.

For all of these virtues, and the continued energy and diversification that are now evident in local history research, there can be no doubt that academics remain reluctant to label themselves as local historians. Rather like the multiple identities that have been recognised in people in the past, many of those employed in history departments who work in local history would prefer to be thought of by their peers as social, cultural or religious historians, or even to be labelled by their period as medievalists or early modernists. Yet the local historian is well placed to transcend the divide between academia and history's recent explosion in popularity among the mass media and the wider public. This divide should exercise all historians more, and local history might take the lead as its sense of place and identity offers an exciting opportunity to encourage the public to more critical understandings of their own environments and communities.

The planning of the 2009 conference began with a 'call for papers'. In the modern style only three plenary lecturers were invited to speak, in order for speakers' places to be open to all comers, allowing equal opportunities without regard to age, gender or background. Would-be speakers were invited to offer papers under various broad themes which had been selected by the organising committee. These were designed to be inclusive, so that anyone working in local history would find an appropriate heading, and indeed some papers could have been accommodated under a number of themes. For this reason the speakers were a blend of university staff, research students and practitioners from outside academia. In order to maximise the number of papers and avoid audiences of unwieldy size parallel sessions were held, which would allow eight themes with seven papers in each. More than eighty offers of papers were received, which forced the organisers to make a selection of fifty-six. They were unevenly spread over the themes, which allows us to suggest some conclusions about the interests of local historians. Traditional subjects such as economic, agrarian and industrial history (which we called 'Making a living in town and country') attracted a good number of offers, as did religious history ('Culture and belief') and demographic and family history. There was much interest also in relatively new themes, or at least themes with new names: those of 'Community' and 'Identity and belonging'. A number of papers were offered on sources and methods, but there was limited interest in the 'History of local history', and 'Local history now'. Fortunately, we were able to invite some extra speakers and persuade others to move from their favoured theme as we wished to give voice to the various doubts and dilemmas surrounding the subject. We suspected that the lack of papers on these controversial subjects did not reflect a lack of interest, but more that speakers needed a great deal of self-confidence to engage in the debates about the nature of the subject and its future development. There were some other notable shortages of offers. Although there was no theme devoted to 'local government' or 'politics', papers on these subjects could have been easily accommodated in the community and identity themes, but few were offered. This is surprising and disappointing given that a recent hallmark of early modern history has been the broadening of the concept of politics through 'micro-history' approaches to particular places. Also, the conference deliberately used the word 'Britain' in its title, a move away from Hoskins's Anglo-centric approach. Yet relatively few papers relating to Scotland and Wales were offered, and some of the would-be speakers on these countries were based in England.

It was very difficult to select the fifteen papers included in this book, but considerations of cost made it necessary to do so, inevitably omitting some excellent papers. They are not classified into the themes selected for the conference programme; rather, the themes have been rearranged and their titles have changed to reflect the papers which are being included in this volume. The essays still represent the wide scope and variety of local history as it is practised in the early twenty-first century.

W.G. Hoskins provided a starting point for the conference and for this book, as this admired figure, many of whose writings are still directly relevant to a contemporary readership, played a major part in establishing local history as a distinct sub-discipline. He was a pioneer in much of his research, most celebrated now for his seminal work on the history of the landscape and his assertion that the ordnance survey map was a historical source in its own right. He also developed the use of such neglected sources as parish registers and probate inventories, and was writing demographic history and urban history before these terms were invented. People below the aristocracy were his principal concern, and he had a particular interest in the yeomen. This led him to warn against an excessive preoccupation among local historians with the lords of the manor. He played an important role in the period between 1948 and 1967 in stimulating and initiating various historical projects, not just in local history but also in agrarian history and vernacular architecture. Professor John Beckett has shown in, for example, his plenary lecture to the Leicester conference, that Hoskins helped to push the *Victoria County History* to move in new directions, above all by embracing economic and social history. In spite of his importance, it is not the purpose of this book to pay homage at length to Hoskins, nor to provide a detailed analysis or critique of his work, nor to trace the chequered history of his legacy over the last fifty years. The authors gathered together between these covers were not expected to indulge in nostalgia or express their reverence for the great man, but rather, as he would have expected, to write about the local history that they know and practise, thereby reflecting the current state of the subject, and sometimes cast an eye forward to future developments.

The remainder of this introduction will survey the diverse collection of subjects, periods, places and approaches that the various authors have presented, and indicate occasionally the gaps which would have been filled in an ideal world of many volumes and numerous essays.

The most obvious new development in local history is the inclusion of the twentieth century. This is not just the natural result of the onward march of time, but a change in the culture, as traditionally local historians were concerned with a more remote past, and Hoskins himself rejected the ugliness and barbarism of recent decades. In this book Caunce has focused on the period 1950–2005 in his analysis of voting in parliamentary elections as a guide to the political consciousness of the north of England, and his analysis connects with current, or at least very recent, concerns such as regional devolution of government. Dick also brings us up to date by considering the settling of large numbers of immigrants from the new commonwealth in English cities since the Second World War. He provides, however, a long-term perspective typical of local historians, because he traces the migration into Birmingham by the Irish, Jews and others from the eighteenth century, and the reaction of the authors of books about the city to these minorities. Two other authors deal with the twentieth century through the continuation of themes with a starting point in the nineteenth. Chase emphasises the connections between labour history and local history: the study of organised labour begins with the movements of the early and mid-nineteenth century, with many local studies of Chartism, but continues into the twentieth century, in which events such as the General Strike and the hunger marches deserve more profound local treatment than they have so far received. The heated religious arguments in the Church of England are usually associated with the nineteenth century, but Smith shows how the suburbs of north Oxford were still disputed territory after 1900. Lastly, the intellectual history of the twentieth century is explored by Lewis in his review of the state of local history between the world wars, in which he shows that a period often regarded as fallow saw much activity in many branches of the subject and prepared the way for expansion after 1948.

'Identity' is a concept which has come into general use in recent years. It assists Caunce in his analysis of the outlook prevalent in the north, the inhabitants of which have little interest in regional self-government, but who still assert their distinctive culture. As class loyalties in the nineteenth and twentieth centuries have diminished in significance for labour historians, Chase suggests that identity was shared by those who pursued a particular occupation or were employed in the same work place. Religion has been an important means of defining or reinforcing identities, as a number of these essays demonstrate.

Watson shows the strength of Catholic loyalties in defining the attitudes of a section of the northern gentry in the late sixteenth century, while in the northern towns of the eighteenth and nineteenth centuries the various branches of nonconformity, as revealed by Royle, wrestled with the problem of expressing their identity through the architecture of their buildings. We might expect that those occupying the large suburban houses in the northern suburbs of Oxford would have a strong common identity, but Smith shows that their support of different branches of the established church divided them into warring camps. Their identity was defined by Anglo-Catholicism and Evangelicalism, rather than by their Anglican affiliation. Identity runs as a thread through many of these essays – among ethnic groups in twentieth-century cities, for the townspeople of medieval Hythe and informing the mentality of the islanders of Skye in the eighteenth century.

Local history has become more inclusive by dealing with the whole spectrum of society. Hoskins was thought to be a radical because he sought to broaden the scope of the parish histories in the *VCH* beyond their traditional fixation with the lords of the manor. Some of these essays follow his interest in the 'middling sort'. Sweetinburgh's study of the butcher–graziers of fifteenth-century Hythe demonstrates the difficulty of pigeon-holing entrepreneurs who had a foothold in the country as well as in the town and profited from more than one occupation, just as Hey reveals a wealthy group of seventeenth-century lead smelters and lead merchants living in the countryside of north-east Derbyshire. Other essays deal with the industrial working class and with such disadvantaged people as the immigrants of Birmingham and the crofters of Skye. The assumption behind much traditional local history was that only the gentry and higher aristocracy could make the decisions that brought about important changes, and it was they who built the great houses, improved farming and dominated politics. But Hey shows that the houses of people below the gentry could be built in an impressive style and still survive, and Sweetinburgh has found that her butcher–graziers had considerable political influence. Miller shifts the explanation for the rural depopulation of the Scottish highlands from the great aristocratic estates to the pressure of a rising population that could not support itself on the sparse local resources.

Gender has become an important theme in local history, just as in other branches of historical inquiry. The traditional expectation that Victorian wives devoted themselves to reading novels and perfecting their cultural accomplishments is dispelled by Howells's analysis of the working lives of many married women in the cathedral city of Salisbury. Some shared in their husband's occupation, while others had their own trade or profession. Their earnings were often essential elements in the family's economy. The cases selected from the records of the court of kings bench by Paley include examples of the great disadvantages facing women in eighteenth-century society and in the courts. In other essays women are depicted as essential contributors to society, as participants in the religious life of Salisbury in the sixteenth century and as holders of property, business women and fraternity members in fifteenth-century Hythe.

A remarkable feature of local history in the twenty-first century is the flourishing of religious history in spite of the secularisation of the age and the diminishing participation in formal religious practice. One feature of the subject has been a move away from the institutional preoccupations of its predecessor, ecclesiastical history, and the greater interest in the experience of the laity, which includes attempts to explain the links between belief and social and cultural developments. The essays in this book reflect the intensity of religious conflict. Cross shows how difficulties and controversies characterised the Reformation in Salisbury, while Watson depicts the struggle of the authorities to deal with religious conservatism in the north of England. One is impressed by the tenacity of adherence to the old beliefs in both places. Smith documents the battles within an Anglican church faced with adding new parishes in an expanding town with adherents of opposing wings sharing the same suburb. In Royle's account of the architectural decisions made by nonconformists conflict lies in the background, as the denominations wished to make clear the differences between themselves and the Church of England, but more apparent is the way that impressive buildings demonstrated the strength and self-confidence of the congregations.

We have seen that local historians have shown much interest in past identities, but now they have their own sense of identity, which is expressed when they write about the history of their own subject. Hoskins and others in the 1950s wrote about the county historians of the sixteenth and seventeenth centuries, and in this volume Dick has followed the different phases of writing about the history of Birmingham since the eighteenth century, highlighting the successive authors' treatment of minorities. Here the main contribution to the past practice of local history is Lewis's survey of the 1920s and 1930s, which demonstrates the vigour of the subject in those decades and in particular shows how local history benefited from its association with economic history and historical geography. Chase has traced the interconnections between local history and labour history, both of which were favoured subjects for adult education classes.

New techniques and methods have had an impact on local history and we can be confident in predicting continued changes. Some of the characteristic features of the subject, such as its connections with other disciplines, are not especially new, but it is still worth drawing attention to the links with architectural and building history, as demonstrated in this volume by Hey and Royle. Buildings figure in many historical publications, but often in order to reinforce a point which derives from written documents. In local history the buildings, like the landscape, are themselves a primary source, providing evidence of past societies quite independently of the documents. Local historians are adept at digging out new sources, such as the remarkable archive for Hythe which has been put to such good use by Sweetinburgh. There is also much benefit from the systematic use of sources for which it is necessary to understand the processes that lie behind their creation, as is well represented here by Paley's explanation of the successive stages of eighteenth-century trials and their documentation in the court of kings bench. Dick makes reference to the use of oral history in the study of the recent past of ethnic minorities. Local historians are practised in the application of computer technology to their work, as, for example, in the use of databases and by accessing sources or archive catalogues, but Ell here explains the great range of data and analytical techniques available. He looks forward to a future of ever-expanding digital resources which might bring to an end some of the trusted methods of research, including the use of conventional paper archives. He gives a new twist to the old debates about professionalism and expertise raised by Dymond and in this introduction – items published on the Internet are not selected or edited, so that information can be placed there which is of dubious quality or reliability. Local historians are bound to debate if that is a development that we should welcome.

These essays provide a glimpse of a lively and very diverse subject at one point in time. The subject could not be covered as a whole, and many subjects and themes are not represented. We have no doubt that others will fill these gaps in future publications.

1. Does local history have a split personality?[1]

David Dymond

John Beckett's recent survey has highlighted the deep amateur origins of local history.[2] For several centuries educated gentlemen and leisured professionals (such as clergy, lawyers and schoolmasters) explored the history of rural parishes, towns, major cities, counties and various kinds of region. They were motivated, as the word 'amateur' implies, by strong emotional attachment to their human and physical surroundings. Then, in the later nineteenth century, academic history based on the critical interpretation of primary sources took root in English universities. It concentrated principally on political affairs at national and international level, an emphasis which it has retained to this day, but at the same time developed a strong separate tradition of economic history. This inevitably carried local dimensions and made use of knowledge already won by amateurs.[3]

Thus were born the two streams of local-cum-regional history which survive today. The older and much larger one is amateur and largely based on personal lifetime experience and allegiance. Often descriptive and discursive in style, it tends to rate the accumulation of evidence more highly than its critical and imaginative use.[4] By contrast, the younger and smaller tradition is professional, university-based and dependent on cumulative academic debate. It starts by

---

1. For comments on earlier drafts I am indebted to Mark Bailey, Alan Crosby, Heather Falvey, Frank Grace, David Hey, Jane Howells, Evelyn Lord, Alan Rogers and Kate Tiller.

2. J. Beckett, *Writing local history* (Manchester, 2007), chapters 2 and 3.

3. The foundation of the *Victoria County History* (hereafter *VCH*) in 1899 marks the first appearance of the professional historian in English local history. Soon after 1900 economic historians such as Tawney fostered the study of local history through adult evening classes.

4. Marshall described antiquarianism, perhaps rather unkindly, as 'an inability to distinguish what features of the past are historically significant; an indiscriminately romantic attitude to the past': J. Marshall, *Tyranny of the discrete: a discussion of the problems of local history in England* (Aldershot, 1997), p. 46.

considering questions and problems, is critical and analytical in using evidence, and builds interpretations around general concepts. By the early 1900s these two groups knew of each other's work but showed little appetite for cooperation. The purpose here is to explore this duality over the last 50 years (since Hoskins's *Local history in England* appeared in 1959), how far it has been a serious fracture, or has been successfully mended, and how far it persists today.

Based on lectures given at Oxford, Hoskins's book was written clearly and elegantly, with touches of dry humour.[5] It was obviously intended for the largest possible readership, and acknowledged both approaches to the subject and the value of linking them. We should remember that Hoskins, like all academics, had gone through an amateur phase of personal development.[6] In his youth he had read widely in history and literature and, as importantly, had explored his physical surrounding with questioning eyes.[7] Thereafter, human contacts convinced him that the amateur strand was a source of talent and energy often characterised by a deep knowledge of people and places, subjects and sources. The amateur, he wrote, 'has made a large contribution to English local history in the past, and there is still plenty of room for him (or her) in this vast and still largely unexplored field'. On the other hand, as a result of his university training in economics and in the relatively young discipline of economic history, Hoskins recognised that the study of local life, although restricted geographically, carried wide chronological and thematic dimensions.[8] Furthermore, it provided incomparably rich evidence for use in broad scholarly debates connecting with the rest of human history.

Local history in England was a landmark in the subject's development, for it mapped out major aspects worthy of investigation and ways of pursuing them. It led commentators to talk of 'old' and 'new' local history, before and after Hoskins.[9] The organisers of the 2009 Leicester conference judged that this book 'helped to establish the subject both as an academic discipline, and as a pursuit of thousands of local historians who are not professional academics'. In fact,

---

5. W.G. Hoskins, *Local history in England* (London, 1959). The 1972 edition was little changed, but that of 1984 carried more on the nineteenth century (pp. 270–4).

6. 'I was an amateur long before I became a professional and I don't see a clear distinction between the two stages of my career ...': David Hey (private correspondence, October 2009).

7. My father was first cousin of William Hoskins and his contemporary at Hele's School, Exeter. He well remembered that WGH as a boy spent much of his spare time cycling and walking the lanes of Devon.

8. His doctoral thesis was on the cloth industry of his native city of Exeter, later published as W.G. Hoskins, *Industry, trade and people in Exeter, 1688–1800, with special reference to the serge industry* (Manchester, 1935).

9. K. Tiller, *English local history: the state of the art* (Univ. of Cambridge Board of Continuing Education, Occasional Paper 1, 1998), pp. 1–6.

Hoskins already valued the work of contemporary professionals such as Tate and Emmison, and insisted that the book was 'not written for the specialist, or the professional historian', but for 'the great army of amateurs in this field'. He described how, during each autumn, when 'the evenings grow longer and darker', amateurs reached for their 'exercise books'. His purpose was to persuade members of the public to study the history around them, respecting the standards already established by the *Victoria County History* (*VCH*) and university pioneers of local history at Reading, Hull and elsewhere.[10] Hoskins's approach was based on inclusiveness and encouragement rather than superiority or snobbish withdrawal. To him the word 'amateur' was not pejorative but simply the opposite of 'paid academic'. Nor was he afraid of calling local history 'a hobby which gives a great deal of pleasure to a great number of people'. In addition, because academic history was becoming ever more specialised, he judged that local history was 'likely to remain the stronghold of the amateur'.[11]

Hoskins observed that, by 1959, amateur historians were being recruited from a much wider sample of the general population. The older antiquarian and elitist tradition survived in the shape of the occasional scholarly squire or parson, but was increasingly overshadowed by groups such as teachers, farmers, housewives and the retired. They included, be it noted, growing numbers of women, a trend which has since contributed massively to the quantity, diversity and humanity of modern research.[12] These trends gave rise to two expressions frequently heard today: 'grass-roots' history and the 'democratisation' of history. They both carry a significant double meaning, not often fully articulated, that many more people *in the present* study the lives of many more people *in the past*. In other words, a wider (although still incomplete) cross-section of contemporary society is now committed to this study and, as time passes, newer social, economic and ethnic groups will undoubtedly be recruited. A notable characteristic of local historians is that they yearn to grow in the subject and not to stagnate. Hoskins's book was an early attempt to advance that process, because he himself had frequently reconstructed the lives of 'ordinary' people from the past, and he knew that non-professionals were capable of contributing positively to this work.

In his inaugural lecture at Leicester in 1966, Hoskins addressed the crucial issue of standards. 'The best amateur can equal – perhaps surpass – the

---

10. H.P.R. Finberg and V.H.T. Skipp, *Local history: objective and pursuit* (Newton Abbot, 1967), p. 2. A research fellowship in local history was established at Reading University as early as 1908.

11. Hoskins, *Local history in England*, pp. 3–4.

12. J. Thirsk, 'Women local and family historians', in D. Hey, *Oxford companion to local and family history* (Oxford, 1996), pp. 498–504. This gender revolution needs further study.

achievement of the professional; but … the average standard of professional achievement is likely to be considerably higher than that of amateurs as a whole'.[13] Not only was local history both professional *and* amateur, but wherever possible cooperation between these two groups was to be encouraged. That responsibility has motivated many authors who since 1959 have written newer general works on the nature, themes, sources and methods of local history.[14] They were writing for all those, professional and amateur, who sought deeper involvement with the subject.

Is local history still the 'stronghold of the amateur'? For example, does this judgement of 1959 now apply to the British Association for Local History (BALH), the subject's principal voluntary national organisation? Most of its members, both individuals and societies, are certainly amateur, but the current list of trustees, council members and committees soon reveals a heavy and growing professional presence. For this and other reasons I would argue that, when we probe developments over the last 50 years, we soon appreciate that local history has grown fast on both fronts. The whole scene is now much more complex and tangled, with an amazing panorama of interests, approaches and levels of involvement. The many divisions and sub-groups are inhabited by those who, being on both sides of the old divide, may be paid or unpaid.

Academics, as full-time professionals, are paid to teach, research and write. This group is now larger than in Hoskins's day, and generates much more research. For 30 or so years after 1959 most teaching posts specifically dedicated to local history were in university departments of adult education, but since the 1990s their number has declined markedly because of funding problems and competition from other subjects. The loss has been barely offset by three recent trends: new appointments in new universities; the growth of sub-specialisations such as demography and vernacular architecture; and the way some scholars engaged with local studies prefer to label themselves as specialists in 'micro-history', 'community history', 'heritage studies' or 'public history'.[15] The most important influence, however, has come from academics in major disciplines such as economic, social and ecclesiastical history, who avoid calling themselves local historians but adopt the localised approach when it suits them – which it

---

13. W.G. Hoskins, *English local history, the past and the future* (Leicester, 1966), p. 4.

14. Over a dozen manuals of English local history appeared between 1959 and 2009: West and Emmison (in the 1960s); Rogers and Stephens (1970s); Riden and Dymond (1980s); Tiller, Williams and Marshall (1990s). Many underwent more than one edition.

15. 'Public History' was established in the USA in the mid-1970s to investigate how history is 'sold' to the non-academic public: <http://en.Wikipedia.org?wiki/Public_history> accessed 7 January 2011. Inevitably, public history pays considerable attention to the local dimension.

increasingly does. Their work is driven less by interest in particular communities or places and more by the availability of above-average local sources that open up broader issues.[16] In the last 50 years professionals of this latter kind have produced most of the 'classic' local histories represented by places such as The Blean, Earls Colne, Dorchester, Havering, Morebath, Terling and Whickham.[17] Simultaneously they have promoted new approaches, themes, sources and methods. In turn these developments have strengthened old-established specialisms (such as place-name studies and ecclesiology) and created new specialisms (such as oral history and garden history). Collectively, they show that the local dimension is increasingly important as a tool of investigation and powerfully stimulates new thinking in many historical fields.

On the amateur, non-professional or lay flank, numbers have grown even faster (Hoskins already referred to an 'army'), so that today local history has become a widespread leisure interest in this country and elsewhere. Not only does it engage the interest of large numbers of people, but it often leads them into practical and critical research. With its emphasis on all levels of society, from paupers to aristocrats, and on all kinds of community, from housing estates to large natural regions, local history presents universal themes of human experience. Paradoxically, this makes it wider and more educationally relevant than any other form of history.

Nonetheless, it is patently foolish to lump all amateur local historians together, because they include many different groups with varying backgrounds, interests and values. One helpful, although still crude, distinction is to postulate two main groups whom we can call 'consumers' and 'activists'. Consumers are a very large segment of the general population. Their interest in history leads them, for example, to visit cathedrals, National Trust properties and English Heritage sites, and to follow *Timewatch* and *Who do you think you are?* on television. They may also join conducted trails and excursions, sample lectures organised by local

---

16. Thus, they work *into* localities from outside, whereas local historians tend to work *outwards*.

17. B. Reay, *Microhistories: demography, society and culture in rural England, 1800–1930* (Cambridge, 1996); H.R. French and R.W. Hoyle, *The character of English rural society: Earls Colne, 1550–1750* (Manchester, 2007); D. Underdown, *Fire from heaven: life in an English town in the seventeenth century* (London, 1992); M.K. McIntosh, *Autonomy and community: the royal manor of Havering, 1200–1500* (Cambridge, 1986) and *Community transformed: the manor and liberty of Havering, 1500–1620* (Cambridge, 1991); E. Duffy, *The voices of Morebath: reformation and rebellion in an English village* (New Haven, CT, 2001); K. Wrightson and D. Levine, *Poverty and piety in an English village* (New York, 1979; Oxford 1999); D. Levine and K. Wrightson, *The making of an industrial society: Whickham 1560–1765* (Oxford, 1991). Of course, classics have also come from those professing local and landscape history: D. Hey, *An English rural community: Myddle under the Tudors and Stuarts* (Leicester, 1974); C. Gerrard with M. Aston, *The Shapwick project, Somerset: a rural landscape explored* (Society for Medieval Archaeology, Monograph 25, 2007). Note that the main and sub-titles of these works identify both the local stage *and* the broader historical theme.

Fig. 1.1 W.G. Hoskins in Devon, in the 1970s

societies, and perhaps dip into the big red volumes of the *VCH*. They are not themselves concerned to research or write, but are happy to learn about the past from others.

Professionals should never forget that these consumers are their public and to a large extent their paymasters through taxes, subscriptions and cash registers. They prove that history in general, but particularly history of the local and family sort, is now hugely attractive to the public. We ignore their interests at our peril, and have a duty to see that they get greater choice when spending their leisure: for example, in where to go, what to attend and what to read. Let us remind ourselves that Hoskins not only supported adult education as 'one of the most vigorous growing-points for the serious study of local history'[18] but also believed in reaching wider audiences (admittedly, mainly middle-class) through the use of radio, television and non-academic writing. I guess that his broadcasts on 'Landscapes of England' and resultant articles in *The Listener* were at least as influential as his books.

By contrast, 'activists' are amateurs who spend large parts of their leisure or retirement striving to discover the past for themselves (although *en route* they usually seek help from others). They regularly use record offices, libraries and to a lesser extent museums; they consult printed and manuscript sources and explore local landscapes and townscapes; and they wrestle with problems of interpretation. Some accumulate useful knowledge but do not write; others publish in local periodicals or produce their own books. Within the expanding ranks of amateur activists are a sizeable proportion, perhaps a majority, whom Tiller memorably described as 'local local historians' – those interested *only* in their place of residence or birthplace.[19] That approach reminds us again of the relevance of personal experience, observation and sentiment in local history. Although it has dangers, it can produce memorable and respected results, as it did with great pioneers of local history such as White Kennett (Ambrosden, Oxon), Henry Cowper (Hawkshead, Lancs.), Sir Matthew Nathan (West Coker, Somerset) and Frank Hill (Lincoln).[20]

Of course, the standards of lay historians have varied enormously and always will. Some have proved themselves capable of making real contributions to historical knowledge, and their work is not easily distinguishable from that of

---

18. W.G. Hoskins, *Fieldwork in local history* (London, 1967), p. 12.

19. K. Tiller, 'Local history brought up to date', *The Local Historian*, 36 (2006), p. 156.

20. W. Kennett, *Parochial antiquities attempted in the history of Ambrosden, Bicester and other adjacent parts* (Oxford, 1695); H.S. Cowper, *Hawkshead: (the northernmost parish of Lancashire): its history, archaeology, industries, dialect, etc.* (London, 1899); M. Nathan, *The annals of West Coker* (Cambridge, 1957); J.W.F. Hill, *Medieval Lincoln* (Cambridge, 1948).

professionals (below, p. 21). Moreover, whether or not properly acknowledged, modern academic research is often indebted to the spade-work of part-timers and earlier antiquaries. On the other hand, too many amateurs promote written or spoken history which is deeply flawed. Although keen to give help and encouragement, Hoskins himself wrote acidly about the 'imbecilities' that mark their work.[21] He was referring to those who adopt an uncritical, heaping approach to the finding of evidence and romanticise the past, or simply invent it. Parochial and inward-looking, they are not prepared to question or contextualise what they find, and they do not believe in giving references. Frequently they allow their parish boundaries to become intellectual Iron Curtains by refusing to recognise the outward and inward movements that influence all communities, and they perpetuate troublesome myths (think of all those ships' timbers in local houses, and underground passages leading to bogus religious houses).[22] It is profoundly sad to see local historians publish studies that are real 'labours of love', costly of time and money, and littered with major defects that could have been avoided.

The uneven and frequently poor standards of amateur history provoke much cynical criticism from professional historians, both from those directly involved with local studies and those with national and international interests. Having failed to influence their lay colleagues, some even express despair. On top of that, other academics, overlooking their own forms of myopia, question whether local history has value at all. They do not see it as a worthwhile record of everyday personal, family and communal life, well justified in terms of learning, personal education and social cohesion, but as mere dabbling in trivial 'antiquarianism' and 'parochialism'. Real history, they insist, can only deal with higher matters such as statecraft, national politics, war and peace; David Starkey, for example, described local history as 'a very limited thing'.[23] Most of us working in this field have experienced the disdain of other kinds of historian. In an obituary of 1992, Beresford wrote that even Hoskins had suffered from 'the cruel indifference of the history establishment'.[24] We who believe in local history must therefore defend it – by insisting that we are committed to the *general* value of the localised approach; by concentrating on the best examples of research, both professional and lay; and by constantly pointing out the advantages flowing from a huge

---

21. Hoskins, *Fieldwork*, p. 13.

22. C. Lewis, *A history of Kirtling and Upend: landowners and people in a Cambridgeshire parish, 1000–2000* (Wallasey, 2000) has an appendix on 'Two things that *didn't* happen in Kirtling', contrary to local belief.

23. D. Starkey, 'The English historian's role and the place of history in English national life', *The Historian*, 71 (2001), p. 15.

24. *The Independent*, 5 March 1992.

amateur base, not least in the finding of new themes, evidence and talent.

Examinations of the present state of local history show that relationships between professionals and non-professionals are still problematic. In 1998, nearly 40 years after Hoskins's book appeared, Tiller claimed that the future of local history lay 'in not distancing academic history … from local history as practised outside universities'. She called for a two-way 'lay–professional alliance' nurtured through adult education, group research and the promotion of postgraduate study.[25] Professionals, in other words, needed to find ways of attracting the cooperation of lay historians, to mutual benefit. In 2007, John Beckett, in his assessment of local history (effectively updating Hoskins's work of 1959), gave an even sharper warning. 'The danger remains of the amateur local historian and the professional academic historian viewing each other across a chasm filled with misunderstanding.' This is strong stuff, but most of us in our working lives have experienced such dangers. He called also for 'a shared agenda of academic and lay practitioners', while conceding that many amateurs do not care what academics think of them and contentedly plough their own furrows.[26]

Here we need to acknowledge a factor of great importance, rooted in the one-year MA course in English Local History which Hoskins established at Leicester in 1965. While some active non-professionals remain largely self-taught, others positively seek academic training. Each year, hundreds enrol for certificates, diplomas, masters' degrees and doctorates. In other words, they avail themselves of a ladder of courses, mainly part-time but also full-time, provided by institutions of higher education – a ladder which they can get on, and off, at any point.[27] They are willing to devote to this education considerable sums of money and a great deal of time (as much as 12 or 15 years, while still holding down a job or bringing up a family). They are mature, well-motivated people of different ages (generally beyond the age of 40), who come from varying social and educational backgrounds. Most are graduates, either in history or some other discipline such as classics, modern languages or social science. Others are non-graduates but have backgrounds and experience relevant to the subject. The essential requirements are an intelligent interest in, and some experience of, the study of local communities.

---

25. Tiller, *English local history*, pp. 19–24.

26. Beckett, *Writing local history*, p. 212.

27. Courses in family and community history developed by the Open University (particularly DA301) have similarly encouraged practical research. For courses currently on offer, see 'List of local history qualifications A–Z by institution': <http://www.uall.ac.uk/links.aspx> accessed 7 January 2011. Their number may be shrinking, a trend which could cause an increase of cheaper versions done by correspondence or through the Internet.

After such training these committed activists do not usually gain professional jobs, and as a result some then feel sidelined.[28] However, desiring to stay involved, most remain busy researchers, writers and freelance lecturers, and help to run voluntary societies. They may also meet in university centres of regional history and attend major conferences. As Beckett has remarked: 'Since there are now hundreds of university-trained local historians in the wider community, we can surely expect a greater understanding of what the subject is ... [They] have the basic techniques and skills of researching, understanding and writing local history.'[29] This, surely, is a revolution which bodes well for the future. It means that, for a growing number of individuals, old distinctions are melting and relationships are becoming closer. People who are technically amateur are acquiring academic training, forging personal links within the academic community and finding themselves increasingly at or close to the cutting edge of research.

Another mode of training, growing in scale, is the setting up of group research projects, which are designed by academics but crucially dependent on detailed work done by unpaid volunteers. This approach was pioneered, from the 1960s onwards, in 'participatory' or 'research' classes run by extra-mural departments in different parts of the country, and many resulted in worthwhile publications.[30] More recent projects have exploited the Internet and email. Some are county-wide, such as 'Eighteenth-century Devon: people and communities', the purpose of which was to transcribe a wide variety of sources, such as oath rolls and diocesan visitation returns, and to publish them electronically. This project was supported by the county council, county record office and the University of Exeter, and received £50,000 from the Heritage Lottery Fund.[31] Similar ventures have been organised by the Family and Community History Society, and by the *VCH* through its initiative 'England's Past for Everyone' (with the fiery motto, 'Get Involved'). Central to these developments is professional guidance in defining the project, training volunteers, ensuring

---

28. Academic jobs are in short supply, fewer chances arise to lecture in adult education, and successful post-graduates lose 'the online resources that are available to enrolled students': Heather Falvey (private correspondence, October 2009).

29. Beckett, *Writing local history*, p. 193.

30. For example, B. Trinder and J. Cox, *Yeomen and colliers in Telford: the probate inventories for Dawley, Lilleshall, Wellington and Wrockwardine, 1660–1750* (London, 1980); The Latin Project, *The Blackburns in York: testaments of a merchant family in the later Middle Ages* (York, 2006). See also A. Rogers, *Group projects in local history* (Folkestone, 1977) and D. Dymond, *Researching and writing history: a guide for local historians* (Lancaster, 2009), pp. 46–51.

31. 'Eighteenth-century Devon: people and communities': <http://www.foda.org.uk/main/projects/eighteenth-century.htm> accessed 14 March 2011.

consistency and shaping a final report. Providing that volunteers derive genuine educational benefit from the exercise, such work should not be regarded as selfish exploitation. As Goose says, 'one of the most constructive ways forward is for the amateur and the professional to work together, forming an alliance that combines their respective talents'.[32]

Although these encouraging trends bring non-professionals into academic work, we still see many other activists beavering away on their own. The loneliness of some local historians, which worried Hoskins, is still a problem. To work primarily at home, or in record offices and libraries, is decidedly more solitary than experiencing the camaraderie of lecture and combination rooms or the sweaty matiness of the archaeological trench. Hence the importance, then and now, of providing opportunities for like-minded people to meet, talk and work together. As previously mentioned, those academically active today have ways of socialising through seminars, group projects and regional centres. For non-professionals, however, the most obvious forms of association are local history societies serving individual places and areas. While many members of these voluntary organisations are middle-aged or elderly and want only to listen or be entertained, others can usually be found who are committed to rewarding lines of research.[33]

The standards of local societies vary considerably, as do judgements on their present state of health. Nevertheless, we can all, and I see this as a special responsibility of BALH and county federations, help local societies to become better known and more ambitious, actively proselytising among all age groups. In some areas, successful groups could be encouraged to link with ones that are struggling, or even to merge to cover wider areas and achieve larger memberships. Lectures, excursions and newsletters are standard fare, but other activities which can prove profitable for societies include:

- agreeing on major historical themes worthy of investigation in the locality;
- identifying physical 'monuments' that deserve greater understanding and protection (from earthworks to redundant industrial buildings);
- maintaining a photographic record which is catalogued, dated and regularly exhibited;

---

32. N. Goose, 'Hertfordshire in history: nineteenth-century poverty and early modern probates: local history projects in their historical context', *Hertfordshire Archaeology and History*, 14 (2004–5), p. 167; N. Goose, 'Participatory and collaborative research in English regional and local history: the Hertfordshire historical research project', *Archives*, 22 (1997), pp. 98–110.

33. For an upbeat account of local societies, see K. Tiller, 'Opinion: "Local historians can do this for themselves": a personal view of 2008–2009', *The Local Historian*, 39 (2009), pp. 324–9.

- becoming involved in research projects with the help of professionals and specialists;
- compiling educationally effective guides and trails;
- producing record publications and special glossaries;
- deliberately putting family history into the wider perspectives of local and regional history;
- making links with local schools and pensioners' organisations;
- taking advantage of significant anniversaries and centenaries.[34]

Nor should we forget that local history can genuinely contribute to the life of whole communities. The stimulus may come from the work of individuals or groups,[35] but, whatever its source, when sound local history is published or promoted in other ways the community in question (whatever its size) can never be the same again: it now knows more about itself, its place in history and how it felt to live there in the past. Consequently it can, and surely should, begin to assess how far it shares characteristics with other human groupings, and how far it is unusual or unique. Moreover, remembering that local historians are citizens with civic obligations, societies should not be afraid to lobby planners, councillors and MPs when threats appear and important issues are publicly debated. This is not easy, and frequently leads to disappointment, but the moral and educational obligation is clear and pressing on us all.

To summarise, the 'split personality' mentioned in this paper's title can still be diagnosed. Academics can be heard castigating non-professionals for overlooking key recent publications and for poor referencing, while amateurs bitterly complain that professional history lacks humanity and is unashamedly opaque. There is truth on both sides. We shall always be haunted by this difference of opinion because local history is not only a serious academic study (part of history as a whole) but has its place in everyday life, conversation and natural curiosity. It is inescapably more 'popular' and 'experiential' than other forms of history because it deals with the lives of ordinary individuals and groups. This may unfortunately give rise to tasteless commercial exploitation and the peddling of myths, which can afflict all kinds of history, but the lack of exclusivity and elitism in local history is a source, actually and potentially, of great strength and diversity. As Alan Crosby has commented, 'there are few other

---

34. For the activities of societies, sometimes involving grants from the Heritage Lottery Fund, see 'News from societies' in BALH's quarterly *Local History News*.

35. Groups can work in an educational framework, guided by experienced tutors, or be more democratic and self-regulating along the lines of Marshall's 'people's history': Marshall, *Tyranny of the discrete*, chapter 7.

academic disciplines in which active participation by non-experts is feasible'.[36] Indeed, experienced practitioners can cite hundreds of instances where valuable work and insights have appeared from quite unexpected sources.

As a result of practical forms of cooperation, the academic–amateur divide is beginning to close, with influences and benefits flowing both ways. Such links scarcely existed in Hoskins's day. For example, while some non-professionals now acquire academic training and commit themselves to planned research, a growing number of academics welcome the involvement of lay colleagues in the quarrying of documentary sources and their transcription and analysis. The great 'army' of amateur local historians may remain largely uninfluenced by these trends, but where they are within reach the two groups are beginning to merge and blur, as can already be seen by attendances at conferences and key lectures.

In the early twenty-first century the situation would be significantly improved if we could clarify the terms which bounce around our subject, defining key words with greater care and jettisoning old assumptions and prejudices. In recent decades, unfortunately, many academics have blithely assumed that local history = amateur = bad, and conversely that academic history = professional = good. Such language confuses three important issues: the physical scale of research (local, regional, national, or international), the writer's status (amateur, professional, or somewhere in-between), and the quality of the end-product. Take, for instance, the word 'amateur'. The basic meaning is a person who does something for love, without expecting monetary gain. Obviously, all 'consumers' and 'activists' mentioned earlier (pp. 17–19) come into this category. Yet by strict definition other groups without full-time academic jobs, such as most history graduates, research students (who may later gain lectureships) and retired academics, are also amateur. Similar problems arise with the concept of 'professional'. It should imply someone with a permanent, paid job in local history (now quite rare) or in allied subjects, but what of those who are paid as freelancers, part-timers or as administrators, and what indeed of history teachers in schools? Many key contemporary figures in the world of local history, whatever they call themselves, are amateur by strict definition and yet clearly professional in their research, writing and teaching.

More confusion arises in judging the *quality* of history. Good history, whatever its origin, should be critical, analytical, built around major concepts, comparative and cumulative; it should also be written lucidly and elegantly. This ideal *could* be described as 'academic history' (and its opposite as 'non-academic', exhibiting all the woeful characteristics outlined on p. 20), but that

---

36. Alan Crosby (private correspondence, December 2009).

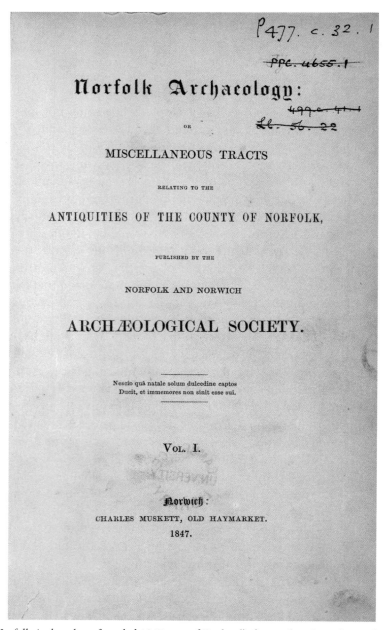

Fig. 1.2 *Norfolk Archaeology*, founded 1847, one of England's first archaeological-cum-historical county journals. Such journals are among the most obvious outlets for committed local historians. Hoskins himself wrote sixteen papers on varied subjects in fifteen years in *Transactions of the Leicestershire Archaeological Society*.

implies that good history can come only from full-time professionals and universities. In fact, as we all know, academic writing is not always first-class, and perhaps it is safer to talk of quality as ranging, straightforwardly, from 'good' to 'bad'. In practice most writing falls between these two extremes, as is routinely indicated by the judgement of examiners and reviewers.

Finally we come to the term 'local history' itself. Current since the late nineteenth century as the opposite of 'national' or 'international' history, it should merely describe the geographical scale of study and carry no implications of a writer's status or quality of work. Local history can be written by high academics and total amateurs; it is both a graduate subject and a widespread leisure interest. In either case it can be illuminating and stimulating, flawed and pedestrian. It is unjust to see it as *necessarily* antiquarian, parochial and of poor quality. Nevertheless, while nearly all amateurs and a few professionals in this field are content to call themselves students of 'local history', most academics avoid the term (as *infra dig*) and prefer to use alternatives such as 'community history' or 'social history'. This may be regrettable but perhaps, in the final analysis, the title preferred by serious researchers matters less than the fact that they are increasingly drawn to the localised or regional approach (Fig 1.2).

Hoskins's book ran to three editions, was available for over 25 years and has been continually referenced. Of course it was not unprecedented, for he himself acknowledged debts to earlier writers such as Maitland and Russell, and it was soon supplemented by works from other authors. Inevitably the book has dated. It was certainly biased against the urbanised, industrialised, suburbanised and commercialised worlds of the nineteenth and twentieth centuries, so it is ironic nowadays that most local historians choose to study this period.[37] Hoskins also assumed that most of his readers were engaged on their own full parish or town histories, adopting the long chronologies that are now largely out of fashion.

Although not so inspirational as his masterpieces, *The making of the English landscape* and *The midland peasant*,[38] Hoskins's *Local history in England* was an effective manual for legions of readers over decades. It gave direction and credibility to a strongly emerging form of practical and democratic history that went on to display the following characteristics:

---

37. Hoskins, *Local history in England*, p. 12. It is sad that, for methodological, linguistic and other reasons, most amateurs avoid the medieval and early modern periods. For many, undeniably, the world since 1800 has a more immediate and personal appeal.

38. W.G. Hoskins, *The making of the English landscape* (London, 1955); W.G. Hoskins, *The midland peasant: the economic and social history of a Leicestershire village* (London, 1957).

- it offers fundamental knowledge about the vast majority of the human race, in all its complexity;
- it seamlessly overlaps with other aspects of the past, such as economic, social and political history, and is therefore part of history as a whole;
- it attracts growing numbers of researchers from other historical specialisations who would never call themselves 'local historians';
- it nurtures, and is nurtured by, new specialisations such as surname studies and industrial archaeology;
- it adds detail, complexity and (paradoxically) breadth to the writing of all kinds of history;[39]
- and, finally, as discussed in this paper, it is unavoidably both academic *and* amateur. If they wish, professionals and amateurs may ignore or even pillory each other, but such negative attitudes ignore the huge advantages which can be gained from open-mindedness, debate and cooperation – as William Hoskins taught half a century ago.

---

39. Neil MacGregor describes the purpose of museums in words which seem better suited to local history: 'to slow down conclusions, to complicate the questions, to make hasty judgement harder': *The Guardian*, 15 January 2009.

2. The great awakening of English local history, 1918–1939

C.P. Lewis

The modern era in English local history is generally believed to have started only after the Second World War, with such developments as the creation of a department for W.G. Hoskins at Leicester in 1948 and the spreading networks of local record offices, adult education classes and local history societies.[1] At first glance, this post-war expansion looks a world apart from local history between the wars, when much evidence for hard times is readily to hand. The *Victoria County History* (*VCH*) – flagship of professional local history and much admired at the time[2] – was a shadow of its Edwardian self: in abeyance until 1922, kept up by an unsalaried general editor until 1933, and only just beginning to renew itself at the Institute of Historical Research in the later 1930s. Whereas the pre-war *VCH* had produced 76 volumes at an average rate of over 5 a year, between the wars it managed only 28 volumes in all (little more than one a year), of which 6 had in fact been finished but not published before 1915, and 8 more were index volumes.[3] Elsewhere the scene was just as bleak. The county historical and archaeological societies had their activities disrupted and memberships reduced by the Great War and faced cripplingly higher printing bills in the immediate post-war years.

---

1. J. Beckett, *Writing local history* (Manchester, 2007), pp. 106–22; J.D. Marshall, *The tyranny of the discrete: a discussion of the problems of local history in England* (Aldershot, 1997), pp. 7–26.

2. *VCH* treated as authoritative: *The Times*, 20 April 1918, p. 7c; 1 September 1925, p. 8a; 9 November 1934, p. 10e; *VCH* contributions noted: *The Times*, 6 December 1922, p. 17d; 6 June 1928, p. 22c; 12 February 1935, p. 1b; 25 September 1939, p. 10d; *VCH*'s wider reputation: cartoon in *Birmingham Daily Mail*, 22 June 1936, reproduced in D.J. Birch and J.M. Horn (comp.), *The history laboratory: the Institute of Historical Research, 1921–96* (London, 1996), p. 48.

3. R.B. Pugh, 'The Victoria History: its origin and progress', in *The Victoria history of the counties of England: general introduction* (Oxford, 1970), pp. 10–16; publication data calculated from 'List of volumes', pp. 31–3. *VCH* volumes hereafter cited as *VCH* with county name.

At least one of them, the Devonshire Association, felt obliged to ask potential authors to help with the costs of publishing their papers.[4] Parish historians of the period have a reputation for being mired in an antiquarian obsession with manorial descents and ecclesiastical trivia, turning out compilations of fact piled up with little method and less art. Emblematic is the industrious but chaotic work of Canon Michael Wood, busy in the early 1920s on the history of Steeple and Middle Aston in Oxfordshire; in despair, his successor as parish historian, the Revd C.C. Brookes, remarked tartly that Wood's notes 'would have been even more valuable had they indicated what sources he had searched'.[5] The much admired Reginald Hine, whose handsome two-volume history of Hitchin (Hertfordshire) attracted over 1000 subscribers in the late 1920s, wrote in a flowery, discursive style which is now unreadable.[6] The standard fare on offer between the wars, indeed, informed such diverse post-war critiques as H.P.R. Finberg's advice on how *not* to write a parish history[7] and Osbert Lancaster's spoof history of fictitious Drayneflete.[8] Finally, it seems that a wide gulf separated local historians of all stripes from the profession of history in the universities. For example, the most prominent and authoritative historical journal, *English Historical Review*, did not review any *VCH* volumes until as late as 1938.[9]

Received opinion is indeed that local history had been 'marginalised' already in the nineteenth century in relation to mainstream history,[10] that it 'struggled to maintain its credibility with … professional historians' down to the Second World War,[11] and that the resurgence of local history in its modern form, distinct from antiquarianism, did not take place until after 1945.[12] Another word used

---

4. H.H. Walker, 'The story of the Devonshire Association, 1862–1962', *Report and Transactions of the Devonshire Association*, 94 (1962), pp. 42–110 at p. 70; cf. L.F. Salzman, 'A history of the Sussex Archaeological Society', *Sussex Archaeological Collections* (hereafter *SAC*), 85 (1946), pp. 3–76 at p. 41.

5. C.C. Brookes, *A history of Steeple Aston and Middle Aston, Oxfordshire* (Long Compton, 1929), p. v.

6. R.L. Hine, *The history of Hitchin*, 2 vols (London, 1927 and 1929), 1, pp. 349–75; 2, pp. 7, 504–9 and half-title verso; *Relics of an un-common attorney* (London, 1951); W.B. Johnson, 'Reginald Leslie Hine of Hitchin, Hertfordshire, 1883–1949', *Amateur Historian*, 7 (1965–6), pp. 28–32; A.L. Fleck, 'Hine, Reginald Leslie (1883–1949), lawyer and author', *ODNB*.

7. H.P.R. Finberg, 'How not to write local history', in H.P.R. Finberg and V.H.T. Skipp, *Local history: objective and pursuit* (Newton Abbot, 1967), pp. 71–86.

8. O. Lancaster, *Drayneflete revealed, illustrated by the author* (London, 1949).

9. *English Historical Review* (hereafter *EHR*), 53 (1938), pp. 521–6; 54 (1939), pp. 698–9.

10. Beckett, *Writing local history*, pp. 70–87.

11. *Ibid.*, p. 106.

12. *Ibid.*, pp. 106–22; G. and Y. Sheeran, 'Reconstructing local history', *Local Historian*, 29 (1999), pp. 256–62; G. and Y. Sheeran, 'Opinion: "No longer the 1948 show" – local history in the 21st century', *Local Historian*, 39 (2009), pp. 314–23, esp. pp. 315–16.

recently of local history in the period is stagnation: 'stagnation reflected the general state of local history in the inter-war period. Whilst parish histories continued to be produced the discipline was of little interest to the academic world … It was not until after the Second World War that new life was breathed into the world of local history.'[13]

It is of course true that the practice of local history was transformed after the Second World War – by being embedded as an academic discipline at Leicester, by much greater public interest, by massive growth in new societies and in membership of the older ones, by the opening up of new sources both physically (in the new record offices) and intellectually, by the proliferation of sub-disciplines such as landscape history, vernacular architecture, industrial archaeology and local population studies, by adult education courses, and by hugely enlarged opportunities for publication. But the inter-war period has been grievously misunderstood and misrepresented. It was not a time of stagnation or marginalisation in local history; rather, it was formative in shaping an emerging discipline, and the new directions taken then laid down the lines of development for the boom years after 1945. This chapter sketches the main aspects of the great awakening of local history between the wars.

Local history activities

The outward signs of health and vitality in local history between the wars can be grouped under four main headings: the county historical and archaeological societies, free-standing parish histories, provision in the universities and the attitude of professional historians.

The county societies, despite their immediate difficulties in 1919, thrived and diversified. In a sample of twelve, of different sizes and dispersed across the country, the membership of the Cumberland and Westmorland grew by 5 per cent between the wars,[14] Bristol and Gloucestershire by 15 per cent,[15] Rutland by 24 per cent,[16] Shropshire by 30 per cent,[17] Birmingham (equivalent of a county

---

13. S. Dunster and E. Edwards, '150 years of local history: local Kentish practice and national trends', *Archaeologia Cantiana*, 127 (2007), pp. 21–38 at p. 24.

14. From 532 in 1918 to 558 in 1939: *Transactions of the Cumberland & Westmorland Antiquarian & Archaeological Society*, new series, 18 (1918), pp. 246–57; 39 (1939), pp. 337–50.

15. From 429 in 1918 to 492 in 1939: *Transactions of the Bristol and Gloucestershire Archaeological Society*, 40 (1917), at end; 60 (1938), at end.

16. From 88 in 1918 to 109 in 1941: *Rutland Archaeological and Natural History Society, 15th Annual Report* (1918), p. 7; *39th–44th Annual Reports* (1942), p. 2.

17. From 125 in 1919 to 162 in 1938: *Transactions of the Shropshire Archaeological and Natural History Society*, 40 (1918–19), pp. xv–xix; 49 (1937–8), pp. xxiv–xxviii.

society) also by 30 per cent,[18] Sussex by 46 per cent,[19] Kent by 51 per cent,[20] London and Middlesex by 54 per cent,[21] Essex by 85 per cent[22] and Dorset by 121 per cent.[23] There were falls only in Chester and North Wales (19 per cent)[24] and Leicestershire (17 per cent).[25] More work is needed on numbers and patterns of recruitment and retention across all the comparable societies, but the trend seems clear. The county societies must have been offering what members and potential members wanted.

Increasingly that was more than the usual late Victorian and Edwardian programmes of lectures, outings and annual *Proceedings* or *Transactions*. The Sussex Archaeological Society lobbied for the preservation of buildings at risk and (through the Sussex Archaeological Trust, set up in 1925) acquired historic properties which it ran as local history museums.[26] New initiatives in the Devonshire Association included a multi-author history of Exeter, a local history essay prize for students at University College, Exeter, and specialist sections on place-names and parochial history, the latter intended to collect material systematically on all the parishes of Devon. Not all those new projects were carried through as intended, and some of the planning was optimistic: the history of Exeter required that the 26 volunteers who had come forward 'should produce monographs, which would be digested by an Editorial Committee' into a history of the city:[27] a recipe for acrimony and wounded pride if ever there was one.

---

18. From 170 in 1918 to 221 in 1939: *Transactions and Proceedings of the Birmingham Archaeological Society*, 43 (1917), p. 134; 63 (1939–40), p. 106.

19. From 794 in 1918 to 1,163 in 1939: *SAC*, 80 (1939), p. [xxxviii]; 85 (1946), p. 41 (for 1918).

20. From 626 in 1918 to 943 in 1939: *Archaeologia Cantiana*, 34 (1920), p. xxxii; 53 (1940), p. xxxv.

21. From 151 in 1918 to 232 in 1939: *Transactions of the London and Middlesex Archaeological Society*, new series, 4 (1918–21), Annual Report 1917, p. xxii; new series, 8 (1938–40), Report 1938, p. xxix.

22. From 380 in 1918 to 704 in 1939: *Transactions of the Essex Archaeological Society*, new series, 15 (1921), p. 258; new series, 23 (1942–5), p. 234.

23. From 287 in 1918 to 634 in 1939: *Proceedings of the Dorset Natural History and Antiquarian Field Club*, 40 (1919), pp. xii–xxii; *Proceedings of the Dorset Natural History & Archaeological Society*, 61 (1939), pp. 6–19.

24. From 187 in 1919 to 152 in 1940: *Journal of the Architectural, Archaeological, and Historic Society for the County and the City of Chester, and North Wales*, new series, 23 (1920), pp. 79–83; *Journal of the Chester and North Wales Architectural, Archaeological and Historic Society*, new series, 34 part 2 (1940), pp. 166–9.

25. From 305 in 1922 to 252 in 1939: *Transactions of the Leicestershire Archaeological Society*, 12 (1921–2), p. viii; 20 (1938–9), pp. xlvi–lii.

26. Salzman, 'History of Sussex Archaeological Society', pp. 45, 50–51; F.B. Stevens, 'The Sussex Archaeological Trust', *SAC*, 85 (1946), pp. 119–37.

27. Walker, 'The story of the Devonshire Association', pp. 72–5, 80; *Report and Transactions of the Devonshire Association*, 52 (1920), p. 28.

Everywhere the content of lecture programmes and published articles was shifting away from older antiquarian interests. Of 245 papers published in *Sussex Archaeological Collections* (*SAC*) between 1919 and 1939, about 40 per cent were archaeological reports (still the work of amateurs, but far more rigorous in approach than previously); about 30 per cent were on traditional topics such as church architecture and manorial and family history; and 7 per cent were transcripts or descriptions of records. That leaves fully a quarter on topics that we might have supposed local historians discovered only after 1945.[28] The largest share was taken by papers on secular buildings (manor houses and farmhouses), at the time called 'domestic' rather than 'vernacular' architecture; this was a development led by the architectural historian Walter Godfrey (resident at Lewes from 1932) and encouraged by the editor of *SAC* throughout the period, L.F. Salzman.[29] Other articles, usually numbering one or two a year, covered place-names, industrial archaeology, agricultural history, topography and the poor law. Elsewhere in the country, the *Transactions of the Historic Society of Lancashire and Cheshire* carried an even wider range of 'modern' local history topics, including fire insurance, early nineteenth-century parliamentary elections, emigration, Liverpool warehousing, the Jewish community in Liverpool and an innovative series on topography and landscape by E.H. and Edna Rideout. By the late 1920s the latter type had almost completely displaced the older sort of antiquarian article.[30] A shift towards new topics, based on new sources, was undoubtedly taking place in the agenda of local history, although it needs to be mapped across a wider range of societies before its extent and impact can be measured.

Outside the county journals, the typical local history publication of the period was the free-standing history of a parish or small town. Any well stocked county or university library holds scores of such works published in the 1920s and 1930s, which are of staggering diversity, ambition, length and sophistication.[31] An indication of the large numbers of local historians active at the time is that W.E.

---

28. *SAC*, 60–80 (1919–39), *passim*. For the amateur status of most serious archaeologists of the period see G. Barker, 'Changing roles and agendas: the Society of Antiquaries and the professionalization of archaeology, 1950–2000', in S. Pearce (ed.), *Visions of antiquity: the Society of Antiquaries of London, 1707–2007* (London, 2007), pp. 383–413 at p. 383.

29. J. Summerson, 'Godfrey, Walter Hindes (1881–1961), architect and antiquary', *ODNB*; Salzman, 'History of Sussex Archaeological Society', p. 73.

30. *Transactions of the Historic Society of Lancashire and Cheshire*, 70–81 (1919–39), *passim*. Articles for all local journals to 1933 listed in E.L.C. Mullins (comp.), *A guide to the historical and archaeological publications of societies in England and Wales, 1901–1933* (London, 1968).

31. e.g. Liverpool University Library, shelfmark DA690 (Library of Congress system).

Tate, beginning to explore the local records which were still to a large degree housed literally in the parish chest, was personally in touch with at least 23 knowledgeable parish historians working in different parts of the country.[32]

Another sign of vigour is the fact that the aspiring parish historian had access to much advice available in print form. The field was led by the enlarged and rewritten fifth edition (1909) of J.C. Cox's *How to write the history of a parish*.[33] Cox died in 1919 and there was no further revision, but the fifth edition was packed with sound practical advice about sources and historical background and retained its value throughout the 1920s and 1930s.[34] Reginald Hine of Hitchin, for one, owned a copy given him by Cox.[35] Cox's advice on sources was complemented by W.P.W. Phillimore's *Parish historian* (1905), a pragmatic guide to planning, writing, printing and publishing a parish history.[36] Another essential textbook, Trice Martin's *Record interpreter*, was sufficiently in demand to be reissued in 1935.[37] For more detailed advice, several of Cox's series of Antiquary's Books (1904–15) retained their value, notably his own contributions on parish registers and churchwardens' accounts and Nathaniel Hone on manorial records.[38] Other volumes in the series provided guidance on prehistoric and Romano-British remains, Domesday Book, castles, royal forests, seals, folklore, medieval schools and a variety of ecclesiastical antiquities (bells, brasses, church furniture and stained glass). What Adolphus Ballard said of his contribution on Domesday held true generally: he had aimed 'to provide an account … which will be of assistance

---

32. W.E. Tate, *The parish chest: a study of the records of parochial administration in England* (Cambridge, 1946), pp. ix–x.

33. J.C. Cox, *How to write the history of a parish: an outline guide to topographical records, manuscripts, and books*, 5th edn (London, 1909; 1st edn 1879); B. Nurse, 'Cox, John Charles (1843–1919), antiquary and ecclesiologist', *ODNB*; E.T. Hurren, 'A radical historian's pursuit of rural history: the political career and contribution of Reverend Dr. John Charles Cox, *c.* 1844 to 1919', *Rural History*, 19 (2008), pp. 81–103.

34. See, e.g., commendation by A.H. Thompson, *A short bibliography of local history*, Historical Association Leaflet, 72 (London, 1928), p. 1. See also Walter Rye, *Records and record searching* (London, 1888; 2nd edn 1897), pp. 14–25 in 2nd edn. On Rye (1843–1929), see C. Kitching, 'A Victorian pioneer in the records: Walter Rye's *Records and record searching* in context', *Archives*, 33 (2008), pp. 126–39. Much less useful were A.L. Humphreys, *How to write a village history* (Reading, 1930) and H.M. Barron, *Your parish history: how to discover and write it* (London, [1930]).

35. In possession of present author, March 2011.

36. W.P.W. Phillimore, *The parish historian: a short initial guide for writing, printing and illustrating the history of a parish* (London, 1905).

37. C.T. Martin (comp.), *The record interpreter*, 2nd edn (London, 1910), facsimile edn with an introduction by D. Iredale (Chichester, 1982), introduction, p. 15.

38. J.C. Cox, *The parish registers of England* (London, 1910); J.C. Cox, *Churchwardens' accounts from the fourteenth century to the close of the seventeenth century* (London, 1913); N.J. Hone, *The manor and manorial records* (London, 1906; 2nd edn 1912).

to those who are studying the history of the place in which they live'.[39] There were clearly hundreds of such local historians active in the 1920s and 1930s.

As Tate's circle of correspondents suggests, personal contacts were at least as useful for local historians as reliable reference books about sources and methods, and there are many signs of friendly and productive relations between amateurs and the small number of academics and other professionals, as the acknowledgements of countless parish histories amply show. The Revd Brookes of Steeple and Middle Aston, a history undergraduate at Oxford 40 years earlier, sought help from two Oxford experts, E.T. Leeds of the Ashmolean Museum for prehistory and the Revd H.E. Salter, research fellow at Magdalen College, for Domesday Book and the twelfth century.[40] Help went both ways, since Tate himself, still a schoolmaster in the 1930s, contributed a meaty 20-page appendix on parliamentary enclosure to the university historian J.D. Chambers's work of regional history on Nottinghamshire.[41]

Local history was taught at several universities and university colleges between the wars, and was researched at virtually all of them, occupying a position appropriate to its standing as an emerging and respectable sub-discipline. In two places the foundations were Edwardian. One was University College, Reading, where in 1908 the principal, W.M. Childs,[42] established a research fellowship in local history and a monograph series, Studies in Local History. The first (as it turned out the only) research fellow was Childs's protégé Frank Stenton, who had recently made a name for himself writing articles on Domesday Book for the *VCH* as understudy to Horace Round. The post lapsed when Stenton was elected to the endowed chair of modern history at Reading in 1912.[43] Stenton's early career with the *VCH* and his continuing interest in local history have been

39. A. Ballard, *The Domesday inquest* (London, 1906; 2nd edn 1923), p. xiii; B. Coghill and A. Windle, *Remains of the prehistoric age in England* (London, 1904; 2nd edn 1909); J. Ward, *Romano-British buildings and earthworks* (London, 1911); A. Harvey, *The castles and walled towns of England* (London, 1911); J.C. Cox, *The royal forests of England* (London, 1905); J.H. Bloom, *English seals* (London, 1906); G.L. Gomme, *Folklore as an historical science* (London, 1908); A.F. Leach, *The schools of medieval England* (London, 1915); J.J. Raven, *The bells of England* (London, 1906); H.W. Macklin, *The brasses of England* (London, 1907; 3rd edn 1913); J.C. Cox and A. Harvey, *English church furniture* (London, 1907; 2nd edn 1908); P. Nelson, *Ancient painted glass in England, 1170–1500* (London, 1913).

40. Brookes, *History of Steeple Aston and Middle Aston*, p. vi; *Crockford's clerical directory for 1940* (Oxford, 1940), p. 163; W.A. Pantin, 'Herbert Edward Salter, 1863–1951', *Proceedings of the British Academy*, 40 (1954), pp. 219–39.

41. J.D. Chambers, *Nottinghamshire in the eighteenth century* (London, 1932), pp. vii–viii, 333–53; K.D.M. Snell, 'Tate, William Edward (1902–1968), teacher and historian', *ODNB*.

42. T.A.B. Corley, 'Childs, William Macbride (1869–1939), educationist', *ODNB*.

43. F.M. Stenton, *The early history of the abbey of Abingdon* (Reading, 1913), p. [iii].

underplayed in the main accounts of his life,[44] but the sort of local history that he undertook as research fellow at Reading continued to inform his work throughout his long and distinguished career as the pre-eminent Anglo-Saxonist of his generation.[45] The Reading monograph series, although running to only four volumes, went beyond traditional topics: Stenton covered the place-names of Berkshire and the early history of Abingdon abbey, and Childs tackled the town of Reading in the early nineteenth century, alongside F.J. Cole's more antiquarian study of Cholsey parish church.[46]

A further point can be made here about the growing scope of local history and its assimilation of advances in other disciplines. Stenton was among the first historians to grasp the significance of the breakthrough in understanding place-names that had been made by philologists of the previous generation,[47] led by W.W. Skeat of Cambridge,[48] Henry Bradley of Oxford[49] and the younger H.C. Wyld and his pupils at Liverpool.[50] The foundation of the Survey of English Place-Names in 1922 and of the English Place-Name Society in 1923 were important departures, the result of philologists and historians working together. Great strides in place-name studies were made before 1939: an inspiring multi-author introduction to the potential of place-names, a pioneering survey of elements, complete publication of fourteen counties and the first edition of Eilert Ekwall's indispensible *Oxford dictionary of English place-names*.[51] Those books equipped local historians with powerful tools for adding significantly to their own work.

44. D.M. Stenton, 'Frank Merry Stenton, 1880–1967', *Proceedings of the British Academy*, 54 (1968), pp. 315–423; J.C. Holt, 'Stenton, Sir Frank Merry (1880–1967), historian', *ODNB*.

45. J. Campbell, 'Stenton's *Anglo-Saxon England*, with special reference to the earlier period', in D. Matthew *et al.* (eds), *Stenton's Anglo-Saxon England fifty years on* (Reading, 1994), pp. 49–59 at p. 53.

46. W.M. Childs, *The town of Reading during the early part of the nineteenth century* (Reading, 1910); F.M. Stenton, *The place-names of Berkshire: an essay* (Reading, 1911); F.J. Cole, *An analysis of the church of St. Mary, Cholsey, in the county of Berkshire* (Reading, 1911); Stenton, *Early history of Abingdon*. I am grateful to Mr David Brown, History Liaison Librarian, University of Reading Library, for bibliographical advice (May 2010).

47. K. Cameron, 'Stenton and place-names', in D. Matthew (ed.), *Stenton's Anglo-Saxon England*, pp. 31–48 at p. 31.

48. K. Sisam (revised C. Brewer), 'Skeat, Walter William (1835–1912), philologist', *ODNB*.

49. W.A. Craigie (revised J. McMorris), 'Bradley, Henry (1845–1923), philologist and lexicographer', *ODNB*.

50. H. Orton (revised J.D. Haigh), 'Wyld, Henry Cecil Kennedy (1870–1945), philologist and lexicographer', *ODNB*; J. Spittal and J. Field (eds), *A reader's guide to the place-names of the United Kingdom* (Stamford, 1990), pp. 3–4, 282–7.

51. Details in *Publications of the English Place-Name Society: catalogue of publications* (Nottingham, 2006; revised periodically), pp. 1–5; E. Ekwall, *The concise Oxford dictionary of English place-names* (Oxford, 1936). Early years of EPNS: 'Introduction', in Spittal and Field (eds), *Reader's guide*, pp. 1–40 at p. 3–4, 12–13; M. Gelling, 'English place-name studies: some reflections', *English Place-Name Society Journal*, 35 (2002–3), pp. 5–16 at pp. 5–8.

The other university where local history was established before the Great War was Liverpool. Coincidentally in the same year as Reading (1908), Liverpool founded a School of Local History and Records to provide 'systematic training in the study, editing and publication of the history and records of the City of Liverpool and adjoining counties' through courses in palaeography, diplomatic, numismatics, the bibliography of and sources for English medieval history, and local records. One of its founding benefactors was the great Lancashire historian William Farrer, who was then heavily engaged on the *VCH* volumes for his native county.[52] The first lecturer (later an associate professor) was J.A. Twemlow (1867–1954), who had been a Liverpool undergraduate before studying medieval history, palaeography and diplomatic at Oxford under Reginald Lane Poole and then in Paris at the École des Chartes. His first position was Assistant Keeper at the Public Record Office (PRO), where he was responsible for calendaring papal letters relating to British and Irish history. Giving up his posting in Rome in 1908 to return to Liverpool, he trained and inspired two generations of local historians through his seminars and edited two huge volumes of the Liverpool town books, the fundamental source for its early modern history.[53]

Other universities taught and actively promoted research in local history between the wars. Manchester emulated Liverpool in starting a local history seminar[54] and Birmingham had a lecturer in local history in the person of Philip Styles.[55] In the mid-1920s the faculty of commerce at Birmingham housed a research fellowship on the city's industrial history sponsored by Cadbury Brothers and held by G.C. Allen, which led to his pioneering book on local economic history.[56] Provision was also made at the new university colleges in Exeter and Hull.[57] At Exeter the Devonshire Association's intended collaborative

52. *University of Liverpool calendar* (1919–20), p. 230. J. Tait (revised H.C.G. Matthew), 'Farrer, William (1861–1924), historian and genealogist', *ODNB*; *The Times*, 29 August 1924, p. 12b.

53. F.J. Routledge, 'Obituary: Associate Professor J.A. Twemlow, B.A.', *Transactions of the Historic Society of Lancashire and Cheshire*, 105 (1953), p. 211; *The Times*, 12 February 1954, p. 11b; biographical notes on Twemlow on Archives Hub website <http://www.archiveshub.ac.uk/news/0606twemlow.html/> accessed 15 June 2009; J.D. Cantwell, *The Public Record Office, 1838–1958* (London, 1991), pp. 344, 389, 405; *Calendar of entries in the papal registers relating to Great Britain and Ireland: papal letters*, 4–14 (HMSO, 1902–60); J.A. Twemlow (ed.), *Liverpool town books: proceedings of assemblies, common councils, portmoot courts, &c., 1550–1862*, 2 vols (Liverpool, 1918 and 1935), esp. 1, p. xxxii.

54. *Bulletin of the Institute of Historical Research* (hereafter *BIHR*), 9 (1931–2), p. 46.

55. Pugh, '*Victoria history*', p. 15.

56. G.C. Allen, *The industrial development of Birmingham and the Black Country, 1860–1927* (London, 1929); E. Ives, D. Drummond and L. Schwarz, *The first civic university, Birmingham 1880–1980: an introductory history* (Birmingham, 2000), p. 208.

57. *BIHR*, 8 (1930–1), p. 169; *The Times*, 24 November 1934, p. 17d; 1 August 1935, p. 10g.

history of the city became instead a History of Exeter Research Group, led by Professor W.J. Harte, which produced six useful monographs before 1939, the best known of which originated as W.G. Hoskins's MSc thesis in the department of economics.[58] In London one of the founding seminars at the new Institute of Historical Research was on the history of London and was conducted by the university's Reader in the History and Records of London (appointed 1921), Eliza Jeffries Davis of University College.[59] The idea that local history 'as a subject … had no place in modern universities' in the 1920s and 1930s is simply wrong.[60] Moreover, many of the growing numbers of postgraduate students in the period were researching local or regional topics in English economic, social, religious, and political history. Including research conducted in other departments and faculties (especially geography), 62 PhDs and 208 MAs (or equivalents like the Oxford BLitt) were awarded for such topics at English universities in the period 1919–39.[61] Most of their authors seem not to have continued as local historians active in research, but they were certainly doing local history of a kind.

Establishing roots in the universities was just one of the ways in which local history was firmly connected to the growing profession of history. The Royal Historical Society, too, was open to local history in its *Transactions* and to amateur local historians in its fellowship throughout the period. The Society was founded in the 1860s by upper-middle-class metropolitan literary dilettanti and only gradually fell under the control of serious historians, a change of regime that was complete by 1918. Throughout the 1920s and into the 1930s its literary director was Hubert Hall of the PRO (who also helped to supervise postgraduate researchers in the University of London) and its honorary secretary H.E. Malden, the leading local historian of Surrey.[62] The rise of university historians among the

58. F. Rose-Troup, *Lost chapels of Exeter* (Exeter, 1923); J.W. Schopp (ed.), *The Anglo-Norman custumal of Exeter, with facsimiles* (Oxford, 1925); A.G. Little and R.C. Easterling, *The Franciscans and Dominicans of Exeter* (Exeter, 1927); B. Wilkinson, *The mediaeval council of Exeter* (Manchester, [1931]); M.E. Curtis, *Some disputes between the city and the cathedral authorities of Exeter* (Manchester, 1932); W.G. Hoskins, *Industry, trade and people in Exeter 1688–1800, with special reference to the serge industry* (Manchester, 1935).

59. *University of London, Institute of Historical Research, annual reports: First*, 1921–2, p. 9; *Second*, 1922–3, p. 10; *Third*, 1923–4, p. 9; *Fourth*, 1924–5, p. 10; *Fifth*, 1925–6, p. 19; *Sixth*, 1926–7, p. 20. G. Parsloe, 'In memoriam E.J.D.', *BIHR*, 19 (1942–3), pp. 185–7; unsigned obituary in *History*, 29 (1944), pp. 1–2.

60. J. Beckett, 'Local history, family history and the Victoria County History: new directions for the twenty-first century', *Historical Research*, 81 (2008), pp. 350–65 at p. 353.

61. Calculated from lists of theses completed, in *History*, 4 (1919–20) to 13 (1928–9); *BIHR*, 7 (1929–30) to 9 (1931–2); *Supplement to BIHR*, 10 (1932–3) to 18 (1940–1).

62. R.A. Humphreys, *The Royal Historical Society, 1868–1968* (London, 1969); J.W. Burrow, 'Victorian historians and the Royal Historical Society', *Transactions of the Royal Historical Society* (hereafter *TRHS*), 5th series, 39 (1989), pp. 125–40; C. Johnson, 'Hubert Hall', *TRHS*, 4th series, 28 (1946), pp. 1–5; *The Times*, 18 March 1931, p. 11a (obituary of Malden).

fellowship and their increasing dominance of Council made the Society more receptive to local history, not less. Of 8 papers read in the 1918 session and published in the 1919 *Transactions* only one had anything like a local focus: Rose Graham on the archiepiscopal visitation of the diocese of Worcester in 1301. The 8 papers read in the 1939 session, by contrast, included 4 explicitly on local topics: Kathleen Major on the Lincoln diocesan records, Hilda Grieve on the married clergy of Essex under Queen Mary, Guy Parsloe on borough government in early modern Newark and R.W. Greaves on the Leicester parliamentary election of 1826.[63] Similarly, while none of the 13 Alexander Prizes awarded down to 1918 (to an historical essay on an approved subject) took a local topic, in the period 1919–39 the count was 4 out of 20.[64] It is difficult to measure the different professional backgrounds among the fellowship in 1939 (since in the published lists fellows indifferently gave professional and domestic addresses), but there were certainly at least 20 schoolteachers drawn from council schools as well as grammar and public schools.[65]

A fuller survey of activity in the world of local history between the wars than is possible here would need to take account of developments in at least seven other areas: record societies, local history societies in towns and suburbs, adult education courses, Historical Association branches, schools, museums and local recording groups. Their activities and personnel overlapped considerably. Six new county (or equivalent) record societies were established during the period, leaving fewer than one in three English counties without a body dedicated to publishing local records.[66] The Norfolk Record Society, founded in 1930 and with 130–140 members during its first decade, can be taken as representative. Its prospectus highlighted the interest of quarter sessions records, ship money and hearth tax lists, records of seventeenth-century religious persecution, cathedral and monastic records, manorial records in private hands, assize records, records of the admiralty courts and maritime trade, churchwardens' accounts, terriers and strip maps (to illustrate the open-field system), archidiaconal court proceedings (to show how ecclesiastical discipline worked in the parishes), municipal and parish records, heraldic visitations, muster rolls and early charters. The list is strikingly eclectic and 'modern', setting an agenda for opening up the materials of local

63. *TRHS*, 4th series, 2 (1919); 22 (1940).

64. 'Alexander Prize', *TRHS*, 4th series, 22 (1940), pp. 255–7.

65. *Ibid.*, pp. 262–84.

66. Oxfordshire Record Society 1919, Dugdale Society (Warwickshire) 1920, Northamptonshire Record Society 1920, Bristol Record Society 1929, Norfolk Record Society 1930, and Buckinghamshire Record Society 1937: Mullins, *Guide*; M. Pinhorn (comp.), *Historical, archaeological and kindred societies in the United Kingdom: a list* (Hulverstone Manor, Isle of Wight, 1986).

history for wider use a generation before Norfolk had a county record office.[67] The founding council of the record society was wholly amateur in composition – of the 13 members, only 4 had university degrees (4 were Fellows of the Society of Antiquaries and one a Fellow of the Royal Historical Society) – yet it set about its business in much the same way as its longer established counterparts in university towns, such as the Chetham Society in Manchester or the Record Society of Lancashire and Cheshire in Liverpool, which could draw on university historians as editors and officers. The parallels suggest the existence of a common local historical culture across England which transcended any supposed divide between professionals and amateurs.

Interest in local history was also increasingly expressed between the wars through societies focused on an individual town. There had been some local antiquarian, archaeological and occasionally historical societies from the late nineteenth century onwards, but more were founded in the 1920s and 1930s, and more often they had the word 'historical' in their name. Their total number is uncertain without much more research, but more than half of the two dozen that can be identified easily were located in the outer London suburbs or the Home Counties, at places such as Southend-on-Sea (1920), Mill Hill (1929) and Chingford (1939).[68]

The story of local history provision through university extension classes, the Workers' Educational Association (WEA) and the Historical Association (HA) remains to be explored in detail, but some pointers can be provided here. The testimony of F.W. Brooks of University College, Hull, is that in the late 1920s 'the subject had not yet caught on with the W.E.A.' but that classes provided in Yorkshire and the East Midlands by the universities and university colleges of Leeds, Sheffield, Hull and Nottingham fed an ever-growing surge of interest.[69] Local history within the HA was led by the branches rather than the central body, and, since at the inter-war peak there were over 90 branches and almost 5,000 full and associate members, there was probably a great deal of activity under way. The centralised local history committee set up in 1925 (initially as the village history committee) struggled to make itself useful or wanted by the branches,[70] but many of them continued to develop strong interests in the history of their own localities. In the 1930s the Nottingham branch, for example, had a local history section

67. Norfolk Record Society, 1 (1931), pp. [ii]–[iii]; J. Barney, *The Norfolk Record Society, 1930–2005* (Norwich, 2005), pp. 19–20; Jean Kennedy, 'Local archives of Great Britain, XXX: the Norfolk and Norwich Record Office', *Archives*, 8 (1967–8), pp. 63–9.

68. Mullins, *Guide*; Pinhorn, *List*.

69. F.W. Brooks, 'Local history 1930–1948', *Local Historian*, 10 (1972–3), pp. 385–9, at p. 386.

70. *The Historical Association, 1906–1956* (London, 1957), pp. 28, 31–4; *The Times*, 21 June 1926, p. 15f; *History*, 21 (1936–7), pp. 331–2, 340.

chaired by J.D. Chambers of the university college's adult education department, and its members were actively researching turnpike roads, enclosure, the settlement laws and early nineteenth-century housing, and had organised a local history exhibition, excavated a medieval site and started both a bibliography of Nottinghamshire history and a survey of documents in parish chests.[71]

More research is also needed on how much local history was taught in schools, and especially on whether the Board of Education's circular of 1908 (requiring that local history be used in secondary schools to illustrate the themes of national history) had widespread or lasting effect.[72] Two certain examples come from the early 1920s. In Staffordshire, the Newcastle-under-Lyme High School Archaeological Society (founded 1913) had lectures on local historical topics,[73] and in Somerset, William Wyndham endowed a series of local history lectures and field trips for secondary schools in five towns, also making provision for the schools to acquire museum exhibits and local history books.[74] Local history activities in schools may have been largely extra-curricular: a little earlier, W.E. Tate had been introduced to local history by his teacher at King Edward VI Grammar School in East Retford (Nottinghamshire) 'despite the time table'.[75]

Current research is showing that small village museums proliferated in the 1920s and 1930s,[76] and indeed in 1930 the Historical Association published a pamphlet about village history exhibitions written by one of Tate's parish chest correspondents and based on an example staged at Cowden (Kent) in 1922.[77] 'Recording schemes' to preserve factual information about village life and recent history were started almost simultaneously in Northamptonshire in 1923 by the county federation of Women's Institutes[78] and in Berkshire in 1924.[79] The idea

---

71. A. Cossons, *The turnpike roads of Nottinghamshire*, Historical Association Leaflet, 97 (London, 1934), p. 2.

72. H.P.R. Finberg, 'Local history', in H.P.R. Finberg and V.H.T. Skipp, *Local history: objective and pursuit* (Newton Abbot, 1967), pp. 25–44 at pp. 25–6.

73. N. Heard, 'School historical societies', *History*, 4 (1919–20), pp. 206–7.

74. L.C. Hayward, 'The study of local history', *History*, 31 (1946), pp. 125–9.

75. W.E. Tate, *Parliamentary land enclosures in the county of Nottingham during the 18th and 19th centuries (1743–1868)*, Thoroton Society Record Series, 5 (1935), dedication.

76. Thesis in progress at University of Gloucestershire by Bridget Yates: B. Yates, 'Volunteer-run museums in market towns and villages', *Rural History Today*, 16 (January 2009), pp. 2–3.

77. G. Ewing, *A village history exhibition as an educational factor … reprinted … from the 'Journal of the Ministry of Agriculture'*, Historical Association Leaflet, 81 (London, 1930).

78. J. Wake, *How to compile a history and present-day record of village life, written for the Women's Institutes of Northamptonshire* (Northampton, 1925), esp. p. [1].

79. M. Simons, 'The local history recording scheme', *Berkshire Local History Association Newsletter*, 84 (January 2006); M. Bayley, 'The Berkshire Local History Association, 1976–2006', *Berkshire Local History Association Newsletter*, 87 (January 2007).

was taken up more widely in the mid-1930s, and from 1937 such schemes were supported by a Local History Fund for Villages set up by the National Council for Social Service's Local History Sub-Committee (itself dating from 1934), with a grant from the Carnegie Trust. Before the war it was in touch with local bodies in 15 English counties, besides 2 Welsh and one Scottish.[80]

Local history activity between the wars was thus diverse, expanding and securely established both in the universities and at several new points in the voluntary sector. It already displayed many of the features which have been thought to characterise local history for the first time only in the period after 1945.

The scope of local history

Attention has already been drawn to how authors writing for the county journals were extending the reach of local history into many new topics. Space does not allow a full discussion of local history's growing intellectual agenda here, but it is clear that three branches of study which are commonly thought of as having enriched local history only after 1945 were in fact already there before: economic history, historical geography and medieval history. Similar points could be made about other sub-fields, such as population studies, landscape history and industrial archaeology.

Economic history has attracted attention because it was W.G. Hoskins's route into local history. It was itself an emerging discipline between the wars, deriving much of its vigour from local studies, not least at Manchester University. The subject was established there before the Great War by George Unwin, appointed in 1910 to the first chair in the subject anywhere in the country.[81] Unwin, significantly, had first become interested through a local topic, the felt-hat industry of his home town of Stockport,[82] and he had two of the essential attributes of the best local historians: he was 'a master of field-work' in the industrial towns of Lancashire and elsewhere, and a serendipitous discoverer and skilful exploiter of records, in his case eighteenth-century business records.[83]

A single example will have to suffice for the work that was being done at Manchester between the wars on local economic history. George Tupling was

80. London Metropolitan Archives, catalogue of LMA 4230 (British Association for Local History and Standing Conference for Local History).

81. [R.H. Tawney,] 'Introductory memoir', in R.H. Tawney (ed.), *Studies in economic history: the collected papers of George Unwin* (London, 1927), pp. xi–lxxiv at p. xliii.

82. *Ibid.*, pp. xxiii–xxiv, xxxvii–xxxix.

83. *Ibid.*, pp. lv, lix–lxi.

then a history master at Haslingden Grammar School, 20 miles north of Manchester. When he fell into Unwin's circle he already had London external degrees in history and economics,[84] and at Unwin's suggestion he undertook a PhD on the economic history of Rossendale before the Industrial Revolution, taking as his locality the larger area around Haslingden. He completed his thesis in 1925 and the Chetham Society published a revised and extended version in 1927.[85] Tupling's preface makes it clear that he saw local history as needing to satisfy local interest as well as contributing to general history,[86] an ambition of the best local history at any time. *The economic history of Rossendale* was taken seriously by the historical profession, being reviewed in *English Historical Review*,[87] *Economic History Review*,[88] the American journal *Speculum*[89] and elsewhere. The one faintly condescending note among reviewers can be discounted, since it came from the pen of a reviewer who later admitted his own lack of interest in original historical research and indeed left the field for sociology (what put him off was 'poring over original documents to the extent demanded by reputable historical research').[90] Other reviewers were full of praise: Charles Johnson of the PRO in *Antiquaries Journal*,[91] Arthur Redford of Manchester University in *Scottish Historical Review*,[92] and Alfred Plummer of Ruskin College, Oxford, in *Economic Journal*.[93]

The success of *Rossendale* drew Tupling, part-time mature student and amateur local historian, into the academic mainstream at Manchester, first as holder from 1929 of the honorary William Farrer Research Fellowship in Local

84. J.S. R[oskell], 'Obituary: George Henry Tupling (1883–1962)', *Transactions of the Lancashire and Cheshire Antiquarian Society*, 72 (1962), pp. 177–8.

85. G.H. Tupling, *The economic history of Rossendale*, Chetham Society, new series, 86 (1927), pp. v–vi.

86. *Ibid.*, p. vi.

87. *EHR*, 43 (1928), pp. 469–70.

88. J. de L. Mann, in *Economic History Review* (hereafter *EcHR*), [1st series] 2 (1929–30), pp. 346–8.

89. N.S.B. Gras, in *Speculum*, 3 (1928), pp. 410–11.

90. T.H. M[arshall], in *EHR*, 43 (1928), pp. 469–70; T.H. Marshall, 'A British sociological career', *International Social Science Journal*, 25 (1973), pp. 88–100, quotation at p. 91; A.H. Halsey, 'Marshall, Thomas Humphrey (1893–1981), sociologist', *ODNB*.

91. He found the book 'corrective of the sweeping historical and economic generalization with which we are only too familiar': *Antiquaries Journal*, 8 (1928), pp. 381–2, quotation at p. 381.

92. He wrote that 'readers nourished on the local histories written in previous generations will feel, indeed, that this is local history of an altogether new kind': *Scottish Historical Review*, 25 (1928), pp. 55–6, quotation at p. 55.

93. 'Such studies of limited areas are very welcome because, apart from the intrinsic interest of the facts and forces that they reveal, they enable us to check accepted generalisations': *Economic Journal*, 37 (1927), pp. 661–3, quotation at p. 661.

History,[94] then from 1935 as Special Lecturer in Local History, where his influence on other amateur local historians in the region is clear enough.[95] His own interests expanded, centring before the Second World War on the markets and fairs of Lancashire.[96] The clearest signal of his personal standing, and also an indication of the high value placed on his approach to local history, is his presence as a contributor to the *festschrift* prepared for James Tait's seventieth birthday in 1933, where the Haslingden schoolmaster formed ranks with professors from 11 universities in 6 countries and fellows of 9 Oxbridge colleges, among them 8 Fellows of the British Academy.[97] Tupling's local history was fully part of the discipline of history between the wars, not on its margins.

Nonetheless there was a tension within economic history between local studies and 'sweeping… generalization', and most economic historians resolved it at the expense of locality, or at any rate by making local studies subordinate to their wider interests. While they tended to recognise that many more local studies were needed, they were not necessarily intending to undertake them personally.[98] The point is well illustrated by one of Tupling's reviewers, Alfred Plummer. In the 1930s he produced an important work of local economic history in a ground-breaking edition of the records of the Witney blanket industry, with a substantial introductory essay,[99] but also a monograph about the new British industries of the twentieth century (electricity supply, motor vehicles, aluminium, rayon, canning, sugar beet and more) which had absolutely no interest in how places were transformed by such industries.[100] The wealth of possibilities that he missed is indicated by later work on Banbury (like Witney in Oxfordshire), where a large aluminium factory was opened in 1933.[101] The main contrary tendency, towards local studies, came in medieval economic history in the very late 1930s, when a new generation of postgraduates, including R.A.L. Smith (d. 1944), Marjorie

---

94. *BIHR*, 7 (1929–30), p. 42.

95. e.g. W. Bennett, *The history of Burnley to 1400* (Burnley, 1946), p. 3; Bennett was history master at Burnley Grammar School (personal knowledge).

96. Bibliography in *Transactions of the Lancashire and Cheshire Antiquarian Society*, 72 (1962), pp. 178–9.

97. J.G. Edwards, V.H. Galbraith and E.F. Jacob (eds), *Historical essays in honour of James Tait* (Manchester, 1933), pp. vii–ix; V.H. Galbraith (revised K.D. Reynolds), 'Tait, James (1863–1944), historian', *ODNB*.

98. N.S.B. Gras, 'The rise of economic history', *EcHR*, 1 (1927–8), pp. 12–34 at p. 31.

99. A. Plummer (ed.), *The Witney blanket industry: the records of the Witney blanket weavers* (London, 1934); also A. Plummer and R.E. Early, *The blanket makers, 1669–1969: a history of Charles Early and Marriott (Witney) Ltd.* (Witney, 1969).

100. A. Plummer, *New British industries in the twentieth century: a survey of development and structure* (London, 1937).

101. M. Stacey, *Tradition and change: a study of Banbury* (Oxford, 1960).

Morgan (later Chibnall), Rodney Hilton and Edward Miller began studying the local estates of monastic houses, the last two visiting the PRO 'with a notebook in one hand and Lenin in the other'.[102]

The second source of enrichment for local history between the wars was historical geography. By 1914 geography was taught in all British universities, but it became a free-standing discipline only after the Great War.[103] Regional geography was its intellectual driving force throughout these early years – a 'thick description' of the physical and human characteristics which defined individual regions – and always had a strong historical dimension. Several of the leading figures in inter-war geography had begun as historians, including P.R. Roxby, who created the influential geography department at Liverpool after 1917.[104]

As the subject grew in the 1930s, historical geography became more clearly defined as a sub-discipline, owing much to the young Clifford Darby's determination to historicise the geography of regions.[105] Darby's projects were national in scope, whether the successive incarnations of the *Historical geography of England* (1936)[106] or the *Domesday geographies* (whose seeds were sown in the later 1930s),[107] but such ambitions could be attained only by building up from local and regional studies. So, although a separate disciplinary space was soon carved out for historical geography, it overlapped deeply with local history in subject matter, sources, and approaches. They shared an eagerness to cover long periods of time, an awareness of topography and spatial differentiation, and a close attention to original sources.

As a result it can be difficult to distinguish one sub-discipline from the other. Instances can be found in several of Roxby's students at Liverpool, but the

---

102. I thank Prof. Christopher Dyer for drawing my attention to this group, and for the quotation. See C. Dyer, 'Rodney Howard Hilton, 1916–2002', *Proceedings of the British Academy*, 130 (2005) [*Memoirs*, 4], pp. 52–77 at pp. 54–5.

103. H.C. Darby, 'Academic geography in Britain: 1918–1946', *Transactions of the Institute of British Geographers*, new series, 8 (1983), pp. 14–26; R. Johnston, 'The institutionalisation of geography as an academic discipline', in R. Johnston and M. Williams (eds), *A century of British geography* (Oxford, 2003), pp. 45–90.

104. Darby, 'Academic geography', pp. 18, 19; E.W. Gilbert, 'Percy Maude Roxby (1880–1947)', in his *British pioneers in geography* (Newton Abbot, 1972), pp. 211–26; R.W. Steel, 'Geography at the University of Liverpool', in R.W. Steel and R. Lawton (eds), *Liverpool essays in geography* (London, 1967), pp. 1–23 at pp. 1–9; R.W. Steel (ed.), *British geography 1918–1945* (Cambridge, 1987).

105. H.C. Prince, 'H.C. Darby and the historical geography of England', in H.C. Darby *et al*, *The relations of history and geography: studies in England, France and the United States* (Exeter, 2002), pp. 63–90; M. Williams, 'Darby, Sir (Henry) Clifford (1909–1992), geographer', *ODNB*.

106. Reprinted with corrections (Cambridge, 1948); H.C. Darby (ed.), *A new historical geography of England* (Cambridge, 1973).

107. H.C. Darby, 'On the writing of Domesday geography', in his *Domesday England* (Cambridge, 1977), pp. 375–84.

example offered here is R.A. Pelham, who started out reading geography at Aberystwyth (BA 1927, MA 1930) under Professor H.J. Fleure, and held appointments as lecturer in geography first at Birmingham (where he was awarded a PhD in 1934 for his published work) and after the Second World War at Southampton.[108] In the 1930s he was a founding and active member of the Institute of British Geographers (1933)[109] and had two chapters in Darby's *Historical geography of England* (1936),[110] but could equally be counted a local historian. He joined the Sussex Archaeological Society as a student in 1928,[111] was elected a fellow of the Royal Historical Society in the mid-1940s,[112] published more than two dozen articles in a string of local historical and archaeological journals[113] and had started work on the history of Birmingham for the *VCH* when the Second World War intervened.[114]

Mainstream medieval history was a third subject which invigorated and shaped a new sort of local history between the wars. This process has been obscured not because medieval history was still finding its feet (as with economic history and historical geography), but because there has been a mistaken idea that the constitutional and administrative medievalism of Stubbs and Tout

---

108. *The Pharos: The Magazine of the Dover County School for Boys*, 76 (July 1934), 'Old Pharosians'; *The Pharos: The Magazine of the Dover County School for Boys*, new series, 80 (July 2001), 'News of Old Boys' both at <http://www.dovergrammar.co.uk/archives/old-pharos/pharos-menu.html/> accessed 23 May 2010; *University of Birmingham: register of degrees, diplomas & certificates, 1900–1935* (Birmingham, 1937), p. 131. I owe these references to the kindness of Philippa Bassett, senior archivist, University of Birmingham Special Collections. P. Gruffudd, 'Fleure, Herbert John (1877–1969), geographer and anthropologist', *ODNB*.

109. *Transactions and Papers of the Institute of British Geographers* (hereafter Transactions), 1 (Transactions, 1935), pp. v, ix; 4 (Transactions, 1936), pp. v–vi; 7 (Transactions, 1937), p. v; 9 (Transactions, 1938), p. v.

110. 'Fourteenth-century England' and 'Medieval foreign trade: eastern ports', in Darby (ed.), *Historical geography of England*, pp. 230–65, 298–329.

111. *SAC*, 70 (1929), p. xxix, and later issues.

112. *TRHS*, 4th series, 24 (1942) [not a fellow]; *ibid.*, 25–9 (1943–7) lack lists of fellows; *ibid.*, 30 (1948), p. 192.

113. *Archaeologia Cantiana*, 44 (1932), pp. 218–28; *SAC*, 75 (1934), pp. 129–35; 78 (1937), pp. 195–210, 211–23; *Sussex Notes & Queries*, 5 (1934–5), pp. 18–19, 33–4, 101–3, 166–71, 205–6; 6 (1936–7), pp. 201–4; *Transactions & Proceedings of the Birmingham Archaeological Society*, 61 (1940 for 1937), pp. 45–80; 62 (1943 for 1938), pp. 32–40; 63 (1944 for 1939–40), pp. 41–62; 66 (1950 for 1945–6), pp. 131–41, 142–9, 150–5; 68 (1952 for 1949–50), pp. 89–106; 78 (1962), pp. 125–38; *University of Birmingham Historical Journal*, 2 (1949–50), pp. 141–62; 3 (1951–2), pp. 16–32; 4 (1953–4), pp. 18–29; 5 (1955–6), pp. 60–82; 6 (1957–8), pp. 161–75; 9 (1963–4), pp. 64–91; *Transactions of the Worcestershire Archaeological Society*, 29 (1952), pp. 50–52; *Collections for a History of Staffordshire* (Staffordshire Record Society) (1954 for 1950–1), pp. 229–42; *Wiltshire Archaeological and Natural History Magazine*, 54 (1951–2), pp. 92–103, 350–60; *Papers & Proceedings of the Hampshire Field Club & Archaeological Society*, 18 (1953–4), pp. 139–53; *The Old Mills of Southampton*, Southampton Papers, 3 (Southampton, 1963).

114. *VCH Warwickshire*, 7 (1964), p. xv.

continued to carry all before them.[115] If attention is paid instead to Maitland and Tait and their admirers between the wars what emerges is a growing concern with topography and with the origins of places and communities, prefiguring an important part of the subject matter of local history since the Second World War. Maitland, who never confessed himself a historian, let alone a local historian,[116] nonetheless wrote a path-breaking local study of a medieval town, Cambridge, which combined close scrutiny of documents and maps, fieldwork, topographical reconstruction and institutional history. His approach amounted to a sophisticated reshaping of the framework needed for writing the history of a medieval town.[117] Maitland was inspiring for professional and amateur historians alike between the wars, leading on the one hand to Helen Cam's work on Cambridge[118] and her protégée Mary Lobel's pioneering monograph on Bury St Edmunds,[119] and on the other to the solicitor Frank Hill's fine book on medieval Lincoln, begun in the 1920s.[120]

Maitland also wrote a remarkable study of social and economic conditions on a single manor, Wilburton in the Isle of Ely, where he justified the purest sort of local history: 'to me it seems that at the present time we have some need for histories of particular manors, for I am convinced that the time has not yet come when generalities about *the* English manor and its fortunes will be safe or sound'.[121] That study set in train the entire field of local and regional manorial

---

115. Their historical interests are succinctly set out in J. Campbell, 'Stubbs, William (1825–1901), historian and bishop of Oxford', *ODNB*; V.H. Galbraith (revised P.R.H. Slee), 'Tout, Thomas Frederick (1855–1929), historian', *ODNB*.

116. S.F.C. Milsom, 'Maitland, Frederic William (1850–1906), legal historian', *ODNB*; C.H.S. Fifoot, *Frederic William Maitland: a life* (Cambridge, MA, 1971); H.E. Bell, *Maitland: a critical examination and assessment* (London, 1965), pp. 17–45; G.R. Elton, *F.W. Maitland* (London, 1985), pp. 19–55.

117. F.W. Maitland, *Township and borough* (Cambridge, 1898). Beckett, *Writing local history*, p. 90, conflates *Township and borough* with *Domesday Book and beyond* (Cambridge, 1897).

118. H.M. Cam, 'The origin of the borough of Cambridge: a consideration of Professor Carl Stephenson's theories', in her *Liberties & communities in medieval England: collected studies in local administration and topography* (Cambridge, 1944), pp. 1–18 (prepared 1933); 'The early burgesses of Cambridge in relation to the surrounding country-side', in her *Liberties & communities*, pp. 19–48 (first published 1938); 'The city of Cambridge', *VCH Cambridgeshire*, 3 (1959), pp. 1–149 (evidently commissioned 1935: *ibid.*, p. xv).

119. M.D. Lobel, *The borough of Bury St. Edmund's: a study in the government and development of a monastic town* (Oxford, 1935).

120. J.W.F. Hill, *Medieval Lincoln* (Cambridge, 1948), pp. [xiii], xv; D. Owen, 'Sir Francis Hill, 1899–1980', in F. Hill, *Medieval Lincoln* (reprinted Stamford, 1990), pp. 1–12; P. Race, 'Hill, Sir (James William) Francis (1899–1980), lawyer and historian', *ODNB*.

121. F.W. Maitland, 'The history of a Cambridgeshire manor', *EHR*, 9 (1894), pp. 417–39, quotation at p. 417; reprinted in H.A.L. Fisher (ed.), *The collected papers of Frederic William Maitland*, 3 vols (Cambridge, 1911), 2, pp. 366–402, and in H.M. Cam (ed.), *Selected historical essays of F.W. Maitland* (Cambridge, 1957), pp. 16–40.

history which began in the Edwardian period and gathered pace between the wars.[122] Others in the inter-war generation of medieval historians took from Maitland a keen awareness of the importance of local studies and of locality as a governing principle of historical enquiry. Helen Cam, who called Maitland 'the historians' historian' and was full of praise for his close knowledge of the history of places,[123] introduced a collection of her own studies from the 1920s and 1930s with an essay 'In defence of the study of local history'.[124]

What of the *VCH* between the wars? There are instructive lessons here about direction and intellectual leadership in difficult times. The *VCH* had two general editors in the period, William Page (d. 1934) and L.F. Salzman (appointed 1935),[125] and, despite its financial difficulties and tiny staff, did not stand still. Page, still operating independently, was able to start or resume work on Huntingdonshire, Kent, Northamptonshire, Rutland and Sussex by securing financial guarantees from wealthy supporters. Salzman, working from the Institute of Historical Research, pushed ahead with Sussex and started work on Cambridgeshire, Oxfordshire and Warwickshire with help from local authorities and other sponsors.[126] All this paved the way for post-war expansion on a much larger scale and with more secure finances.

The inter-war *VCH* tends to be thought of as being of a piece with the Edwardian volumes, where parish histories comprised little more than manorial descents and church architecture. In fact both general editors, prolific scholars of great range in their own right, were fully aware of how the scope and content of

---

122. Including F.G. Davenport, *The economic development of a Norfolk manor [Forncett], 1086–1565* (Cambridge, 1906); F.M. Stenton, 'Types of manorial structure in the northern Danelaw', in P. Vinogradoff (ed.), *Oxford studies in social and legal history* (Oxford, 1910); W. Rees, *South Wales and the March, 1284–1415: a social and agrarian study* (Oxford, 1924); D.C. Douglas, *The social structure of medieval East Anglia* (Oxford, 1927); A.E. Levett, *Studies in manorial history*, ed. H.M. Cam, M. Coate and L.S. Sutherland (Oxford, 1938).

123. H. Cam, 'Maitland: the historians' historian', in her *Law-finders and law-makers in medieval England: collected studies in legal and constitutional history* (London, 1962), pp. 212–34 at pp. 215–16, reprinted with alterations from Cam (ed.), *Selected historical essays of Maitland*, pp. ix–xxix at pp. xii–xiii.

124. Cam, *Liberties & communities*, pp. ix–xiv; K. Major, 'Cam, Helen Maud (1885–1968), historian', *ODNB*.

125. Where not otherwise stated, information about the *VCH* is drawn from Pugh, 'Victoria history', pp. 10–16. C.P. Lewis, 'William Page (1861–1934)', in *Making history: the changing face of the profession in Britain* <http://www.history.ac.uk/makinghistory/resources/articles/william_page.html/> accessed 23 May 2010. For Salzman, I.D. Margary, 'Louis Francis Salzman, C.B.E., F.S.A.: an appreciation', *SAC*, 97 (1959), pp. 1–2; F.B. Stevens, '1896 & 1956: a comparison', *SAC*, 97 (1959), pp. 89–97 at p. 89; F.W.S[teer], 'Louis Francis Salzman, 1878–1971', *SAC*, 109 (1971), pp. 1–3; *The Times*, 6 April 1971, p. 18g; R.B. Pugh, 'Salzman, Louis Francis (1878–1971), antiquary and historian', *ODNB*.

126. *VCH Cambridgeshire*, 2 (1948), p. xiii; 3 (1959), p. xv; *Oxfordshire*, 1 (1939), p. xiv; 3 (1954), p. xv; *Sussex*, 3 (1935), p. xiii; 4 (1953), p. xv; 9 (1937), p. xv; *Warwickshire*, 3 (1945), p. xiii; 4 (1947), p. xiii.

local history were changing, and tweaked the *VCH* formula accordingly. In some respects the *VCH* was at the cutting edge of scholarship. Salzman, for example, put into the newly restarted Sussex series a great deal of what would now be called vernacular architecture at a time when only a handful of enthusiasts were beginning to record lesser secular buildings. More widely, the success of the inter-war *VCH* volumes depended on three things. First, the general editors commissioned authors who had demonstrated that they were capable of research to *VCH* standards and could write in the way that was needed.[127] For the general articles on Huntingdonshire, for example, Page secured the services of such stars as Cyril Fox, author of *Archaeology of the Cambridge region* (and shortly appointed director of the National Museum of Wales),[128] Marjerie Taylor, editor of the *Journal of Roman Studies*, and Frank Stenton. For the topographical articles (parish histories) experiments were made with local amateur authors, but they almost always fell short of the quality needed in research, writing and referencing; most of the Huntingdonshire parish histories were thus written by members of the pre-war team of experienced *VCH* assistants (what Page called his School of Local History): Ada Russell, Dorothy Powell, Maud Simkins and Catherine Jamison. Secondly, Page wrote dozens of letters to local clergymen and other residents asking for information on particular points of parish history, and then tirelessly sent round draft histories (in galley proofs) for comments and correction. The third volume of *Northamptonshire*, for example, thanks well over 50 people for help of that kind. Thirdly, he edited everything himself, bringing to bear his great knowledge of all aspects of English local history and his skill in drafting lucid, economical prose. The high standards of topographical writing that could be achieved in this period are shown best by the article on the borough of Northampton commissioned from Helen Cam, a 'formidably erudite' medievalist of international distinction.[129] She produced a rounded and succinct history of the town, with much fuller treatment of its physical growth and economy than was included in the *VCH* before the Great War, as well as keeping the older staples of borough government, parish churches and municipal charities.[130]

Page's openness to new approaches in local history appeared in many ways. His topographical volume on Rutland, for example, included brief but informative

127. What follows relies on the *VCH* archives at the Institute of Historical Research (hereafter IHR), and summarises an unpublished paper by the present author on the history of *VCH Huntingdonshire*.

128. C. Scott-Fox, *Cyril Fox: archaeologist extraordinary* (Oxford, 2002).

129. C. Robbins, 'Helen Maud Cam, C.B.E.', in *Album Helen Maud Cam*, 2 vols (Louvain and Paris, 1960–1), 1, pp. 1–6 at p. 4.

130. *VCH Northamptonshire*, 3 (1930), pp. 1–67.

comments on village plans.[131] But it is best illustrated by the article on the drainage of the Middle Level of the Fens which appeared in the third volume of *Huntingdonshire*. The idea originated with Granville Proby, an amateur local historian who was backing the county volumes financially, but it was Page who saw its potential. He began by writing to Cyril Fox in 1926: 'I am anxious to get an article in the *VCH* on the reclamation of the Middle Level of the Fen District … Do you happen to know a promising Cambridge student who would care to undertake the work? It struck me that it might be developed further, possibly for a thesis for a Ph.D. degree.'[132] Fox was keen and asked around.[133] Stenton in Reading got to hear of the idea and wrote to Page to recommend a new research student of his, Phyllis Crowther.[134] She completed her doctoral thesis in 1929 and her chapter for the *VCH* was in Page's hands by the end of the year.[135] Being part of a thesis, it needed revision, but there was a delay extending beyond Page's death in 1934 while other articles for the volume were in preparation. When approached by Granville Proby to revise the chapter, Phyllis declined on the grounds that she had lost touch with the subject after marrying and moving to Halifax[136] (where, as Phyllis Ramsden, she was a lifelong member of the Antiquarian Society and much later played an important part in making the remarkable journals of Anne Lister known to scholars).[137] Instead, in circumstances on which the *VCH*'s records shed no light (this was shortly after Page had died and before Salzman was appointed as general editor), revision was handed to H.C. Darby, who had completed his own PhD on the Fens at Cambridge in 1931.[138] He revised her work heavily enough for the chapter to appear under his own name 'with the collaboration of'

---

131. *VCH Rutland*, 2 (1935); cf. 'The origins and forms of Hertfordshire towns and villages', *Archaeologia*, 69 (1920), pp. 47–60; 'Notes on the types of English villages and their distribution', *Antiquity*, 1 (1927), pp. 447–68.

132. IHR, *VCH* Records, A6, Page to Fox, 19 September 1924; 5 October 1926.

133. *Ibid.*, Fox to Page, 7 October 1926.

134. *Ibid.*, Stenton to Page, 18 October 1926; 28 October 1926.

135. *Ibid.*, Crowther to Page, 10 January [1927]; Page to Proby, 10 October 1927; Crowther to Page, 16 December 1927; Crowther to Page, 17 May [1928]; Page to Crowther, 18 May 1928; Page to Proby, 3 October 1929. P.M. Crowther, 'The reclamation of the Middle Level of the Fens' (PhD thesis, Reading, 1929).

136. IHR, *VCH* records, A6, Page to Proby, 31 July 1930; B2, Proby's secretary to Ramsden, 5 March 1934; Ramsden to Proby, 8 March [1934].

137. Member of the Society from 1934: *Transactions of the Halifax Antiquarian Society* (hereafter *THAS*) (1933), at end; (1934), at end; her only publications there were 'Haigh House, Warley', *THAS* (1936), pp. 133–7, and 'Anne Lister's journal (1817–1840)', *THAS* (1970), pp. 1–13. For her role in Lister scholarship: J. Liddington, 'Anne Lister of Shibden Hall, Halifax (1791–1840): re-reading the correspondence', *THAS*, new series, 1 (1993), pp. 62–78. I owe my knowledge of her Halifax years to Dr John Hargreaves, editor of *THAS*.

138. H.C. Darby, 'The role of the Fenland in English history' (PhD thesis, Cambridge, 1931).

Phyllis Ramsden.[139] The intersection of Page's innovative ideas about what the *VCH* should cover – and what local history should comprehend – with Darby's agenda for the emerging discipline of historical geography is very striking.

Conclusion

It would not be right to claim too much for local history as practised between the wars – and calling it a Great Awakening may go too far – but enough has been said to make it clear that post-war developments evolved from pre-war conditions rather than setting off in revolutionary new directions.[140] One aspect notably absent before the Leicester School became established was much in the way of explicit theorising about the scope of local history. It was largely taken for granted that the parish or town was the appropriate unit of study, and most parish and town histories sought to appeal only to a local constituency. One line of thinking occasionally made explicit was the idea that studying in depth the lives of people who were rooted in a locality provided more authentic contact with the national story: local history as English history in miniature.[141] That view had been well expressed by one of the Edwardian pioneers, W.M. Childs, who hoped to establish at Reading 'a living interest in the study of local history *as a means of illustrating the wider study of national history*' (my italics).[142] In the early 1920s George Unwin could plausibly state that 'the generally accepted idea of local history is that it is an account of events of national importance happening within a given locality', only to disagree strongly.[143] Narrow views of local history could still be found among academics in the 1920s and 1930s. Chambers, for example, thought of his well-received book on Nottinghamshire as 'essentially an attempt to use local history in the service of general history', although in reality he was more of a local and regional historian than that unguarded (and youthful)

---

139. *VCH Huntingdonshire*, 3 (1936), pp. 249–90.

140. C. Phythian-Adams, 'The department of English local history (1948–1998): contexts and evolution', in M. Tranter, K. Hawker, J. Rowley and M. Thompson (comp.), *English local history: the Leicester approach. A departmental bibliography and history, 1948–1998* (Leicester, 1999), pp. 1–28.

141. e.g. Sir H. Lambert, *The value of local history: an inaugural address given [to the Mid-Surrey Branch of the Historical Association] on 25th May, 1934* (Epsom, 1935), esp. p. 3; H.C.M. Lambert, *History of Banstead in Surrey* (London, 1912–31); *Who was who*, 1929–1940, 2nd edn (London, 1967), p. 773.

142. Quotation in Stenton, *Early history of Abingdon*, p. iv.

143. Review in *History*, 6 (1921–2), pp. 114–17 at p. 114.

144. Chambers, *Nottinghamshire*, p. vi; 2nd edn (London, 1966), p. xxiv; commendatory reviews include *EHR*, 48 (1933), pp. 716–17, and *EcHR*, [1st series] 4 (1932–4), pp. 365–7. For Chambers's approach: Marshall, *Tyranny of the discrete*, pp. 12–13; E.L. Jones and G.E. Mingay (eds), *Land, labour and population in the Industrial Revolution: essays presented to J.D. Chambers* (London, 1967), pp. [ix], [xiv]–xvii; *Who was who*, 1961–1970 (London, 1972), p. 193.

statement allowed,[144] and the more ambitious ideals for local history as pursued by George Tupling or Helen Cam pointed the way firmly to future developments.

The different worlds of local history encountered in this chapter were not sealed off one from another. Many interconnections will have been apparent, as historians mentioned here in one context then reappeared in another. More work is needed on scholarly networks of all kinds, but one among dozens of examples will suffice to underline how changing ideas about the scope and practice of local history could spread. The squire of Aldermaston in Berkshire who supported Stenton's fleeting local history fellowship at Reading before the Great War was C.E. Keyser, himself an active and distinguished antiquary who published two important books and many articles on ecclesiastical architecture and wall paintings. His contacts straddled several different worlds since, besides his support for University College, Reading, he was an active Fellow of the Society of Antiquaries in London, was involved in several other national bodies and three different county archaeological societies, and assisted the *VCH* by reading the proofs of Aldermaston and other parishes and lending photographs of churches for reproduction.[145]

This paper has only scratched the surface of a complex story of intellectual links and cross-currents between different fields and different groups of people who were interested in local history between the world wars. But it shows that some of the ways in which we think of post-war English local history as lively, 'modern' and intellectually rigorous – creativity in exploring new sources, interest in the origins of settlements and communities, a concern with topography and buildings, a sense of spatial relationships between places – were developing already in the 1920s and 1930s, in some cases on foundations laid even earlier. Some of the scholars involved would not have defined themselves primarily (or even at all) as local historians, but they were shaping a new intellectual agenda for English local history which studied places for their own sake but also because they shed light on wider problems. This was, after all, the period and the milieu in which W.G. Hoskins himself served his apprenticeship as a historian. He, too, straddled many of the different sub-worlds of local history outlined here. Heavily influenced as an undergraduate and postgraduate at Exeter by two men trained in the Manchester school of economic history (Joseph Sykes and W.J. Harte),[146] attached to the Exeter Research Group, employed from

---

145. *Who was who*, 1929–1940, 2nd edn (London, 1967), p. 750; his main works were *A list of buildings in Britain and Ireland having mural and other painted decoration*, 3rd edn (London, 1883) and *A list of Norman tympana and lintels* (London, 1904); Mullins, *Guide*, p. 821 indexes his journal publications from 1901; *VCH Berkshire*, 3 (1923), pp. xxi, 390.

146. I owe this point to Dr R.B. Peberdy, who is writing a biography of Hoskins.

1931 in a department of commerce headed by a geographer, active in his county archaeological society in Leicestershire and involved in teaching extramural classes,[147] Hoskins was one among many who shaped the great awakening of local history in the inter-war years.

---

147. J. Thirsk, 'William George Hoskins, 1908–1992', *Proceedings of the British Academy*, 87 (1992), pp. 339–54 at pp. 341–2.

3. Twentieth-century labour histories

Malcolm Chase

During the late 1950s and 1960s labour history established itself as a distinctively specialist field within history. It sought (as it continues to do) to illuminate and analyse the culture and movements of working people, particularly those movements and institutions whose momentum crucially derived from their members' shared perception of their interests as workers. A powerful disposition among labour historians towards local studies shaped this academic endeavour. Indeed, labour history in its formative phase seemed at times almost a specialist field of local history; it emerged exactly as Hoskins's influence was extending and its impact was profound both within and beyond the academic study of history.

The formation of the Society for the Study of Labour History in 1960 did much to define and extend the field's distinctiveness from its mightier cognate disciplines of economic and social history. Some of the most influential and widely read of any historians in the past half-century have written extensively on labour history, the most obvious examples being E.P. Thompson and Eric Hobsbawm. This has undoubtedly enhanced the reputation of labour history. Yet it has also always been rooted in the study of locality, despite the considerable standing of those lofty names and, more particularly, labour history's strong inclination towards the grand and generalising narrative of Marxism. This essay seeks to tease out why this is so before considering some aspects of the labour history of the twentieth century itself where local studies still have a critical role to play.

Labour history in its formative period – and for a long time thereafter – was particularly the province of the historian working in adult education, specifically university extra-mural classes. A defining feature of extra-mural education was a commitment to academic rigour combined with a distinguished history of reaching out 'beyond the walls' to students in their own communities. A local historical perspective therefore became a powerful educative tool with which academic labour historians reached out to their primary audience, recognising with Hoskins that 'the bigger and more incomprehensible the modern world grows the more people will turn to study something of which they can grasp the scale and in which they can find a personal and individual meaning'.[1]

Thompson's classic book *The making of the English working class* (1963) was precisely a product of this world. Written while Thompson was a lecturer for the University of Leeds' extra-mural department, it is essentially a study of the industrial revolution as seen from the textile regions of the Pennine uplands, and was dedicated to two stalwarts from the author's Cleckheaton evening class. Hobsbawm's whole academic career was spent at Birkbeck, London University's college for part-time mature students. In the 1950s and 1960s, young extra-mural historians would find themselves suddenly immersed in unfamiliar localities amidst earnest students whose command of recent – and not-so-recent – labour movement history was often remarkable and compelling. 'One was conscious of being part of a tradition', the distinguished social historian J.F.C. Harrison recalled of his extra-mural career at Leeds. He was particularly influenced by one student, a woolpacker, who 'talked about Ernest Jones, the Halifax Chartist leader, as if he had died yesterday, instead of in 1869'. Another 'rising star' among labour historians, Royden Harrison of the Sheffield extra-mural department, dedicated his first book to the Derbyshire miners' leader 'Bert Wynn and all my friends and comrades in the coalfields of Derbyshire and Yorkshire'.[2]

Much labour history in this early period was avowedly provincial. In his contribution to the seminal 1960 collection *Essays in labour history* Thompson paid 'Homage' to an obscure Leeds–Irish socialist, opening with a vigorous assault on national histories that disregarded local evidence as 'dubious ... unless required for "colour"':

> The national historian ... tends to have a curiously distorted view of goings-on 'in the provinces' ... Provincial leaders are commonly denied full historical citizenship ... labour historians tend to fall into a double-

---

1. W.G. Hoskins, *Local history in England* (London, 1959), p. 8.

2. D. Goodway, 'E.P. Thompson and the making of the English working class', in R.K.S. Taylor (ed.), *Beyond the walls: 50 years of adult and continuing education at the University of Leeds, 1946–1996* (Leeds, 1996), pp. 138–9; J.F.C. Harrison, *Scholarship boy: a personal history of the mid-twentieth century* (London, 1995), pp. 127, 175; R. Harrison, *Before the socialists: studies in labour and politics, 1861–1881* (London, 1965), p. v. My analysis here and in the following three paragraphs draws on M. Chase and J. Allen, 'Great Britain, 1750–1900', in J. Allen, A. Campbell and J. McIlroy (eds), *Histories of labour: national and transnational perspectives* (Pontypool, 2010), pp. 64–98.

vision; on the one hand, there are mass movements which grow blindly and spontaneously under economic and social pressures: on the other [there are] leaders and manipulators ... who direct these elemental forces into political channels.

Thompson then went on to argue that the 'superficial national approach is beginning to give way to a more mature school of local history'.[3] This development was significantly expedited by many of the landmark studies in labour history published around this time, notably the collection *Chartist studies*, edited by Asa Briggs, which appeared in 1959, the same year as Hoskins's *Local history in England*.[4] Hoskins's works were part of the mental furniture of those who contributed to labour history's coming of age. While they did not share his distaste for modernity, Hoskins's influence arguably shaped their concern to root their investigations in the familiar and the local. Like Hoskins, the dedicatee of *Essays in labour history*, G.D.H. Cole (*doyen* of the earlier generation of labour historians) 'never cared much for abroad' and was a keen rambler.[5] A similar temperament can be discerned in several of the post-1945 generation of labour historians.[6]

The remarkable flowering of labour history during the 1960s was, of course, not solely the consequence of its connection with adult education and its sensitivity to the significance of local history. It reflected broader intellectual trends (of which Hoskins's writings were also part). 'Economic history is beginning to escape from the clutches of the economist', wrote the medievalist Herbert Hallam in 1958, reflecting that 'the best economic historians are beginning to see the major factors in economic history which are not really economic at all'.[7] In his illuminating historiographical survey *Modernising England's past* Michael Bentley has delineated the emergence of social history around this time from a convergence of *Annaliste* influences, the increasing synthesis of economic, social and geographic elements and an older tradition of historically grounded, 'humanistic social

---

3. E.P. Thompson, 'Homage to Tom Maguire', in A. Briggs and J. Saville (eds), *Essays in labour history* (London, 1960), pp. 276–7.

4. A. Briggs (ed.), *Chartist studies* (London, 1959).

5. Gaitskell also affectionately described Cole as 'really a little Southern Englander', with 'a certain nostalgia for pre-industrial Britain': see H. Gaitskell, 'At Oxford in the twenties', in A. Briggs and J. Saville (eds), *Essays in labour history* (London, 1960), pp. 12–13.

6. For example, Ian Dyck makes a conscious parallel in an appreciation of Harrison, in M. Chase and I. Dyck (eds), *Living and learning: essays in honour of J.F.C. Harrison* (Aldershot, 1996), pp. 6–7.

7. Quoted in M. Bentley, *Modernizing England's past: English historiography in the age of modernism, 1870–1970* (Cambridge, 2005), pp. 132–3.

commentary' epitomised by the Hammonds.[8] Reinforcing these factors was the capacity of local history to provide a human and familiar face to the impersonal forces of class which, inevitably, dominated much of labour history's analytical and conceptual frameworks.

Labour history's attachment was especially evident in studies of Chartism, the great mass movement for parliamentary reform that dominated domestic politics in the first decade of Victoria's reign. *The making of the English working class* helped here: Thompson's thesis was that the English working class was made by 1832, and thus chronologically the book stopped short of the emergence of Chartism. Meanwhile, the author's bravura performance left those who contemplated writing about the Chartist period with a sense that his was an impossibly hard act to follow. For a time its impact was so great that large-scale labour history of mid-nineteenth-century England was effectively stalled.[9] Instead, the localising trend initiated by *Chartist Studies* was powerfully reinforced. Of the approximately 140 local histories of Chartism that have been produced, only a dozen appeared before *Chartist Studies*. Briggs and his colleagues (who included three extra-mural lecturers and none other than Reginald Pugh, the editor of the *Victoria County History*) contributed 6 more. Fifteen further local studies appeared in the 1960s, 44 in the 1970s and 48 in the 1980s. However, the flow then dwindled to a mere 13 in the 1990s.[10] In part this phenomenon was driven by the material circumstances of higher education from the 1960s, as an expanding number of institutions and professional historians turned out growing numbers of students who needed dissertation topics at undergraduate, master's and doctoral level. Chartism also benefited from its location at the convergence of three separate historiographical trends: the broad growth of interest in 'history from below' and similar surges of interest in the pursuit of local history and in the Victorian period generally.

However, it can be suggested that something else was happening here. 'There are not many [other] points in modern British history at which the historian can profitably speculate whether a revolutionary situation might have developed but did not', observed J.F.C. Harrison, the author of the Leeds and Leicester chapters in *Chartist Studies*.[11] Harrison went on to argue that Chartism in 1839

---

8. *Ibid.*

9. For a detailed analysis of this theme see Chase and Allen, 'Great Britain, 1750–1900', pp. 67–71.

10. Figures based on J.F.C. Harrison and D. Thompson, *Bibliography of the Chartist movement* (Hassocks, 1978) and O. Ashton, R. Fyson and S. Roberts, *The Chartist movement: a new annotated bibliography* (London, 1995), plus subsequent annual bibliographies in *Labour History Review*.

11. J.F.C. Harrison, *Early Victorian Britain, 1832–51* (London, 1979 edn), pp. 185–6.

and the spring and summer of 1848 constituted two such points. He might have added a third, the summer of 1842. In a happy quotation from the Roman poet Horace, W.G. Hoskins defined locality thus: 'it is that corner of the world above all others which has a smile for me'.[12] But smiling corners can be emotionally and politically defined, as well as spatially. What also stimulated the flood of local studies of Chartism was a form of revolutionary antiquarianism – historiography as a form of comradeship with the past, and the writing of history almost as consolation for political failure. It was also a historiography which – sometimes overtly and sometimes subconsciously – speculated over why revolutionary situations almost developed but did not. Both local and national histories of Chartism provided a kind of platform from which to interrogate Marxist theories of social and political change.

The collapse in the fashion for local studies of Chartism from the late 1980s partly reflected a broader historiographical trend: Britain's avoidance of revolution was no longer the key question it once had seemed to be. However, this was also the decade of post-modernism and the linguistic turn. Local history was largely untouched by these broader intellectual developments.[13] However, their impact on social history was considerable, and this applied especially to labour history, whose attachment to the certitudes of Marxism was, at least in the hands of some practitioners, almost filial in its piety. One consequence of diminished confidence in the Marxist paradigm was a critical reappraisal of what Chartism really was. A powerful argument emerged that the plethora of local studies had atomised understanding of Chartism, obscuring both the movement's strengths and weaknesses.[14] There ensued a profound shift in the trajectory of nineteenth-century labour history, as local studies were supplanted by other 'niche', biographical and thematic studies.[15] Local histories in this latest phase of Chartist studies have been rare and, where they occur, have taken the form of substantial longitudinal studies that achieve a depth of contextualisation (and engagement with the key issues of continuity and change in labour politics) unmatched in the earlier tradition of local

---

12. Hoskins, *Local history in England*, dedication page.

13. Despite the best efforts of G. and Y. Sheeran, 'Reconstructing local history', *The Local Historian*, 29 (1999), pp. 256–62. See also their article 'Discourses in local history', *Rethinking History*, 2 (1998), pp. 65–85.

14. The pivotal text in shifting the historiography of Chartism was 'Rethinking Chartism', the principal chapter in G. Stedman Jones, *Languages of class: studies in English working-class history, 1832–1982* (Cambridge, 1982), pp. 90–178. For a detailed critique see Chase and Allen, 'Great Britain, 1750–1900', pp. 72–5.

15. See especially O. Ashton, R. Fyson and S. Roberts (eds), *The Chartist legacy* (London, 1999); J. Allen and O. Ashton (eds), *Papers for the people: a study of the Chartist press* (London, 2005); K. Flett, *Chartism after 1848: the working class and the politics of radical education* (Monmouth, 2006); P. Pickering, *Feargus O'Connor: a political life* (Monmouth, 2008).

Chartist studies.[16] In short, they look beyond Chartism and the years 1838–48 as a putative site of revolutionary confrontation and investigate instead the rich civic and voluntary associational cultures of the later Victorian period in which those who called themselves Chartists continued to be active.

While Chartism dominated local studies within labour history until the 1990s, it was far from the only topic area where local history was the dominant mode of approaching the subject. Labour historians have, understandably, always been interested in popular protest, and such protest of its very nature is typically localised in form and function.[17] Trades councils of necessity are organised within a particular urban locale and have been historically investigated accordingly.[18] The extent and depth of the socialist revival of the 1880s, so easily overstated in institutional histories and biographies of leadership, has been dissected by local studies that reveal its profoundly localised patterns. Estimates of early Social Democratic Federation (SDF) membership suggest an organisation with rarely more than 3000 members, often many fewer, with heavy concentrations in Lancashire, London and, to a lesser extent, West Yorkshire.[19] The Independent Labour Party, established in 1893, enjoyed greater support than the SDF, but its reach, too, was restricted and geographically concentrated in Lancashire, Yorkshire and Clydeside, with isolated outposts such as Merthyr Tydfil and Leicester.[20] Here, however, we come to one of the paradoxes of twentieth-century political history: the energy expended on the history of the labour movement at the local level dwarfed all effort similarly to capture the

16. J. Allen, *Joseph Cowen and popular radicalism on Tyneside, 1829–1900* (Monmouth, 2007); R.G. Hall, *Voices for the people: democracy and Chartist political identity, 1830–1870* (Monmouth, 2007).

17. See, for example, J. Rule and R. Wells, *Crime, protest and popular politics in southern England, 1740–1880* (London, 1997), a compendium of regional and local studies by the two authors, including Burwash (Sussex) and Truro (Cornwall).

18. The sole national study is itself chronologically narrow: A. Clinton, *Trade union rank and file: trades councils in Britain, 1900–1940* (Manchester, 1977). On the other hand there is a plethora of local histories, for example: J. Corbett, *The Birmingham Trades Council, 1866–1966* (London, 1966); D. Large and R. Whitfield, *The Bristol Trades Council, 1873–1973* (Bristol, 1973); A. Durr (ed.), *A history of Brighton Trades Council and labour movement, 1890–1970* (Brighton, 1974); A. Tuckett, *Up with all that's down!* (Swindon, 1971); R. Lewis (ed.), *For the public good: studies to commemorate the centenary of Stockton and District Trades Council* (Middlesbrough, 1990).

19. M. Crick, *The history of the Social Democratic Federation* (Keele, 1994); P. Watmough, 'The membership of the Social Democratic Federation, 1885–1902', *Bulletin of the Society for the Study of Labour History*, 34 (1977), pp. 35–40.

20. D. Howell, *British workers and the Independent Labour Party, 1888–1906* (Manchester, 1983); B. Lancaster, *Radicalism, cooperation and socialism: Leicester working-class politics, 1860–1906* (Leicester, 1987). See also D. James, A. Jowitt and K. Laybourn (eds), *The centennial history of the Independent Labour Party* (Halifax, 1992).

experience of Liberalism and Conservatism. For example, membership of the Conservatives' Primrose League, founded in 1883 to build grassroots support for the Party, soared to over a million within a decade, rivalling the total membership of all Britain's trade unions at the time. By 1899 there were more Primrose Leaguers in Bolton alone (6227) than in the Independent Labour Party nationally.[21] Yet local historians are largely oblivious to the Primrose League and even the local historiography of the Conservative Party generally remains in its infancy. The reasons for this are complex and largely lie beyond the scope of this study. However, a 'whiggish' attachment to a teleology of progress impelled historians of a certain political bent to the history of labour, with its profound emphasis upon change and the path to modernity. For the reasons outlined above, local studies proved a valuable medium through which to explore that theme. Historians of a contrasting political inclination, though, were drawn to issues that underlined continuity, not change, in both locality and nation. Continuity, at least in the modern period, seldom provides the stuff of satisfying local history.

Continuity and change provide a useful optic through which to consider local historical treatment of the 1926 General Strike. Just as local histories of Chartism tended to approach their subject as a case study in extreme social tension (frequently unmindful that social cohesion, not tension, has been the abiding feature of modern British social history), so local histories of 1926 are apt to decouple the strike from its broader context. To a considerable extent this is understandable. It was an episode during which social tension reached a very 'un-British' level. Eight decades later, the General Strike still retains a firm place in the public's historical imagination. Local histories of 1926 generally enshrine the widely held collective memory of the strike, namely that it was betrayed by the leaders of the Trades Union Congress (TUC) and failed because it was never given a proper chance of succeeding. The persistent reluctance of the TUC leadership to commemorate the General Strike, its preference instead being to memorialise the safer and far less contentious Tolpuddle Martyrs, has reinforced this perspective. The formal commemoration of these six Dorset farm workers, transported in 1834, and indeed the very terminology of martyrdom, was effectively the invention of the TUC General Council as it sought to rehabilitate public regard for the labour movement in the wake of 1926 and the collapse in 1931 of the second Labour government.[22]

Few local histories contextualise 1926 within the prevailing industrial relations

---

21. M. Pugh, *The Tories and the people 1880–1935* (Oxford, 1985), pp. 2 and 241.

22. C. Griffiths, 'Remembering Tolpuddle: rural history and commemoration in the inter-war labour movement', *History Workshop Journal*, 44 (1997), pp. 145–69.

system of the post-1918 years, or pursue its consequences into the workplace; labour historians are perversely reluctant to investigate what actually happened in the workplace, with the result that the perspectives of industrial archaeology dominate local histories of work. And, absorbed in the sheer fact of the strike, few studies investigate which workers did not strike, or who did strike but returned hastily to work. Given the consistency with which contemporary accounts of the General Strike, both supportive and critical, commented on the depth and solidity of popular support for it, it is also astonishing how few local studies investigate what happened when it was so peremptorily concluded. Were there viable alternative leaderships to the TUC at the local level? If not, why not? Why were local voices attempting to call the TUC to account so feeble? Why were there no attempts to continue to strike in solidarity with the miners? Local historians have hardly begun to consider if, or how, 1926 may actually have accelerated processes of fragmentation within working-class communities and culture. It is beyond dispute that the General Strike was an epochal episode, but, in all but the short term, it was one which necessitated that trade unionists set aside militancy and pursue instead strategies of moderation.[23]

In short, the situation regarding local studies of 1926 is broadly similar to that which once confronted the historiography of Chartism. There is a compellingly written and richly researched corpus of local studies, but each is largely decoupled from a deep understanding of the key issues of long-term context, change and continuity. And, as with Chartism, few studies of 1926 are comparative in any meaningful way. Local histories of 1926 do not yet match the quantity we have of Chartism, despite the slowdown in the latter mentioned above.[24] However, the pressing need is not for more local case studies *per se* but for locally textured regional, and ultimately national, narratives, for the General Strike has been ill-served in recent general accounts. This partly reflects, perhaps, the relative paucity of local studies of 1926. A substantial, and in many ways admirable, history of British trade unionism skates over 1926 in barely a page, while a popular history published to capitalise on the eightieth anniversary conjured, on the basis of limited original research, a picture of solid national loyalties triumphing over fringe extremism and misjudgement in high places.[25]

---

23. This paragraph draws heavily on the following two articles: J. McIlroy, 'Memory, commemoration and history: 1926 in 2006', *Historical Studies in Industrial Relations*, 21 (2006), pp. 65–108 and K. Laybourn, 'Revisiting the General Strike', *Historical Studies in Industrial Relations*, 21 (2006), pp. 109–20.

24. See 'The General Strike and mining lockout of 1926: a select bibliography', *Historical Studies in Industrial Relations*, 21 (2006), pp. 183–206. On pp. 188–91 this lists 72 local studies of the General Strike and, on p. 197, 15 of the mining lockout.

25. A. Reid, *United we stand* (London, 2004); A. Perkins, *A very British strike* (London, 2006).

The relative paucity of local studies of the General Strike, compared to Chartism, reflects the still under-developed nature of twentieth-century local history. A great deal of what purports to be local history of twentieth-century work and workers is conceptually thin: much of it is quasi-autobiographical or biographical, drawing its authority and reader-appeal from the immediacy of experience but typically framed as an uncritical narrative of nostalgia or (equally suspect) steady progress. Much of it is driven by the ready availability of photographic sources, which in many publications constitute the text, supported by captions noting a world that has been lost. There is a profound tension here between, on the one hand, the celebration of craftsmanship and workplace and community solidarity, seemingly so elusive in the twenty-first century, and on the other hand an informed understanding of the exhausting, exploitative and dangerous character of work in the past. And do not historians of every hue tend to use visual evidence largely uncritically, seldom contemplating the extent to which photographic depiction is likely to have been contrived in a 'painterly' fashion?

In terms of local studies, labour history of the twentieth century therefore still has some ground to cover before it can match – in critical engagement and analytical vision – the corpus for earlier centuries. This is doubly unfortunate, not least because we are letting crucial oral source material quite literally die around us. Recently this struck me forcibly as I finally assembled a study of inter-war unemployment among Cleveland ironstone miners based mainly on research material gathered when a local history tutor in the late 1980s: poignantly, I suddenly realised that every one of the 16 people I had interviewed had since died.[26] This matters because popular historical understanding of the 1930s is largely reached by looking through a telescope labelled 'Jarrow', or – for the more critical – through a telescope marked 'the myth of the slump'. Since the 1980s an important revisionist element within the historiography has sought to replace or temper the image of the hungry thirties with that of a dynamic prosperous Britain, epitomised perhaps in the example of the car manufacturing centre of Coventry. This is hardly a novel concept: J.B. Priestley's *English journey* (1934) forcibly stated, 'I saw two Englands'. Contemporaries spoke consistently of the 'depressed areas', meaning geographically discrete concentrations of heavy industry on Clydeside, in northern England and south Wales, afflicted by systemic structural unemployment. Figures for unemployment among the

---

26. M. Chase, 'Unemployment without protest: the ironstone mining communities of East Cleveland in the inter-war period', in M. Reiss and M. Perry (eds), *Unemployment and protest: new perspectives on two centuries of contention* (Oxford, 2010), pp. 265-82.

insured workforce amply bear this out – 68 per cent for Jarrow in 1934 compared to 5 per cent in Coventry, for example.

In what sense can local labour histories be said to have neglected Britain in the 1930s? There are several ways. For example, the concept of a prosperous English midlands and south derives much of its weight from a reading back of post-war indicators into the 1930s. The attention paid to Coventry, for example, frequently overlooks the endemic housing shortages and overcrowding that went hand in hand with being an area of high in-migration. The idea of the hungry thirties may be a caricature, but the revisionist interpretation of the slump itself needs more local nuance. The emphatic consistency with which Jarrow is invoked is also a caricature. Without in any way detracting, one hopes, from the human cost of the slump in Jarrow, it should be noted that when unemployment among insured workers in that shipyard town hit its peak of 77 per cent in 1933, in the East Cleveland ironstone-mining communities of Yorkshire's North Riding it nudged 90 per cent.[27] Why is Jarrow remembered and East Cleveland not? In the intra-regional north-east context, part of the answer (I suggest) may lie in ready access to an economy of makeshifts: allotments, strategically organised smallholding schemes, casual employment and poaching.[28] These softened the depression in the North Riding but were practically non-existent on south Tyneside.

But the bigger question is why is the Jarrow Crusade remembered at all? It is even depicted in a sculpture in the car park of Jarrow's Morrison's supermarket. The town's iconic status derives from a hunger march that has been allowed to eclipse – indeed was meant from its inception to eclipse – a much longer tradition of direct action by the unemployed. This included hunger marches, many much larger in scale than Jarrow's, stretching back to 1921. I say *meant to eclipse* because the Jarrow Crusade's avowed non-political stance was intended to differentiate it sharply from the National Unemployed Workers' Movement, closely associated with the Communist Party. It paid off: it led to the marchers being entertained on their way to London by local Conservative Constituency Parties and to Jarrow attaining a place in the national historical consciousness

27. *Ministry of Labour Gazette*, 38:2 (February, 1930) and 41:1 (January, 1933); M. McCann, 'Organised labour and the unemployed on Teesside, 1930–36' (MA thesis, CNAA/Teesside Polytechnic, 1985); M. Chase and M. Whyman, *Heartbreak Hill: a response to unemployment in East Cleveland in the 1930s* (Redcar, 1991), p. 7.

28. The concept of 'an economy of makeshifts', widely applied to survival strategies of the early modern and nineteenth-century poor, is no less apposite in the context of 1930s East Cleveland. See particularly S. King, *Poverty and welfare in England, 1700–1850* (London, 2000); A. Tomkins and S. King (eds), *The poor in England, 1700–1850: an economy of makeshifts* (Manchester, 2003); S. Williams, 'Earnings, poor relief and the economy of makeshifts: Bedfordshire in the early years of the New Poor Law', *Rural History*, 16 (2005), pp. 21–52.

almost on a par with Agincourt, the Great Exhibition or Dunkirk.[29]

This is a considerable paradox, because from a national perspective the inter-war unemployed of north-east England were noticeably quiescent about their lot compared to other 'depressed areas', especially south Wales. The similarity between the two regions in the 1930s is striking: in both, overwhelmingly working-class industrial communities had mushroomed in the nineteenth century; in both, trade unionism was deeply implanted in workplace and residential communities; in both, Liberalism and Protestant nonconformity had thrived; and both had been captured as strongholds for the Labour Party after 1918. Yet in south Wales militant resistance to the regulation of unemployment and its relief through the hated Means Test was endemic. In Durham and Northumberland, protest and resistance was spasmodic and piecemeal. Where does the answer to this paradox lie? Is it in the contrasting pace and intensity of industrialisation in the two regions? Is it in the persistence of employer paternalism in the north-east and an aversion to collective action? Or, to touch on a theme raised earlier, does it lie in the greater resilience of Welsh trade unionism's response to the defeat of 1926? Only detailed local comparative studies will answer such questions.[30] Embedded within each local response to mass unemployment were micro-histories of depression and resilience and communal cohesiveness in the face of desperation. Local historians would do well to reclaim them, and not leave the field to the continual dominance of Jarrow (in many ways atypical), or to remain an adjunct to historical debate about inter-war communism, which is where, at a national level, the history of responses of the unemployed to their plight largely rests.

Finally, it is pertinent to point to two more general developments that underline the case for a close and fecund relationship between labour history and local history. Firstly, as the introduction to this essay noted, the generalising narrative of Marxism has been a powerful influence upon labour history. However, the past two decades have seen this diminish steadily. One consequence of this process has been a reaffirmation of the strategic importance of local and regional historical research, as labour historians turn increasingly to comparative history as a means to make sense of their field.[31] Second, labour historians are no

---

29. R. Croucher, *We refuse to starve in silence: a history of the National Unemployed Workers' Movement, 1920–46* (London, 1987); M. Perry, *The Jarrow crusade: protest and legend* (Sunderland, 2005).

30. See the important comparative study by S. Ward, 'The means test and the unemployed in south Wales and the north-east of England, 1931–9' (DPhil thesis, Aberystwyth, 2008).

31. See, for example, these volumes in the influential *Studies in Labour History* series, published under the auspices of the Society for the Study of Labour History: S. Berger, A. Croll and N. LaPorte (eds), *Towards a comparative history of coalfield societies* (Aldershot, 2005); M. van der Linden, *Transnational labour history: explorations* (Aldershot, 2003); M. Worley (ed.), *Labour's grass roots: essays on the activities and experiences of local Labour Parties and members, 1918–1945* (Aldershot, 2005).

longer so comfortable talking about class consciousness, when once most if not all defined their purpose as the study of class formation and of working-class politics, and thus of class struggle itself. That certainty was undermined from the late 1970s by two important developments in the historiography of modern Britain. The first emphasised the evolutionary nature of economic change; the second stressed the extent and influence of social, occupational and gender stratification within 'the working class'. This has led to growing suspicion that, however useful it may be as a shorthand description, class is too wide or too elusive to constitute a cohesive entity deserving historical scrutiny in its own right.

The redrawing of the map of social identities that has accompanied the demotion of class points to a need for greater attentiveness to local and regional variations in workers' lives. What it does not do is detract from the centrality of labour to human experience. Since part of the collapse of class as an explanatory device derives from increasing appreciation of occupational stratification within 'the working class', appreciation of the contribution of work to self-identity may actually be said to have increased. At the risk of stating the obvious, work has long been a defining feature of self-identity, as much as residence, family life or religious commitment. It is difficult in our so-called 'post-industrial' society fully to understand the centrality of labour to ways of constructing self-identity, so used are we to being seen – and seeing ourselves – as consumers rather than producers. This is not to argue that work above all other factors has consistently determined identity. In particular gender, and the social and cultural processes accompanying child bearing and rearing, have always been critical. The ways in which work, gender and the associational life of workers interplayed in the past, in the evolution of, for example, the male breadwinner ideal, are an important reason why labour history is so central to our understanding of the past. Local variations in the employment experience of both sexes, however, remain under-researched,[32] as are the ways in which labour and locality often mutually reinforced one another: how shared perceptions of a community of interest, derived from being workers in a particular trade or industry, might have been strengthened by common experience of residence. Thus the interplay of labour and locality looks set to remain a powerful element in labour history.

---

32. For an illuminating insight into the possibilities here see M. Williamson, '"The iron chancellors": the dynamics of the domestic economy in ironstone-mining households, 1918–1964', *Journal of Family History*, 28 (2003), pp. 391–410.

4. Parliamentary elections, 1950–2005, as a window on Northern English identity and regional devolution

Stephen Caunce

Northern England has a well-established and widely acknowledged sense of itself, and the past four decades has seen the region develop deep grievances about British economic policy-making.[1] Roy Hattersley argued in 2000 that English regional devolution had consequently become inevitable, and a leader in *The Guardian* endorsed this three years later.[2] Before 1970 the financial and service economy of the metropolitan South seemed able to co-exist to mutual benefit with the manufacturing and mining of the North, and most other parts of the UK, but throughout north-western Europe such fusions have come under great stress since then. In England the deputy prime minister John Prescott became a determined if not particularly effective champion of several Northern initiatives, including a campaign for regional assemblies.[3] No popular supportive groupings emerged in response, so of three referendums planned to cover the whole region only that in the north-east actually occurred. In November 2004 slightly less than half the electorate there voted 'no' in every district. Overall only 22 per cent voted

1. Significant recent examples include M. Wainwright (northern editor, *The Guardian* newspaper), *True North: in praise of England's better half* (London, 2010); S. Maconie, *Pies and prejudice: in search of the North* (London, 2007); D. Russell, *Looking North: Northern England and the national imagination* (Manchester, 2004); N. Kirk (ed.), *Northern identities: historical interpretations of 'the North' and 'Northernness'* (Aldershot, 2000); R. Samuel, 'North and South', in *Island stories: unravelling Britain, theatres of memory*, vol. 2 (London, 1998), pp. 153–71.

2. *The Guardian*, 21 August 2000 and 17 June 2003.

3. *The Westmorland Gazette*, for instance, reported 'an impassioned speech' by him to 250 people in Kendal, 23 April 2004. *The Guardian* reported several months later on his spending 'three days on the campaign trail pushing his pet project', 15 October 2004.

'yes'.[4] A potential break with centuries of English constitutional history thus became the dampest of squibs: this was evidently not an issue that the overwhelming majority comprehended, much less cared about. Afterwards, *The Scotsman* summed up the general feeling that 'devolution in England is dead, if not forever, certainly for a generation'.[5]

In contrast, elsewhere within the UK and its neighbouring dependencies, Scotland and Wales had demanded and won devolution and Scots today discuss separation; Northern Ireland is slowly working out its own tortured version; the Isle of Man and the Channel Islands have exploited their anomalous constitutional status to the full; and even the conurbation of London accepted a regional administration thrust upon it by government.[6] Belgium, it should be noted, became temporarily ungovernable in 2007 owing to similar tensions.[7] Northern England thus stands out in apparently preferring a system of local councils too small and weak to plan strategically or exert influence nationally, and members of parliament who show no collective regional awareness or commitment. This situation provides an excellent opportunity to investigate the practicalities and limits of regional identity within a long-standing nation state by analysing selected general election results since 1950.[8] The intention is to reveal attitudes to the North's sense of its place within the nation, and thereby to use statistical evidence to buttress a long-term study of cultural attitudes within Northern England, aspects of which have already been published.[9] For many

---

4. The Electoral Commission website published detailed results which are no longer accessible. See instead <http://en.wikipedia.org/wiki/Northern_England_devolution_referendums,_2004#The_result> accessed 8 December 2010.

5. *The Scotsman*, 6 November 2004.

6. J. Cook, 'Relocating Britishness and the break-up of Britain', in S. Caunce, E. Mazierska, S. Sidney-Smith and J.K. Walton (eds.), *Relocating Britishness* (Manchester, 2004), pp. 17–37; D. Stewart, *The path to devolution and change: a political history of Scotland under Margaret Thatcher* (London, 2009); C. Fowler, 'Welsh national identity and the British political process', in Caunce, Mazierska, Sidney-Smith and Walton (eds.), *Relocating Britishness*, pp. 196–216; 2010 nearly saw Channel Island and Manx separation undo reciprocal medical treatment deals with the UK, <http://www.gov.im/dhss/reciprocal_agreement/faqs.xml> and *Health Service Journal*, 24 January 2010. A clear brief version of Manx constitutional change is found in C. Kerruish, 'The Manx constitution: an outline', in *The Isle of Man official yearbook, 1986* (Douglas, 1986), pp. 33–45.

7. See, for instance, 'Belgium approaches 150 days without government', *The Independent*, 5 November 2007, and 'Belgian separatists seek way out after poll win', *The Guardian*, 15 June 2010.

8. The dates show either key turning points or illuminate periods of consistent voting, with the emphasis on the devolutionary years. The election of 1945 was highly unusual, so results from 1950 stand for the period of Labour ascendancy; 1951 recorded the highest ever Labour vote but saw a Conservative victory; 1959 is from the solid period of Butskellite consensus; 1983 and 1997 saw huge swings and changes of government; 2005 records Labour in decline, but still winning.

9. S. Caunce, 'Regional identity in Lancashire and Yorkshire: hunting the snark', *Journal of Regional and Local Studies*, 20 (1999), pp. 25–50.

people the locality and the region have the greatest day-to-day cultural reality, so understanding identity requires engagement with them even though nations, or potential nations, are easier to research. This remains a much-neglected aspect of academic history within the UK.

This investigation will also contribute to the extensive enquiries over the last few decades into the general nature of group identities in the modern world, following the final abandonment of Victorian notions of racial origins of nationalism.[10] Specifically, this study engages with 'othering', the sense of difference, and often fear, which has become widely accepted as the root of many identities. Colley's important study of Britishness is particularly relevant here.[11] This concept has limited explanatory power, however, since such analyses usually raise the question of how, why and when hostile groups first began to perceive themselves as separate, competing collective entities to which individuals were prepared to commit to the point of death. Moreover, while the drama of war, rebellion and discord understandably form the obvious point of entry to many investigations, identities that persist need a purchase during peaceful times as well. Northern England provides a perfect case study for investigating such issues, especially as it also forms a potentially disaffected part of England, a much more solid and historic identity than that of Britain.

There is no assumption here that the apparent passivity of the North is somehow incorrect, but it must not be seen as inevitable either. If Ireland and Scotland can be taken seriously as independent political entities then it has at least the same potential, especially within the European Union.[12] The North covers the geographical heart of Great Britain, from Scotland to a line at or south of the Mersey and Humber rivers. Where that line runs is disputed, but here we largely follow that created fortuitously by the sequence of short-lived metropolitan counties enacted by central government in 1972, since they were devised specifically to define areas of obvious common economic interest.[13] A regional population of approximately 14 million people is a third more than in the recently devolved UK 'nations' combined, and is nearly equal to the

---

10. This essay grew from an unpublished contribution to the conference which produced S. Caunce, E. Mazierska, S. Sidney-Smith and J.K. Walton (eds), *Relocating Britishness* (Manchester, 2004).

11. L. Colley, *Britons: forging the nation, 1707–1837* (London, 1992).

12. M. Keating, *The new regionalism in western Europe: regional restructuring and political change* (Cheltenham, 2000).

13. B. Rodgers, 'Manchester: metropolitan planning by collaboration and consent: or civic hope frustrated', in G. Gordon (ed.), *Regional cities in the UK 1890–1980* (London, 1986), pp. 41–57; R. Lawton and C. Pooley, 'Liverpool and Merseyside', in Gordon (ed.), *Regional cities*, pp. 60–82. The precise line chosen does not significantly affect the statistical analysis.

Netherlands. It is physically about half as big as Scotland, and larger than Wales and Northern Ireland combined. It contributes significantly to British industrial production and exports, although less than previously.

Finally, the UK as a whole forms a distinctive and under-used environment for comparative internal study.[14] Even in the early 1960s the grandest version of that multi-layered and very diverse identity called Britishness, as a concept of an active, unifying and global force, was not quite dead. Yet, in a new millennium, it is both unclear and debatable what *being* British means for the bulk of the people to whom that term used to be fairly unthinkingly applied. There is even doubt as to how many residents would now include themselves within it, while devolution and the recent reforms of the House of Lords have shown that this is one of the most weakly entrenched constitutional settlements in the world. Outside Ireland political change has been largely evolutionary in character since the seventeenth century, which implies enough enduring consensus to contain, and even to harness to constructive effect, those centrifugal forces of group rivalry that clearly remained active within it. The lack of either a large peacetime standing army or an armed national police force has reinforced this tendency. Even so, tactics used to redefine constitutional relationships over the twentieth century ranged from successful armed rebellion, in Ireland, to the use of existing but neglected powers in the Channel Islands and the Isle of Man. Thus, while the UK remains a diverse collection of individual, pragmatic unions of varying completeness under what was originally the English crown, it also continues to be divided along quite different lines by religion, class and language, as well as emerging ethnic differences due to immigration. Many internal forces therefore exist which can disrupt apparently coherent regions or form unifying bonds across potential geographical divisions.

Northern voting patterns, 1950–2005

General election votes may seem a crude analytical device but they do record actual and self-aware choices, whereas people's stated beliefs may conflict with what they do, individually and collectively. Modern UK elections have operated within a simple and unchanging system of first-past-the-post voting among a few serious candidates, in which voters generally select the candidate that they really want to win. If a first preference cannot win, they may vote tactically against another they oppose strongly, but such action was rarely apparent in the North and still

---

14. C. Harvie, 'English regionalism: the dog that never barked', in B. Crick (ed.), *National identities: the constitution of the United Kingdom* (London, 1991), pp. 105–18. B. Deacon, 'County, nation, ethnic group? The shaping of the Cornish identity', *International Journal of Regional and Local Studies*, 3 (2007), pp. 5–29, deals with the one region generally seen as a base for potential ethnic separatism.

Table 4.1 Number of MPs for the North of England and Britain as a whole, 1950–2005

Election year	North	National
1950	107L/58C/1Lib	396L/189C/25Lib
1951	100L/66C/4Lib	296L/320C/6Lib
1959	88L/74C	258L/365C/6Lib
1983	90L/56C/6A	209L/397C/23A/21other
1997	132L/14C/5LD	418L/165C/46LD/30other
2005	126L/17C/10LD	355L/198C/62LD/30other

Key: L = Labour; Lib = Liberal; A = Social Democratic Party and Liberal Party Alliance; LD = Liberal Democrat; C = Conservative.

generally indicates a basic preference for left or right. Of course, no tenable conclusions could be drawn unless significant and enduring patterns emerged from Tables 1, 2 and 3, but they are evident there. Moreover, overt nationalism is only a ghost in this particular analysis; the evident satisfaction with the pre-existing party system is still among the most significant, if least spectacular, outcomes. If new parties emerged successfully in Scotland and Wales they could also have done so here, especially as the North had previously played a large part in establishing both the Independent Labour Party and the Labour Party.

Since 1945 overall Northern voting patterns can be seen (in Table 4.1) to have changed both internally and relative to national trends. The assumption held by many that, shortly after its rise, the Labour Party achieved near-total control of Northern politics is immediately shown to be wrong. Even with Labour recording its highest ever total votes, the Conservatives held 35 per cent of Northern seats in 1950, equivalent to 54 per cent of the Northern Labour total, and in 1951 the figures were 39 per cent and 66 per cent respectively. The North did prefer Labour, but this was no one-party region and Conservatives could hope to increase their share. Indeed, British politics then constituted a genuine national system on the mainland with all three major parties fighting seriously in all regions, and nationalists and radical parties of both left and right barely registering even in local government.[15] By 1997, in contrast, national voting patterns indicate fragmentation into several regional systems. Within the North, what had been a false stereotype of universal Labour dominance became reality, despite a general perception that class-based politics was collapsing. Building a parliamentary majority, and even more a real governmental mandate, thus became a much more complex business, though news organisations today deal only in national swings.

15. D. Tanner (ed.), *Debating nationhood and governance in Britain, 1885–1939* (Manchester, 2006).

Table 4.2 MPs according to metropolitan county boundaries, by party, 1950–2005

Election year	Merseyside plus Cheshire fringe	Greater Manchester	West Yorkshire	South Yorkshire	Tyne and Wear
1950	7L/11C	19L/11C	17L/4C	16L/2C	11L/1C/1Lib
1951	7L/11C	15L/15C	17L/4C	15L/3C	11L/2C
1959	7L/12C	14L/14C	13L/7C	12L/3C	9L/4C
1983	11L/6C	14L/10C/1A	6L/10C/2A	18L/0C/1A	11L/2C
1997	15L/0C/1LD	22L/2C/1LD	18L/0C	17L/0C/1LD	13L/0C
2005	15L/0C/1LD	20L/1C/4LD	16L/1C/1LD	17L/0C/1LD	13L/0C

Key: L = Labour; Lib = Liberal; A = Social Democratic Party and Liberal Party Alliance; LD = Liberal Democrat; C = Conservative.

Tables 4.2 and 4.3 reveal the internal complexity within the regional voting pattern, primarily by comparing the short-lived metropolitan counties of 1972 to each other and collectively to the rural North and other areas. Labour, predictably, always proved strongest in the large cities, the industrial towns and the coalfields, but only the last were overwhelmingly Labour throughout. Wigan, for instance, has always elected a Labour MP since 1918, but textile towns have a long tradition of three-party politics. The election of 1951 saw Liverpool represented by five Conservative members and four Labour; Manchester was the reverse; and Newcastle had three Labour and one Conservative. In 1959 Manchester remained the same, but the Conservatives had seven seats in Liverpool to Labour's three and Newcastle was evenly split.[16] Northern rural areas, in contrast, have persistently shared a national cross-class identity based on a sense of difference from the towns, or even exploitation by them. The urge to vote Conservative was more powerful in this group than the expected Labour reflex generally was elsewhere, although it could be masked where small industrial or mining settlements outvoted a thinly scattered agricultural population. The suburbs have been the most difficult group to classify over time, but they had a clear tendency at first to vote Conservative where they were dominated by the middle class, a not insignificant category given the entrepreneurial nature of Northern economic development until recently. It had been a wealthy Northerner, Sir Robert Peel, after all, who turned the old Tory party into the modern Conservatives and maintained their nationwide appeal.

---

16. *Whitaker's almanack* (1953), p. 333.

Table 4.3 MPs in Northern England, 1950–2005: conurbations, rural constituencies, remainder

Election year	Northern Conurbations	Rural North*	Rest of North**
1950	70L/ 29C/1Lib	2L/19C	35L/10C
1951	65L/ 35C/0Lib	2L/19C	33L /12C
1959	55L/ 37C/0Lib	2L/20C	31L/14C
1983	60L/ 27C/4A	0L/18C/1A	30L/11C/1A
1997	85L/ 2C/3LD	7L/12C/1LD	42L/0C/1LD
2005	81L/ 2C/7LD	7L/12C/1LD	38L/3C/3LD

Key: L = Labour; Lib = Liberal; A = Social Democratic Party and Liberal Party Alliance; LD = Liberal Democrat; C = Conservative.
* All Labour seats in this category, including 1997, contain either a substantial non-market town, or coal mining as well as large rural tracts.
** Seats containing substantial industrial, mining and urban elements, but not part of major conurbations.

The elections of 1983 and 1997 receive special attention here as disasters for Labour and for the Conservatives respectively, in which waverers clearly switched allegiance away from the unpopular party *en masse*, revealing the underlying bedrock of political geography, to left and right, beneath the more malleable upper layers.[17] The brief emergence of the Social Democratic Party (SDP) in the 1983 election also illustrates that the system was not inherently closed. Its impact exaggerated the Northern Conservative vote, with four victories in Greater Manchester apparently resulting entirely from strong SDP/Liberal Party Alliance showings.[18] However, this increases the significance of the fact that Liverpool elected five Labour MPs and one Alliance, and Manchester four Labour and one Conservative, while Newcastle was entirely Labour. Merseyside and Greater Manchester counties together elected twenty-four Labour members, fifteen Conservatives and one Alliance, with Tyne and Wear electing twelve Labour members to one Conservative.

In contrast, many of Labour's English victories outside the North were concentrated in inner London, with the industrial Midlands giving Thatcher many surprising wins. South of a line drawn from the Mersey, around Staffordshire and Derbyshire and then up to the Humber, but disregarding Greater London and West Midlands metropolitan county, Labour won just Ipswich, Bristol South and Leicester West, together with Thurrock on the Greater London border. By 1997 it still held only a handful of southern constituencies,

---

17. Random examples are Bolton North East, Conservative vote of 19,632 defeated Labour's 17,189, because of an Alliance vote of 8,311; Bradford North, Conservative vote of 16,094 beat Labour's 14,492 because of an Alliance vote of 11,962, plus 4,018 for Independent Labour. Both rapidly returned to Labour.

18. Stockport, Conservative vote of 18,517 defeated Labour's 12,731 because of an Alliance vote of 12,129. Bolton West, Bury North and Manchester Withington were similar.

almost all urban and completely isolated.[19] Thus, the Thatcherite revolution alienated the North as much as Scotland or Wales, where Labour also dominated, but, whereas this alienation initiated a transformation of their politics, the North opted for more of the same. Within England, Labour during these years became more reliant on Northern votes than ever before, though London and the West Midlands prevented the English party being owned entirely by the North.

In 1997 the national political pendulum swung to the opposite extreme, and the Alliance's collapse after 1983 also reasserted, and must have stemmed from, a preference for conventional politics. The Northern Conservative tally reduced from a poor 44 to a disastrous 14, while Labour won 132 seats in the region. The Liberals seized agricultural Berwick-upon-Tweed, where Scottish influence was very strong, as well as four traditionally Conservative urban seats. The election of 2001 proved that the surge of anti-Conservativism was no short-term protest vote, and the patterns established in 1997 thus persisted in their essentials down to 2005. Even among apparently rural seats a third contained enough non-agricultural votes to go, and stay, Labour. The remaining rump, a large share of the northern landscape which contained only a tiny and self-evidently atypical fraction of its population, constituted a diagonal swathe of diehard Conservatism running from the Humber to the western and central Scottish border, leaving Hull and its suburbs as a Labour island. Two seats in the most salubrious parts of Manchester's Cheshire commuter fringe represented all the Conservatives retained elsewhere, and one other such preferred Liberal to Labour.

In areas where devolution campaigns took root, in contrast, enough rural electors also abandoned the Conservatives to deny them any Scottish seats in 1997. It was no protest vote, for only Galloway and Upper Nithsdale returned in 2001, and then by just 74 votes. One seat in this vicinity (boundaries were then redrawn) remained the only Conservative toehold north of the border after the 2010 election. Rural areas are usually portrayed as the repository of traditional values and identity, so this pattern has more significance than mere counting indicates.[20] In Scotland such former Conservative seats created the nationalist and Liberal pressure on two-party politics which provided a platform solid enough to bring a vote on devolution. Welsh Conservatism always had less success in rural areas, so the situation there was more complex, but the nationalist core was rural.

---

19. The Forest of Dean might seem rural but was a remnant mining area.

20. It would be instructive to research the regional membership and activity of the Countryside Alliance, founded in 1997, in this sense. It is reported to have mobilised around 400,000 marchers in London on 22 September 2002 to protest about country sports legislation.

Nationally in 1997 Labour won an overwhelming victory in all the major conurbations as well as gaining the suburbs and mixed constituencies that included small towns and some industry. Wigan might have delivered a record majority of 22,643, but the tenacity of such Northern loyalty, and its significance, was somewhat obscured to a party that could now win seats in all parts of the UK except Northern Ireland. The voting system exaggerated the electorate's change of heart, of course, but clear, absolute Conservative majorities emerged only in Huntingdon (the then Prime Minister's seat), Hampshire North East and Kensington and Chelsea. There were bare absolute majorities in another 13 constituencies, all in the heartland except Staffordshire South and Sutton Coldfield.[21] Conservatives retained a more widespread local government presence, gained representation in the new devolved institutions and even won the European elections when turnout fell right away, but outside southern England general support for them had dropped below the threshold that delivers parliamentary representation proportionate to votes. On the other hand, it maintained a broad geographical base for recovery if the party could reconnect to popular concerns.

Under William Hague the Conservative revival strategy did not achieve this: subsequent by-elections, especially that in Hartlepool, proved not only that there was indeed no hope among the working class but also that the individualistic Conservative vision of a national development strategy, overtly focused on the metropolis, had persuaded very few others to return.[22] Even though Conservatives remained the party of business, its public agenda was summed up by John Major's Orwell-derived image of an old lady riding a bicycle to church past a village green. This identified it overwhelmingly with the home counties and rural England, and Peel's work had been undone.[23] Outside south-eastern

---

21. Bare majorities were secured in Arundel and South Downs; Chesham and Amersham; Horsham; New Forest West; Ruislip Northwood; Staffordshire South, Surrey East, Surrey Heath, Sutton Coldfield; and Wokingham.

22. The larger constituencies are the clearer divisions become. Thus, European elections in 1994 elected one Conservative and no Liberals north of a line running due west from the Wash to Wales, and only two more Conservatives east of London, with none in the metropolis. The remainder of their seats lay in south–central and south-west England, where Labour had only one seat, compared to 53 elsewhere. For local elections, only a handful of councils showed a near-monolithic character, such as Gateshead (co. Durham), with 60 Labour councillors, 4 Liberals and 2 Conservatives, or Bracknell Forest (Berkshire), with 39 Conservatives to 1 Labour. In Eden (Cumbria), 34 of 37 councillors called themselves Independent (plus an Independent Conservative). In East Yorkshire, 20 Conservatives faced 7 representatives of the other major parties, 10 Independents, and 6 'others'.

23. In 1992 the north Midlands were roughly equally divided between the two main parties, with no Liberals. In 1997 the industrial areas went solidly Labour, with a patchwork of 7 Conservative seats in rural niches. Lincolnshire was divided equally along predictable rural/urban lines, but its Conservative members all sat for southerly constituencies. *The Times*, 9 October 1975, quoted Harold Macmillan regretting the loss of national acceptability, from Stewart, *Path to devolution*, p. 225.

England it was only agricultural constituencies that maintained a presence in Parliament, thus shadowing the stereotyped concept of Englishness traditionally propounded by heritage publications just as the North now also played up to traditional misrepresentations of itself. The generalised but limited national swing against the Conservatives was thus turned into a rout by strong and persistent nationalist and regional trends.

The new and lasting dominance of Labour in the North that emerged in 1997 was not due to short-term factors, therefore, but rather to a commitment that was atypical even when compared with other erstwhile heartlands. Indeed, after the 2005 election, when enthusiasm for Labour was visibly waning in national terms and the invasion of Iraq had detached some convinced supporters, the concentration of committed Labour voters in general terms, but particularly in the North, is indicated by the fact that the 30 safest seats in Parliament were all held by Labour, and 23 of them were Northern, compared to 6 where nationalists were challenging. Taking the 100 safest seats, 83 were Labour, and 53 of those were Northern, while extending the survey as far as the 150 safest seats, 106 were Labour and 64 of those were Northern.[24] Despite this, no distinctive collective voice for Northern Labour constituencies resulted as it did in Scotland and Wales when devolutionary pressure built up, and overt Northern regionalism would certainly have alienated the other conurbations, especially London. Indeed, Northern English Labour seats provided havens for government ministers, including Tony Blair, who in December 1999 explicitly denied that the North had a regional case to make.[25]

The extent of Northern passivity was amply demonstrated by two contrasting episodes in the 2001 general election. First, Arthur Scargill had launched the Socialist Labour Party in 1996, avowedly to challenge Labour over its new attitudes. Though it was never a regional party in either intention or impact, the lasting bitterness in Yorkshire coalfield seats might have been expected to challenge existing loyalties most effectively there. However, in Barnsley East and Mexborough it received just 722 votes, in Don Valley 466, and in Wakefield 634.[26] Meanwhile, across the Pennines, Conservative renegade Shaun Woodward was imposed by the Labour leadership at the last minute on St Helens South, and won there despite an almost total mismatch of origins, personal lifestyle and previous beliefs with this extremely introverted, working-class and ex-mining

---

24. <http://news.bbc.co.uk/1/hi/uk_politics/vote_2005> accessed 8 December 2010.

25. Reported in *The Independent* and *The Times*, 8 December 1999. *The Yorkshire Post* and *The Northern Echo* treated the claim with derision, 7 December 1999.

26. Nationally it polled only about 3% in the seats it contested.

constituency.[27] Only the significantly renamed *British* National Party ever created an image as a possible Northern mould-breaker, but it is important to recognise how very limited and localised its gains were even within local government before it suffered a severe rebuff in 2010.[28]

Perhaps such attitudes derived from the lesson of the SDP experiment, which showed that splitting the Labour vote could create a Conservative majority out of a low share of the popular vote. In any case, the alienation produced by Labour's self-evident unwillingness to change Thatcherite policies on the decline of the old Northern economic base led only to falling turnouts in parliamentary elections. Disaffection did lead to more turbulence in local politics, however. In Sheffield, erstwhile heart of the 'People's Republic of South Yorkshire', the city council in 2010 consists of 44 Liberal Democrats, 36 Labour, 3 Green and 1 Independent. Moreover, the leader of the Liberal Democrats in the coalition government represented Sheffield Hallam.

Labour thus safely neglected Northern concerns over many years in search of nationwide appeal, despite the growing centrality of the region to its ability to survive should that appeal dwindle. Threatening the Conservatives on their home ground seemed more strategically important; nationalist parties also had to be dealt with; and manufacturing seemed outdated and largely irrelevant to the party's leaders. The North was thus co-opted into underpinning a project aimed at building a national majority which offered it very little directly, which it might theoretically have wrecked but never did, and which it therefore could not even influence.

Northern identity
The imaginary lines drawn on maps between Scotland, Wales and Northern England have thus proved very real and persistent for people, despite obvious shared experiences and interests that spanned them. The North's notoriously indefinable southern edge also reflects a cultural reality in that Northerners show no desire to define and retire behind it. Growing ethnic diversity means that those residents who do not feel rooted in Northern England as a region often prefer alternative identities that may well be only conditionally British, weakening any possible arguments about incipient nationhood. *The Yorkshire Post*, however, wrote in 1999 that Yorkshire has 'a strong sense of regional identity … It isn't nationalist. There never was a king of olde Yorkshire after all.

27. H. Young, 'What Shaun Woodward really means', *The Guardian*, 15 May 2001.

28. A poll of non-voters suggests most would have voted Labour if forced to choose, *The Guardian*, 9 August 2001, p. 10.

But the identity is real. It has shaped Yorkshire and its people in unique ways. And still does.'[29] Such a statement, coupled to the North's passive political character, must turn our attention to issues of realisation and expression.

Arthur Conan Doyle famously pointed out that a dog that sleeps through a burglary may indicate something more significant about the nature of the crime than one that predictably barks its head off. The North forms a most determinedly non-barking dog, for, when its preferred political party departed from its traditional policies, the North's involvement with it was so strong that the expected dramatic protest was heavily muted despite the very real detrimental consequences of the new direction. Indeed, political quiescence persisted despite the apparent rewards of investment and self-determination that protest brought elsewhere. Scotland raises so little interest in most of the North that this overriding Northern sense of Englishness cannot be written off as just an exercise in 'othering'. The Northern regional version of that more general identity therefore forms a more difficult and interesting cultural construct which exists within a dynamic system, conditioned by a long historical process, whose many components interact constantly with each other. Explaining such cultural patterns definitively is notoriously hard, but some elements of causation can be teased out from all this, especially by comparing the probable agents with those suggested by Stewart for Scotland.[30]

The localism of Northerners is a persistent theme of most cultural analyses and must form the essential starting point in explaining why northern identity does not cohere across the region, or at any level higher than the county. Even the compact new metropolitan counties of 1972 failed utterly to engage their inhabitants, despite the undoubted economic logic underlying their creation. In fact, people consciously rejected that logic owing to a fear of being subsumed into units that swallowed up or broke down those units with which they identified.[31] Locality is very real for most individuals in such areas, even though for most modern intellectuals this feels anachronistic. To someone who lives in or very near the place where they and their relatives spent their whole childhood, who has not gone away to university, and who has a stable core group of friends who speak with a common accent and share many attitudes, identity is usually accepted unconsciously as a ready-made pattern.

Localism in this setting did not lead to fragmentation, however, but rather to a willing and successful involvement as localities in national and global relationships dealing with all aspects of life, political, trading, industrial and

---

29. *The Yorkshire Post*, 15 January 1999.

30. Stewart, *Path to devolution*, pp. 225–32.

31. Rodgers, 'Manchester: metropolitan planning' shows the depth, extent and consequences of such tensions throughout the twentieth century.

sporting. The region, especially one that spanned several counties, felt largely irrelevant, a feeling reinforced by strong, close economic linkages with parts of the Midlands and north Wales. The Victorian economic system of market co-ordination that the region's entrepreneurs consciously promoted had undercut any practical need for regulation and definition other than that offered by the national parliament. As a result, the regional elites that emerged across the North recognised the existence of some kind of Northern cultural unity, but otherwise never developed those lasting social mechanisms that make people become formally committed to a common enterprise, as opposed to acting in similar but apparently uncoordinated ways, and copying each other when it suited. Even the Co-operative Movement was based around the same network principle.

Many of the national elite clearly perceived Northern culture as a spoiled version of Englishness, moreover, rather than something of its own with its own virtues. Northerners have long recognised and lived with this, and it rarely made a direct impact on their lives before the Thatcherite assault on their economic base. New regional grievances then arose, but we have seen that even they did not transmogrify this region into a nascent nation, any more than the Scots, Welsh and Irish had ever let their ancient nationalisms decay into mere regionalism, however useful a British overlay may have sometimes been to them. Identity thus evidently does need history, institutions and cultural underpinning to give it purchase within the real world. These factors can certainly be manipulated and given or denied significance, but there must be something of substance with which to work.

Selecting a capital in which to base regional institutions is a prime example of the problems of creating a coherent Northern region. None of the Northern industrial cities stands out as Cardiff does in Wales, despite that city's relatively recent growth to importance. None has ever exercised any political authority outside their own immediate boundaries either, and Manchester, Newcastle and Liverpool all actually had a substantial part of their own, apparently cohesive, urban area managed by a twin 'city' administration. As regards Manchester and Newcastle, although Salford and Gateshead had few facilities or other real indicators of genuine autonomy, such as Bradford had in relation to Leeds, for instance, their independence was rooted in history and they retain local loyalty even now. No Northern city has ever been prepared to accept leadership from any other.

Thus, the region had no universities until the late nineteenth century, but, once the idea caught hold, all the cities wanted their own, with none able to rise above the group and form a natural social and educational centre for an elite.[32]

---

32. J. Walsh, 'The university movement in the north of England at the end of the nineteenth century', *Northern History*, 46 (2009), pp. 113–32. No university library has ever been granted copyright status, for instance.

The cities in general terms never achieved a social and cultural status as separate entities in line with their economic and demographic strength. The integration of high-order urban functions between them is almost non-existent, and London has actually always exercised the highest in ways the North could accept.[33] The recent loss of Manchester's twentieth-century Northern media supremacy destroyed the one dimension where a tangible Northern primacy did seem possible, but most of the newspapers published there were really always London-based, and those that were not aspired to achieve that goal.[34] Granada Television ultimately also shared the same value system. Finally, no historic centre outside the major cities had enough cultural status to gain wide acceptance by them all as a compromise candidate. York might seem a possibility, but even in medieval times its influence was almost entirely restricted to Yorkshire.

The asymmetrical fragmentation of the urban pattern means that collective Northern influence, however threatening in appearance in the nineteenth century, actually has no reality.[35] Southern England has one tight-knit conurbation standing at the functional heart of the southern quarter of the UK, which achieved its dominance for very practical, and still important, reasons. Nationally it monopolises most high-order functions in a way that has few parallels around the world. It is the leading port, the financial and commercial centre, the centre of national government and justice, the religious centre in practice, the media centre and has the main airports. In Scotland, the Central Belt, and especially Greater Glasgow, is only marginally more dispersed, and its dominance over Scotland is more complete and obvious even if the administration is in Edinburgh. In contrast to both, the old Northern industrial complexes remain as five separate conurbations, although four are contiguous and closely linked. Hull forms a further substantial city and a major port that complements and competes with Liverpool.

Devolution rouses far more divisive fears than hopes within such a system. The highly visible displaying of Northumberland flags over the past three decades may apparently echo Scottish campaigns for constitutional change, but the referendum result of 2004 showed that it merely reflected particularly intense localism.[36] The potential gains from devolution of any kind for any one place are

33. S. Caunce, 'Urban systems, identity and development in Lancashire and Yorkshire: A complex question', in N. Kirk (ed.), *Northern identities: historical interpretations of 'the North' and 'Northernness'* (Aldershot, 2000), pp. 19–41.

34. R. Waterhouse, *The other Fleet Street* (Altrincham, 2004).

35. S. Caunce, 'Northern English industrial towns: rivals or partners?', *Urban History*, 30 (2003), pp. 338–58.

36. A. Green and A.J. Pollard, *Regional identities in North-East England, 1300–2000* (Woodbridge, 2007).

unclear, but the overwhelming preponderance of the Mersey–Humber corridor within the whole North is obvious to all. The linguistic and cultural divide between the far north and Lancashire and Yorkshire is deep and reinforces this.[37] Within the north-west the obvious dominance resulting from the enormous populations of the Merseyside and Greater Manchester city-regions frightens the rest, especially in what is now Cumbria. Yorkshire's rural areas have similarly always resented the superior economic status of the old central and southern West Riding. Given the enormous social and economic problems of the old industrial belt, fears of neglect felt elsewhere cannot be dismissed. Effective intra-regional or sub-regional alliances that can gain lasting general commitment in any policy area remain therefore just a dream. Development bodies like *Yorkshire Forward* exist, but few have heard of them, or know anything about their structures, or feel any civic involvement, as there is no popular right to observe and approve their actions.

In this setting other things that might provide fuel for nationalism also do not do so, especially as there is a kind of diffidence and self-deprecation that lurks behind the apparent assertiveness of the North. Thus, Northern English speech patterns are, like the urban pattern, diverse. Lancashire and Yorkshire speak differently from each other as well as from the counties near the Scottish border, even if far less noticeably to outsiders.[38] No single respected version of a possible standard Northern speech has emerged even within one of these sub-regions, so the elite have expressed local superiority by moving towards Received Pronunciation. Dialects and associated accents are still robust and form a focus of much interest and pride, but paradoxically they are also generally accepted as markers of lower status.[39] The 'guides' to Northern speech that are now widely sold are all clearly humorous and nothing else.[40] Dialect literature exists, but as a distinct minority interest. In Northern universities the locally born manual and

---

37. Tyne Tees Television was the last ITV station, apart from the Midlands-based ATV, to take up *Coronation Street*: Graham Turner, *The North country* (London, 1967), p. 408.

38. R. Lass, *The shape of English: structure and history* (London, 1987), pp. 243–50; D. Crystal, *The Cambridge encyclopaedia of language* (Cambridge, 1987), pp. 24–33; K. Wales, *Northern English: a cultural and social history* (Cambridge, 2006). See also *The Sunday Times*, 3 January 2010, for a survey of academics that concludes that 'Regional Accents Thrive Against the Odds in Britain': <http://www.timesonline.co.uk/tol/news/uk/article6973975.ece> accessed 8 December 2010.

39. For an in-depth review of *The Guardian*'s current attitude to the use of accents in its own output see: <http://www.guardian.co.uk/commentisfree/2007/dec/17/comment.britishidentity> accessed 8 December 2010.

40. For instance, D. Dutton, *Lanky spoken here: a guide to the Lancashire dialect* (London, 1978). Illustrations were provided by Bill Tidy, the famous cartoonist who specialises in affectionate northern stereotypes, notably *The Cloggies, an Everyday Saga in the Life of Clog Dancing Folk*, which ran in *Private Eye* and then *The Listener* between 1967 and 1986.

clerical workers, and many local students, speak Northern English, but it largely fizzles out somewhere in the middle ranks, and most of the academics and higher management speak Standard English. In Belgium, for instance, language continually provides the detonator that sets off disunity between different economic and cultural zones, but here it leads to very little real action.

Burns has played an enormous symbolic role for Scottish unity, and Wordsworth is another internationally acclaimed poet, with *Daffodils* possibly the most popular and recognised poem in England. However, he is seen as either an Englishman or as a defender of a rural Lakeland against the industrial North, and so not relevant to the whole North as a region. Similarly, Lakeland attracts tourists from all over the world, including southern England, and it is universally praised for its scenery and views, yet here again its very attractions form an honorary opt-out from Northernness as it is generally perceived. This is even more remarkable given the plentiful evidence of its own industrial past, especially extensive mineral extraction. In contrast, L.S. Lowry has maintained a Northern identity as an artist while acquiring an international reputation, but the portrait of the North conveyed by this success is very stylised and perpetuates the standard image of ugliness and squalor.

In modern popular culture the evident huge and creative regional interest in music has produced little that celebrates the North – indeed, George Harrison's *Only a Northern Song* has an interesting title and words from this point of view. Similarly, Mike Harding's highly successful *Rochdale Cowboy* was even more affectionately self-mocking about the disjunction between local and global culture. Gerry Marsden's *Ferry Cross the Mersey* and Lindisfarne's *Fog on the Tyne* were simply celebrations of local community strength. The bedrock of Northern culture has always been, and continues to be, ordinary life, and surviving it in good shape, rather than the spirit of *Braveheart* or *Flower of Scotland*.[41] Thus, the *Lancashire Hotpots* were a surprise hit at the 2009 Glastonbury Festival, since previously

> few people had heard of [them] and those who had thought it was just
> four blokes having a bit of a laugh in their spare time … Bernard Thresher
> [a band member] admits he gave them three months before the jokes
> would start to wear thin. But somehow singing about sat navs, chippy
> teas, emos and pints of mild has won them fans not just across Lancashire

41. V. Williamson, 'Regional identity: a gendered heritage? Reading women in 1990s fiction', in S. Caunce, E. Mazierska, S. Sidney-Smith and J.K. Walton (eds), *Relocating Britishness* (Manchester, 2004), pp. 168–83. This was true even in the hands of a writer like Arnold Bennett, if we stretch the northern boundary a little.

but the length and breadth of the country – and it has even caught on in the celebrity world.[42]

Peter Kay also maintains this tradition in wry comedy based on everyday existence, a Northern strength, which could be said to differentiate the immensely successful *Coronation Street* most clearly from its rival *EastEnders*.[43] In December 2010 it reached its fiftieth anniversary and was the longest-running drama of its type still transmitted. While some post-war films apparently set in the North have achieved recognition the theme that runs through almost all, down to *Billy Elliot*, is that achieving cultural aspirations means moving out, probably to London. *Billy Liar* showed those who stay as essentially too scared to seize opportunities they desperately desired.

Conclusion

The political North of today is in practice moving away from self-assertion. The faceless business corporations and quangos that have come to dominate modern public life (even if the Coalition government is dismantling a good number of the latter) have no local or regional commitment, and few of their senior staff have strong connections with the locality they operate in, or expect to stay there for a significant portion of their lives. Localism no longer forms an adequate base for connecting with new general business opportunities, and the resources of the region are managed from outside with little concern for local consequences. Local politics now certainly attracts few who could be called established leaders with the connections and influence to drive communities forward over a long period. The old desire for local recognition seems inadequate now as the main reward for such activity. Moreover, widespread if unfocused dissatisfaction with the region's current status is offset in practice by the benefits of living within a rich country. While the quality of life is often perceived as having declined in intangible ways, Northerners mostly enjoy far higher purely material living standards than its 'glory days' actually delivered to their ancestors. No real and widespread sense of desperation therefore exists.

The consequence of all this is that, far from gaining autonomy and respect in the devolutionary decades, Northern England in 2010 has probably never had less of either. Much of this analysis has used categories that have essentially lost

---

42. <http://www.prestoncitizen.co.uk/leisure/music/4377084.Interview__Bernard_Thresher_of_The_Lancashire_Hotpots/> accessed 8 December 2010.

43. *The Guardian*, 13 February 2010, devoted the cover of its weekly television guide to a cartoon representation of *EastEnders*, characterising it as a mass of insulting and violent personal confrontations with one lonely figure in a corner offering an irrelevant cup of tea.

anything but historical meaning during the period under study, with the transformation of both the economy and the local government framework. Today it is generally characterised as a backward-looking problem area, appealing for protection from the very economic forces that once brought it success, and it receives little attention except at flashpoints over ethnic tensions. Its preferred relationship to the rest of the nation remains much as it always was, and if the general election of 2010, with its slogan of 'a new politics', may seem to have put an end to the distinctive patterns described above, this is very debatable. The election occurred after this analysis was completed so no detailed treatment has been attempted, but in the hypothetical new Northern parliament there would be 104 Labour MPs (40 per cent of all Labour representation) to 43 Conservatives and 11 Liberal Democrats. This forms a Labour preponderance similar to that in Wales but less than in Scotland.[44] The conurbations, where most of the people live, remained very solidly Labour and many Conservative victories (though not all) owed at least something to a limited revival of traditional three-party politics reminiscent of 1983 outside them. Only 15 Northern seats produced an overall Conservative majority, most of them their perpetual strongholds.

Those really disaffected with Labour thus have not turned to nationalism of any kind, and only marginally to the Conservatives. In terms of seats won, nationalisms of all kinds actually did very poorly in 2010 right across the mainland, with only nine MPs returned. Indeed, what emerges most sharply is a huge divide in political outlook between all the conurbations, including London outside the wealthy zones, and the rest of the country. That seems very dangerous for national cohesiveness in a time of fierce government retrenchment, but regionalism still seems unlikely to flourish as a result. Identity will surely alter, but no sharp break with past patterns is likely, and we can only wait to see how it will happen.

44. <http://news.bbc.co.uk/1/shared/election2010/results/> accessed 8 December 2010.

5. Locality and diversity: minority ethnic communities in the writing of Birmingham's local history

Malcolm Dick

This chapter considers how local historians have represented the nature and experiences of minority ethnic communities whose origins derive from outside mainland Britain.[1] Using Birmingham as the focus of study, it illuminates how these communities appear or fail to appear in texts and what light this throws on the ways in which historians have portrayed urban localities. In so doing, the exploration provides a means of drawing attention to different voices and ways of characterising localities by examining how published historians since the eighteenth century have represented ethnic minorities.

The author's interest in this subject began in 2000 while working for 'The Millennibrum Project' (2000–2002), which aimed to create a multimedia archive of printed and manuscript materials, artefacts, photographs and film for Birmingham Libraries and Birmingham Museums and Art Gallery. The project reflected the City Council's awareness that its heritage collections did not fully represent the growth in Birmingham's cultural diversity since 1945.[2] Work on this project led to a series of questions. How far was the history of ethnic minority communities in

---

1. I am grateful to Dr Sally Baggott and the editors of the book for commenting on an early draft of the text.

2. This project was a partnership between Birmingham City Council, The Birmingham Post and Mail Group and the University of Central England (now Birmingham City University). The project was largely financed by the Millennium Commission. See <http://www.thefreelibrary.com/Millennibrum%3A+Bringing +Birmingham's+history+to+life.-a065007512> accessed 6 January 2011. The outputs of the project (oral histories, video histories, films, photographs, archival collections and artefacts) are held by Birmingham Archives and Heritage in Birmingham Central Library and Birmingham Museums and Art Gallery.

the city reflected in historical publications? What light did the publications throw on the experiences of these minorities: for example, how they came to Birmingham, patterns of settlement, their work and family life, the formation of communities, their influence on civic life and relationships with other groups? Were they ignored by writers? If so, what did this absence reflect: a lack of evidence or an unwillingness to consider different ways of viewing the past?

For some years historians have been looking at the history of the UK as a collection of diverse nationalities and ethnicities. The best known general survey is Norman Davies' 2000 publication *The Isles*.[3] Such a representation is not new. M. Dorothy George, in her history of London in 1925, devoted a substantial part of one chapter to the presence of overseas migrants, including Irish, Jews, Africans and Asians in London.[4] Important books on Manchester, Bristol and London have been published which chart aspects of the history of minority ethnic communities over a long timespan.[5] In their different ways they provide models of how local studies might proceed. However, the way in which ethnic minorities have been represented in the histories of towns over a long timespan has not been explored, although historians have started to consider the evolution of the writing of urban histories.[6] David Parker and Paul Long have written a relevant article which addresses how Birmingham has been represented in recent public discourse, including examples of popular history.[7] Birmingham provides a useful case study of how historians of localities have represented the nature and experiences of minority ethnic communities partly because there is a rich tradition of local history writing since William Hutton in the eighteenth century, and partly because it has an equally long ethnic minority presence. How the two have interconnected forms the subject of this chapter.

The chapter proceeds as follows. Firstly, it provides an overview of the history of ethnic minorities in Birmingham; secondly, it considers the ways in which ethnic minorities have been represented in the work of eighteenth- and

---

3. N. Davies, *The Isles: a history* (London, 2000).

4. M.D. George, *Life in eighteenth-century London* (Harmondsworth, 1976), pp. 120–45.

5. B. Williams, *The making of Manchester Jewry 1740–1875* (Manchester, 1976); M. Dresser and P. Fleming, *Bristol: ethnic minorities and the city 1000–2001* (Chichester, 2007); K. Chater, *Untold histories: black people in England and Wales during the period of the British slave trade, c. 1660–1807* (Manchester, 2009). Chater's book explores the black presence in London.

6. For an overview of the history of urban histories within the context of local history writing see W.G. Hoskins, *Local history in England*, 2nd edn (London, 1972), pp. 17–27, and K. Tiller, *English local history: an introduction* (Stroud, 2002), pp. 7–23. R. Sweet, *Antiquaries: the discovery of the past in eighteenth-century Britain* (London, 2004), explores the beginning of published local histories.

7. D. Parker and P. Long, 'Reimagining Birmingham: public history, selective memory and the narration of urban change', *European Journal of Cultural Studies*, 6 (2003), pp. 157–78.

nineteenth-century historians: William Hutton (1723–1815), John Alfred Langford (1823–1903) and John Thackray Bunce (1828–1899); thirdly, it explores the three volumes in the Oxford University Press *History of Birmingham* series, published in 1952 and 1974; and, fourthly, it examines how work produced within and outside the academy has extended the range of published material on the history of local ethnic minorities.

Ethnic minorities in Birmingham

Parish registers, local newspapers (including *Aris's Birmingham Gazette*, first published in 1741[8]), photographs, private papers and official sources (such as council documents and census returns) provide evidence of a long history of migration into Birmingham from outside England, Scotland and Wales.[9] The process of population movement included Jewish and Irish newcomers in the eighteenth, nineteenth and twentieth centuries, continental Europeans, notably Italians, from the late eighteenth century and a small black presence before 1914.[10] The relative prosperity of Birmingham, compared to other industrial towns in the late 1930s, encouraged economic migration. The first Asian community in Birmingham was composed of Yemeni men who were employed as lascars on merchant ships and settled in British coastal towns including Cardiff and South Shields. In the late 1930s a number settled in Birmingham, probably to work in the expanding metal industries. By 1941 the Yemenis had an organisation and religious leadership based on a *zawiya*, or centre for prayer, which was created in Balsall Heath.[11] At the same time there were also a small number of settlers from the Indian subcontinent, some of whom were doctors, although it is not easy to

---

8. 'Economic and social history: social history before 1815', in W.B. Stephens (ed.), *A history of the county of Warwick: volume 7: The City of Birmingham* (London, 1964), pp. 209–22. This volume in the *Victoria County History* series can also be viewed electronically on British History Online: <http://www.british-history.ac.uk/>.

9. Birmingham Archives and Heritage in Birmingham Central Library provides a range of relevant printed, manuscript and visual material: <http://www.birmingham.gov.uk/archivesandheritage> accessed 9 December 2010.

10. Z. Josephs, *Birmingham Jewry 1749–1914* (Birmingham, n.d.) and *Birmingham Jewry – more aspects, 1740–1930* (Birmingham, 1984); J. Moran, *Irish Birmingham: a history* (Liverpool, 2010); D. Hopwood and M. Dilloway, *Bella Brum: a history of Birmingham's Italian community* (Birmingham, 1996); I. Grosvenor, 'Never again will a single story be told as though it's the only one', in I. Grosvenor, R. McLean and S. Roberts (eds), *Making connections: Birmingham black international history* (Birmingham, 2002), pp. 19–30; A study of Peter Stanford, a nineteenth-century African-American pastor who lived in Birmingham, is provided in P.F. Walker, 'The Revd Peter Thomas Stanford (1860–1909): Birmingham's "coloured preacher"' (PhD thesis, Manchester, 2004).

11. M. Dick, 'Yemenis: the Yemeni community', in M.A. Chishti (compiler), *Lok Virsa, cultural voyage, exploring the Muslim Heritage* (Studley, 2008), pp. 48–50.

identify the establishment of organisations serving these migrants which would indicate that communities had been formed.[12] African-Caribbean and South Asian migration after 1945 is better known and was larger in scale. During the 1930s and 1940s there were also movements of refugee populations from Central Europe, Serbia and Poland, as a result of Nazi and Soviet persecution, and in the late twentieth and early twenty-first centuries from Vietnam, the former Yugoslavia, Iraq, Iran, Afghanistan and several African states (including the Democratic Republic of the Congo, Eritrea, Ethiopia, Somalia, Sudan and Zimbabwe).[13]

It is not easy or even possible to measure the size of minority populations during most periods of time in the past. The census of 2001, however, which included a section in which people could tick a box to indicate their ethnicity, provided a substantial statistical snapshot of ethnic diversity in Birmingham. Out of a total population of 977,099, those who described themselves as white numbered 687,406, of whom 641,345 were British and 31,467 were Irish. Of the other categories, 27,954 described themselves as 'mixed'; 190,689 were of Asian or Asian British background; 59,835 were Black or Black British; and 11,215 were either Chinese or a member of another ethnic group.[14] The categories in the census were broad, so that it was not possible to identify the precise national origins of people from, for example, Iraq or Somalia. Moreover, census returns tend to under-record the presence of single males, who frequently escape being recorded by enumerators. The importance of the census, however, was that it showed that Birmingham was a very ethnically diverse city at the beginning of the twenty-first century, a diversity that was the result of centuries of population movement from overseas. Historians were aware of Birmingham's ethnic diversity from the late eighteenth century, but sometimes this dimension was ignored and, even when it was recorded, perspectives varied considerably.

Eighteenth- and nineteenth-century histories

William Hutton, acknowledged to be the first historian of Birmingham, published his celebratory and substantial *History of Birmingham* in 1781. It went

---

12. D.R. Prem, *The parliamentary leper: a history of colour prejudice in Britain* (Aligarh, India, 1965); M. Dick, 'Travelling through time: migration and the black experience', in Grosvenor, McLean and Roberts, (eds), *Making connections*, pp. 35–6.

13. M. Dick, *Birmingham, a history of the city and its people* (Birmingham, 2005), attempts to integrate the experience and contributions of minority ethnic communities within the history of Birmingham. See also M. Dick, *Celebrating sanctuary: Birmingham and the refugee experience 1750–2002* (Birmingham, 2002), which describes the history of refugees in the city.

14. Census 2001 provided a snapshot: see Table KS06, p. 65, at <http://www.statistics.gov.uk/downloads/census2001/KS_LA_E&W_part1.pdf> accessed 9 December 2010.

through several editions and remained the standard history of Birmingham until John Langford's publication of 1868.[15] Hutton was a poor migrant from Derby and in Birmingham he established himself as a bookseller, paper maker and writer.[16] He included many contemporary observations in his book and, unlike some of his twentieth-century successors, he was aware of ethnic minorities in Birmingham. Birmingham people who came to the town, he claimed, liked the place: 'a predilection for Birmingham, is entertained by every denomination of visitants'.[17] As evidence, he drew attention to the experience of an Irishman:

> A paviour, of the name of Obrien, assured me in 1750, that he only meant to sleep one night in Birmingham, in his way from London to Dublin. But instead of pursuing his journey next morning, as intended, he had continued in the place thirty-five years: and though fortune had never elevated him above the pebbles of the street, yet he had never repented of his stay.[18]

In this anecdote the subject is presented as an individual who found work and enjoyed his stay. There did not appear to be an Irish community with institutions and leaders at this time, and large-scale Irish migration only came later.

For Hutton, an individual outsider who connected with the locality was not a problem, but he portrayed an alien community with a different culture negatively; he presented this alternative perspective when he described the Jews of Birmingham:

> We have also among us a remnant of Israel. A people who, when masters of their own country, were scarcely ever known to travel, and who are now seldom employed in anything else. But, though they are ever moving, they are ever at home: who once lived the favourites of heaven, and fed upon the cream of the earth; but now are little regarded by either: whose society is entirely confined to themselves, except in the commercial line.
>
> In the Synagogue situated in the Froggery, they still preserve the faint resemblence of the ancient worship. Their whole apparatus being no more than the drooping ensigns of poverty. The place is rather small, but

---

15. C.R. Elrington, 'Introduction', in W. Hutton, *An history of Birmingham* (Wakefield, 1976), pp. v–xxv; reprint of 1783 edition. See also C.R. Elrington, 'Hutton, William (1723–1815), historian', *ODNB*.

16. Elrington, 'Introduction', p. x.

17. Hutton, *An history of Birmingham*, p. 62.

18. *Ibid.*, pp. 62–3.

tolerably filled; where there appears less decorum than in the christian churches. The proverbial expression, 'as rich as a jew,' is not altogether verified in Birmingham, but perhaps, time is transferring it to the Quakers.

It is rather singular, that the honesty of a jew is seldom pleaded but by the jew himself.[19]

How do we interpret this text? Hutton used various labels which communicate a negative picture: 'remnant', 'little regarded' and 'less decorum'. Jews are described as poor and, according to the insinuation of the last line, dishonest. This disparaging extract does show, however, that there was a local Jewish community with an institution and a synagogue, and this is supported by other sources. Since the 1740s Birmingham had been a home to a Jewish community from central Europe which had settled in the Froggery, a badly drained part of Birmingham, where New Street station is now located. The community's synagogue was also located there.[20] However, Hutton's critical portrait is a selective one, as it does not draw on other possible ways of representing the Jews which were available at the time. As a trader in Birmingham, Hutton would have known that there were businesses owned by Jews. Sketchley and Adams' *Directory* of 1770 listed several individuals with Jewish names who were wealthy enough to pay to be listed. These included Asher Barnet, a spectacle grinder; Moses Aaron, a pencil and necklace maker; Mordecai Solomon and Abraham Sampson, also pencil makers; and Michael and Barnett Frideberg, glass cutters, flowerers and toymen.[21] Also among them was Mayer Opnaim (also known as Mayer Oppenheim), described as a merchant in the directory but who had established a glassworks in 1762 and taken out a patent for making red glass.[22] Hutton had a choice of how he represented a community which was contributing economically to Birmingham's development, and he chose to present a negative view. Later sources offer other perspectives on the local Jewish community. Rabbi Isaiah Phillips was appointed minister and reader of the synagogue in 1785 and died in 1834; his obituary in *Aris's Birmingham Gazette* drew attention to his charitable work, not least in collecting money for the relief of the wounded and the relatives of those who died at the battle of Trafalgar: 'In him his family are bereft of a kind and indulgent parent; the poor, a sincere friend; and the

---

19. *Ibid.*, pp. 128 and 123 (the pagination in this part of the book is confusing).

20. Josephs, *Birmingham Jewry 1749–1914*, pp. 10–11.

21. *Sketchley and Adams' tradesman's true guide and universal directory of the streets and inhabitants of Birmingham* (Birmingham, 1770).

22. A. Engle, 'Mayer Oppenheim of Birmingham', in A. Engle (ed.), *Readings in glass history* (Jerusalem, 1974).

Israelites, a most excellent preceptor.'[23] A later writer in 1885 commented on Hutton's observations: 'No modern historian would think of using such language nowadays respecting the Jews who now abide with us, whose charitable contributions to our public institutions may bear comparison with those of their Christian brethren.'[24] Hutton recognised diversity in Birmingham, but his portrayal of an Irish individual contrasted markedly with his representation of the Jewish community.

A second historian who drew attention to a minority presence in Birmingham was John Langford, whose *A century of Birmingham life* was first published in 1868. Unlike Hutton, Langford was born in Birmingham, but, like Hutton, he was able to achieve status in the town. He began his career as a chair maker and became a teacher, bookseller, writer and journalist before he published his history. He was also active in local political life, becoming secretary of Birmingham Co-operative Society, a supporter of Hungarian and Italian nationalism and an elected member of the Birmingham school board.[25] Langford's history was, as he modesty described it, 'a compilation' of local subjects based on extracts from *Aris's Gazette*.[26] His chronicle was not a work of history in the traditional sense of the word, but was creative, comprising selected extracts from the newspaper and providing commentaries on events and passages from other sources to offer insights into how he saw Birmingham's past. The book drew attention to the presence of ethnic minorities in Birmingham and there are several references, for example, to events affecting the Jewish community after 1783.[27] Langford's selected extracts from *Aris's Gazette* presented a positive picture: the opening of a new synagogue in 1791, for instance, was accompanied with psalms and songs which were sung 'with great judgement and melody',[28] while the laying of the foundation stone in 1809 for another synagogue in Severn Street was a public ceremony which 'was conducted in a manner that reflects the highest honour on the manager of the festival'.[29] Langford also charted the presence of black people. His first reference was to an advertisement for the sale of a slave in Lichfield in 1771, in which the 10- or 11-

---

23. *Aris's Birmingham Gazette*, 22 December 1834.

24. *Showell's Dictionary of Birmingham* (1885).

25. C. Chinn, 'Langford, John Alfred (1823–1903), writer and journalist', *ODNB*.

26. J.A. Langford, *A century of Birmingham life: or, a chronicle of local events from 1741 to 1841*, 2 vols (Birmingham, 1870), 1, p. v.

27. *Ibid.*, 1, pp. 369–70; 2, p. 234.

28. *Ibid.*, 1, p. 370.

29. *Ibid.*, 2, p. 234.

year-old boy for sale was described in detail: 'He is remarkably straight, well-proportioned, speaks tolerably good English, of a mild disposition, friendly, officious, sound, healthy, fond of Labour, and for Colour, an excellent fine Black.'[30] Langford's sympathies were clear – 'Could a Southern slave auctioneer dwell more lovingly on the qualities of this specimen of a human chattel?'[31] – and his history also included information on Birmingham's involvement in the abolition of the slave trade in the 1790s and slavery in the 1830s.[32] He noted how 'this town took an active part in the noblest philanthropic labour of the age – the Abolition of the Slave Trade',[33] and outlined the visit of the former African slave and campaigner against slavery, Olaudah Equiano, to the town in 1790.[34] Langford's comments and selection of newspaper sources show that he was aware of the abolitionist movement and the Black presence in Birmingham in the late eighteenth and early nineteenth centuries. Only recently have historians and archivists taken his investigations further.[35]

Another nineteenth-century historian who deserves examination is John Bunce, who was a member of Birmingham's civic elite, edited the *Birmingham Daily Post* and supported local initiatives, including Birmingham's new museum and art gallery and Birmingham School of Art.[36] He was responsible for a two-volume official history of Birmingham published by the Corporation of Birmingham in 1878 and 1885. Like Langford's history, it contained a large collection of primary source material but, in his case, this was derived from survey reports and official documents rather than newspapers. Bunce covered the evolution of Birmingham's local authority in great detail from 1760 to 1880 and was scathing of opposition to increasing the power and influence of Birmingham's elected council. He described improvements in the town, including the building of the Town Hall, the removal of slums and the creation of Corporation Street, and he ascribed these to effective leadership in Birmingham, culminating in the 'brilliant administration of Mr

---

30. *Ibid.*, 1, p. 151.

31. *Ibid.*, 1, p. 152.

32. *Ibid.*, 1, pp. 434–43; 2, pp. 555, 558–60.

33. *Ibid.*, 1, p. 434.

34. *Ibid.*, 1, p. 440. On Equiano's visit to Birmingham to sell his autobiography, *The interesting narrative of the life of Olaudah Equiano, or Gustavus Vassa, the African. Written by himself* (1789), see V. Carretta, *Equiano, the African: biography of a self-made man* (New York, 2005), pp. 337–9.

35. Birmingham City Archives, *Black history sources in Birmingham City Archives* (Birmingham, 2004), text by Fiona Tait.

36. J. Marsh, 'Bunce, Kate Elizabeth (1856–1927), painter', *ODNB*: Kate Bunce was a painter and daughter of J.T. Bunce.

Chamberlain'.[37] Bunce made only two references to ethnic minorities. One, a descriptive remark, concerned the appointment of David Barnett, the first Jewish member of Birmingham Corporation, as an alderman in 1839, when he was allowed to take his oath of office without having to use the words 'on the true faith of a Christian'. The second, which is more revealing, occurred in his description of the Murphy Riots of 1867, the only time when the 'general peace of the borough' had been 'disturbed since its government has been in the hands of the Corporation'.[38] William Murphy was an Irish Protestant who toured England between 1866 and 1871 making anti-catholic speeches; while in Birmingham he faced vigorous local opposition.[39] Bunce wrote:

> The solitary case of serious riot happened on the evening of the 16th June, 1867, when William Murphy, an anti-papal lecturer, came to deliver a course of addresses in the town. A wooden tabernacle was built for his accommodation ..., and as he was addressing a large audience inside, a crowd of infuriated Irishmen assembled round the building. One of these in a drunken state, being arrested, a general riot was provoked, stones being thrown in all directions, and many persons being injured.[40]

Bunce's description of the disturbances contained a portrayal of the Irish as angry, drunk and violent. As Patsy Davis showed in 2006, a negative view of the Irish as ignorant, living in disease-ridden slums and active in crime was common in both official and unofficial texts in nineteenth-century Birmingham.[41] The Irish did not form part of Bunce's vision of Birmingham's onward progress; instead, where they appeared in the historical narrative, he represented them as a disruptive element.

Eighteenth- and nineteenth-century historical writing, therefore, recognised the presence of ethnic minorities in Birmingham, but the ways in which they were represented differed. Both Hutton and Bunce provided negative portrayals, while Langford offered a more positive picture. Another set of representations is provided in twentieth-century historical writing.

37. J.T. Bunce, *History of the corporation of Birmingham; with a sketch of the earlier government of the town*, 2 vols (Birmingham, 1878–85), 2, pp. xxxiv–xxxv.

38. *Ibid.*, 1, pp. 162–3; 2, p. 292.

39. J. Wolffe, 'Murphy, William (1834–1872), public lecturer', *ODNB*.

40. Bunce, *History of the Corporation*, 2, p. 292.

41. P. Davis, 'Birmingham's Irish community and the Murphy riots of 1867', *Midland History*, 31 (2006), pp. 37–64. Davis' thesis and article remain two of the few substantial histories of an ethnic minority community in Birmingham.

The Oxford University Press histories of Birmingham

In the twentieth century much written work on Birmingham's past could be characterised as belonging to the 'onwards and upwards' school of history, which perpetuated Bunce's Whiggish initiative by charting the progressive political activities of Birmingham's municipal councils. The first two volumes in the Oxford University Press *History of Birmingham* series by C. Gill and A. Briggs respectively, both published in 1952, represent this perspective.[42] Social history received very little treatment, although religious diversity secured some attention. Gill claimed that 'In the middle years of the nineteenth century Birmingham became an important centre of Roman Catholicism.'[43] His evidence, based on the presence of churches, including St Chad's, which became Birmingham's first cathedral, supports his case, but he did not mention that the dramatic growth in the catholic population was largely the result of migration from Ireland. Unlike his nineteenth-century predecessors, Briggs also ignored the presence of minorities from overseas. For both Gill and Briggs minority communities did not form a part of the march of progress in Birmingham.

Ethnic minorities did appear, however, in the third volume in the *History of Birmingham* by A. Sutcliffe and R. Smith in 1974: this is still the most substantial and well-researched history of the twentieth-century city. The book, which covered the years 1939–1970, contained an explanation of the economic reasons for migration and a chapter on post-war migration (chapter 11) entitled 'The impact of coloured immigration'.[44] The first three sentences of this chapter presented newcomers as creating difficulties for the city:

> Coloured People formed only a minority of the total of immigrants into Birmingham in the years 1939–70. They were, however, the most noticeable, and in some ways they created more problems than white immigrants from other parts of the British Isles and from abroad. Not only were they marked out by the colour of their skin, but frequently, too, by their language difficulties.[45]

The authors thus drew attention to the skin colour of the newcomers and suggested that this 'noticeable' difference and 'their language difficulties' created 'more problems' than were occasioned by white migrants to Birmingham. By

---

42. C. Gill, *History of Birmingham, vol. 1: manor and borough to 1865* (London, 1952); A. Briggs, *History of Birmingham, vol. 2, borough and city 1865–1938* (London, 1952).

43. Gill, *History of Birmingham*, p. 375.

44. A. Sutcliffe and R. Smith, *History of Birmingham, vol. 3: Birmingham 1939–1970* (London, 1974), pp. 209–10.

45. *Ibid.*, pp. 363–98.

focusing on the 'problems', Sutcliffe and Smith drew attention away from any positive impact which migrant labour had on the city's economic life. Much of the chapter concentrated on political controversies up to 1970 and the pressures that immigration placed on housing and education, but, surprisingly, there was no mention of Enoch Powell's famous 'Rivers of Blood' speech, which was delivered in Birmingham on 20 April 1968 and had a considerable impact both locally and nationally.[46] Nevertheless, the chapter offered a few descriptions of minority experiences, albeit presented as unusual events which 'excited interest and curiosity'. Immediately before and during the Second World War, 'People were amused to read of three Sikhs who refused to remove their turbans when being taught how to put on gas masks during the Munich crisis in 1938; and later they were sorry to hear of the death by suffocation of a whole Arab family in an air-raid shelter in Holloway Head after the collapse of a wall of sandbags.'[47] The descriptions raise tantalising questions which the authors did not consider. Why were Arabs (presumably Yemenis) and Sikhs living in Birmingham? How long had they been in the city?[48] How did they make a living, to what extent were they able to retain their culture or religion and what was the nature of their relationship with people of other communities? These are still questions which a contemporary historian of early migratory experiences needs to explore.

These twentieth-century historians of Birmingham either ignored the presence of ethnic minority communities, as in the case of Gill and Briggs, or, as with Sutcliffe and Smith, they represented them as problems or as interesting anecdotes. Volume 7 of the *Victoria County History of Warwickshire*, which is devoted to Birmingham, provides detailed sections on political, social and economic history, but it also ignored the experiences of ethic minorities from overseas.[49] In the late twentieth century, starting with the work of John Rex, sociological studies began to explore race and ethnicity in Birmingham,[50] but historians were slower than sociologists in addressing these issues.

Recent historical writing from within and outside the academy

By the 1990s popular histories of Birmingham by Carl Chinn and Chris Upton

---

46. <http://www.bbc.co.uk/white/rivers_blood.shtml> accessed 9 December 2010.

47. Sutcliffe and Smith, *History of Birmingham*, p. 363.

48. On the origins of the Yemenis in Birmingham see Dick, 'Yemenis', pp. 48–50. On the early settlement of Sikhs in Britain see G. Singh and D.S. Tatla, *Sikhs in Britain, the making of a community* (London, 2006), pp. 43–50.

49. *VCH Warwickshire*, 7.

50. J. Rex, *Race, community and conflict: a study of Sparkbrook* (Oxford, 1967); T. Abbas, *The education of British South Asians: ethnicity, capital and class structure* (Basingstoke, 2004).

presented information on local ethnic minorities, but their work was descriptive with limited referencing. They offered few analyses of ethnic experiences. The ways in which minorities were represented by these two historians have also been criticised by Patsy Davis (Upton) and Parker and Long (Chinn).[51] Eric Hopkins produced two substantial and well-researched histories of Birmingham in 1989, but, although they described economic and social experiences, ethnic minorities were, as in the histories of Gill and Briggs, absent.[52] One exception, which did focus on minority experiences, was a study of the interplay of race and educational policy in post-war Birmingham by Ian Grosvenor.[53]

Outside the academy, however, individuals and community groups began in the 1980s to uncover aspects of ethnic minority history. The pioneer of local work is this area was Zoë Josephs, who, using archival primary sources and oral history interviews, drew attention to the long history of Jewish people in Birmingham from the eighteenth century to the arrival of many refugees from the Nazis.[54] The Black Oral History Project, based in Handsworth, 'was set up in 1990 by a group of organisations and individuals, concerned to preserve the memories of an older generation of black and Asian migrants to Birmingham'. It published a collection of tape recordings in 1992 which, among other things, presented memories of hostility and racism.[55] Yousuf Choudhury, a Birmingham-based migrant from Bengal, described the lives of Bangladeshi settlers in a series of books published after 1993 and substantially based on interviews he had conducted.[56] Birmingham City Libraries also published a series of short books, beginning in 1996 with a scholarly study of local Italians by Doreen Hopwood and

---

51. C. Upton, *A history of Birmingham* (Chichester, 1997), pp. 100–106, 206–9. C. Chinn, *Birmingham: the great working city revised edition* (Birmingham, 2001), pp. 76–106. On Upton's treatment of the Irish, however, see Davis, 'Birmingham's Irish community' and on Chinn's approach to multi-culturalism see Parker and Long, 'Reimagining Birmingham'.

52. E. Hopkins, *Birmingham: the first manufacturing town in the world, 1760–1840* (London, 1989), republished as *The rise of the manufacturing town: Birmingham and the industrial revolution* (Stroud, 1998); E. Hopkins, *Birmingham: the making of the second city 1850–1939* (Stroud, 2001).

53. I. Grosvenor, *Assimilating identities: racism and educational policy in post-1945 Britain* (London, 1997).

54. Josephs, *Birmingham Jewry 1749–1914* and *Birmingham Jewry – more aspects*; Z. Josephs, *Survivors: Jewish refugees in Birmingham 1933–1939* (Birmingham, 1988).

55. <http://www.bbohp.org.uk/> accessed 9 December 2010. The published selection of interviews on audio cassette was entitled *The land of money*.

56. Y. Choudhury, *The roots and tales of the Bangladeshi settlers* (Birmingham, 1993), *Sons of Empire* (Birmingham, 1995) and *The book of Indian sub-continental cooking in Britain* (Birmingham, 2002). See also M. Dick, 'Yousuf Choudhury and Britain's Bangladeshi heritage', in M.A. Chishti (compiler), *Lok Virsa, cultural voyage, exploring the Muslim Heritage* (Studley, 2008), pp. 20–21. A DVD of Choudhury's life had been produced: M. Choudhury, *A son of empire: a documentary on Yousuf Choudhury* (Bangla Connection Production, 2004), available via banglaconnection@yahoo.co.uk.

Margaret Dilloway.[57] Later publications varied in depth and quality, but in their different ways they drew attention to the history of ethnic minority communities in Birmingham.[58] The advent of funding from the Heritage Lottery Fund and local projects such as 'Making Connections', 'Lok Virsa' and 'Connecting Histories' have attempted to extend the work of the 'Millennibrum Project' (itself funded by the Millennium Commission) by deepening collections of archives, publishing books and, in the case of 'Connecting Histories', developing a sizeable website.[59] Interestingly, these projects involved collaboration between community historians, academics and heritage professionals, including individuals from ethnic groups.

Conclusion

Unlike a number of twentieth-century historians, Birmingham's two earliest historians, Hutton and Langford, did address the presence of minority communities in Birmingham. Hutton's perspective reflected two approaches: a welcoming approach to individuals (in his case a sole Irish migrant), but a more critical approach to an alien Jewish community. His critical account, based on personal observation, occurred at a time when there were, as additional sources of evidence revealed, other ways of seeing Jewish people as contributors to local business and charity. Langford, whose publication was based on primary sources, also provided a diverse portrayal of the Birmingham area through his references to anti-slavery and the presence of black people and Jews, but, unlike Hutton, he presented a positive picture of the local Jewish community. Bunce's publication was the first of many that pursued a Whiggish agenda associated with a forward-looking local authority; his book avoided complicating this vision of a Birmingham led by a progressive elite. His depiction of the Irish provided a negative image of this minority during the Murphy Riots in 1867, as their behaviour was alien to that of the political culture he celebrated. Bunce's progressive approach was perpetuated in the twentieth century through the works of Gill, Briggs, Sutcliffe and Smith.

The range of works about minority communities has grown substantially since the 1980s, particularly resulting from community groups outside the academy, but there are challenges posed by new perspectives. Oral histories provide a way of gaining an insight into the experiences of different peoples, but, like all sources, they need to be used critically to make sense of the past. Historians of communities

---

57. Hopwood and Dilloway, *Bella Brum*.

58. P.L. Edmead, *The divisive decade: a history of Caribbean immigration to Birmingham in the 1950s* (Birmingham, 1999); Y. Choudhury and P. Drake, *From Bangladesh to Birmingham: the history of Bangladeshis in Birmingham* (Birmingham, 2001); C. Chinn, *Birmingham Irish: making our mark* (Birmingham, 2003).

59. I. Grosvenor, R. McLean and S. Roberts (eds), *Making connections: Birmingham black international history* (Birmingham, 2002); Chishti, *Lok Virsa*, <http://www.connectinghistories.org.uk/> accessed 9 December 2010.

might be unwilling to confront issues which cast minority individuals or communities in a critical light. This is understandable when those communities have been excluded from mainstream historical writing, but, as the present author's own experience revealed when working for a local Muslim history project, there can be a tension between the moral imperatives of a project organiser and the concerns of a professional historian. This occurred during the editing of the publication *Lok Virsa, cultural voyage: exploring the Muslim heritage*, which was an outcome of a project led by the 'Social Unity Foundation of Innovation (Sufi) Trust'.[60] The leader of the project was reluctant to include material which presented Muslim communities negatively, so that, for instance, during the finalising of text for the chapter on the Albanian community (pp. 13–15) references to the forced conversion of Christian Albanians by the Ottoman Turks had to be removed. This chapter was part of a larger section on Muslim communities which was edited by the present author, who was acting as historical consultant to the project. It was possible for the project leader and consultant to agree on appropriate linguistic compromises in most cases of disagreement, but the process of compromise revealed how the interpretation of evidence is affected when participants in a project have different perspectives. Community histories, as well, can be tainted by nostalgia, which can lead to a decontextualised celebration of lives, traditions and practices which are fast changing. Moreover, the old Whiggism might be replaced by a new Whiggism: multi-culturalism in history can become a selling point for the 'saris and samosas' syndrome, which presents the contributions of ethnic communities in making the urban environment vibrant, colourful and interesting while the existence of poverty, alienation and hostility is downplayed.

These issues show the importance of collaboration between universities and communities, where both can learn from each others' expertise and knowledge. This has happened, most notably, in the production of the publication on Bristol by Madge Dresser and Peter Fleming, which was supported by the Heritage Lottery Fund, the Victoria County History and the Institute of Historical Research, and included contributions from community historians.[61] In *Local history in England*, which was first published in 1959, W.G. Hoskins recognised that non-professional and professional historians could both contribute to the effective study of local history.[62] This lesson is one which we can emphasise when encouraging research into and the writing of ethnic minority histories in the future.

---

60. Chishti, *Lok Virsa*.

61. Dresser and Fleming, *Bristol*, pp. viii–ix.

62. Hoskins, *Local history*, pp. 4–5.

6. Hythe's butcher–graziers: their role in town and country in late medieval Kent

*Sheila Sweetinburgh**

Studies of the interconnection between town and countryside in medieval England have proliferated over recent decades, not least because it has become apparent that towns exercised considerable influence over their hinterlands. As Galloway, among others, has noted, 'towns served or exploited an increasingly commercialised countryside, moulding flows of goods, money and people, and dividing space into spheres of influence', and the processes whereby this took place have been of particular interest to historians.[1] Furthermore, studies of small towns in the later Middle Ages have explored social structural changes, especially matters such as greater polarisation and the incidence of familial and other networks that cross the rural/urban divide, as well as adding significantly to our knowledge on living standards and on production and consumption at the level of the household.[2] In some cases this research has been aided by an interdisciplinary, or at least multidisciplinary, approach that has drawn on documentary, topographical, architectural and archaeological sources as a means of providing a more holistic understanding of the relationships between urban communities and their hinterlands as seen through the actions of the townsfolk

*I would like to thank Justin Croft for permission to use his masters' dissertation and doctoral thesis, and Andrew Butcher for introducing me to the Hythe archive. I am grateful to Hythe Town Council for permission to photograph the maletote book.

1. J.A. Galloway, 'Urban hinterlands in later medieval England', in K. Giles and C. Dyer (eds), *Town and country in the middle ages: contrasts, contacts and interconnections, 1100–1500* (Leeds, 2005), p. 111.

2. For the latter the classic studies are C. Dyer, *Standards of living in the late Middle Ages* (Cambridge, 1989) and *Making a living in the Middle Ages: the people of Britain, 850–1520* (London, 2002).

and their rural neighbours.[3] Where possible, this would seem to be the way forward, but for many towns such a package of resources is sadly lacking, so requiring us to use parallels and analogies. Nevertheless, some of these problems can be overcome where there are particularly rich archival sources, which is the case for late medieval Hythe, in Kent.

The late medieval street pattern of Hythe is largely preserved in the cluster of roads and lanes below the church of St Leonard, itself a far grander and spacious building than its status as a daughter church of the parish church at neighbouring Saltwood would seem to warrant.[4] This preservation has resulted partly from Hythe's subsequent decline as a port and the later building of the 'new town' on the extended shoreline at the base of the earlier settlement. As one of the original head ports of what would become the Cinque Ports confederation, it enjoyed certain royal privileges from perhaps as early as the eleventh century. Yet many of these privileges were not particularly unusual by the later Middle Ages, and the town government comprised the bailiff, traditionally the archbishop of Canterbury's appointee, and twelve jurats.[5] The latter were elected annually by the freemen (barons) of Hythe. Nonetheless, close ties among the ports had fostered ideas about their political importance as a group, exemplified by their role as carriers of the royal canopy at coronations, and as a result the leading citizens had a keen regard for their status as special urban communities.[6] One aspect of this concern was the production and preservation of a civic archive that included the town's custumal and various administrative, judicial and financial town books. As well as aiding the survival of the medieval fabric of the town, Hythe's early modern decline was probably also instrumental in the continued existence of much of its medieval archive. Of particular interest here are the local taxation records.

The Cinque Ports employed a system of civic taxes called 'maletotes' that can most easily be described as forms of income and sales tax levied on each freeman dwelling in the town and at double rate on resident strangers. Only those considered to be paupers were given exemption. The scale of charges to be levied

3. The new study of medieval Sandwich exemplifies the value of this approach: H. Clarke, S. Pearson, M.E. Mate and K. Parfitt, *Sandwich: 'The completest medieval town in England': a study of the town and port from its origins to 1600* (Oxford, 2010).

4. J.F. Barker, *The parish of Hythe: St Leonard's church, a historical and architectural guide* (Hythe, 1994).

5. Although the exact circumstances are not clear, in 1455 the freemen acquired the right to appoint the bailiff but their success was relatively short-lived and Archbishop Morton reasserted successfully the Church's position: J.P. Croft, 'Hythe MS 1061: the making of an urban archive' (MA dissertation, Kent, 1992), pp. 22–7.

6. K.M.E. Murray, *The constitutional history of the Cinque Ports* (Manchester, 1935). See, in particular: A.F. Butcher, 'The functions of script in the speech community of a late medieval town, c.1300–1550', in J. Crick and A. Walsham (eds), *The uses of script and print, 1300–1700* (Cambridge, 2004), pp. 157–70.

was laid out in very detailed maletote lists in both Anglo-French and English, especially regarding the fishing industry, and almost equally for those engaged in the butchery trade.[7] For example, each ox sold or slaughtered was taxed at 2d, while cows and steers were a penny each, yearlings a halfpenny and calves a farthing. The trade in sheep similarly employed a sliding scale: those designated simply as 'sheep' (sold or killed) were taxed at a halfpenny each, the same rate as was applied to sheep called 'wollefells' (sold or killed); younger animals called sheep 'pyltys' (sold or killed) in the returns but 'scheylyngs' in the maletote list were charged at a farthing each; the sale or slaughter of two lambs contributed a farthing to the town's coffers. Hides, various skins and woolfells were also taxed at different rates, although pigs killed and horses sold were each charged at a fixed rate per animal, and a wey of tallow sold was taxed at $1\frac{1}{2}$d. In addition, other fines, such as sheep illegally grazing on 'le slip' at the haven, might be added to the assessment, but an individual's tax burden could be reduced by claiming allowances such as providing gifts given on the town's behalf to important people or working for the good of the town.[8]

Among the ports the most common extant maletote records are lists of those living in the town and the final sum due, but some of the tax returns are more detailed. The Hythe records are exceptional, as there is a largely complete 40-year run of very detailed returns from the early 1440s, in addition to a couple of years around 1420.[9] The arrangement, listed by ward, suggests that the head of each household went to the 'Common Hall', often in January (the end of the civic year), and before a panel of senior jurats stated what s/he had made and sold during the previous twelve months and what might be allowed against this sum (Fig. 6.1). Space was often left in the town book for the later entry of reports from those temporarily away from the town.

Of the various residents in late fifteenth-century Hythe, some worked as porters, labourers, masons, carpenters and coupers, but a sizeable majority were involved in the cloth and leather industries and in fishing and trading, which included importing wine; many gained at least part of their income from other victualling trades, such as brewing. Farming provided another source of income; in 1468 Robert Down sold various cereals including 14 quarters of wheat, 12 sheep, 6 lambs and 2 steers, and also received rent from land valued at 38s per

---

7. East Kent Archives (hereafter EKA), Whitfield, H1061, fos. 1–3; 6v; 7–8v; 9–9v. For an assessment of this manuscript, especially the maletotes: Croft, 'Hythe MS. 1061', pp. 37–43.

8. For example, in 1446–7 Richard Sellyng received an allowance for the scarlet cloth produced for the queen's coronation: EKA, H1055, fo. 85.

9. The three surviving maletote books cover the periods 1441–56, 1454–65 and 1467–84 respectively, though none are complete: EKA, H1055; H1019; H1058.

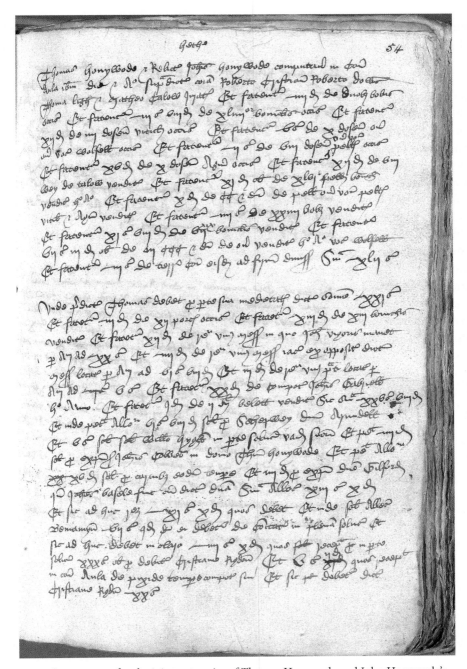

Fig. 6.1 Maletote return for the joint enterprise of Thomas Honywode and John Honywode's widow, 1470–71. Source: EKA, Whitfield, H1058, fo. 54.

annum.[10] Robert was living in Hythe's Middle Ward at the time but, according to his will, made five years later, he also had another house in the town, a windmill at Saltwood, other lands and a considerable number of cattle, including cows.[11]

As elsewhere in England in this period, the town's livestock trade was stimulated by the burgeoning demand for meat, which provided opportunities not only for rural farmers and urban butchers but also for urban livestock producers, such as Robert Down, and urban butcher–graziers.[12] Nevertheless, the shift away from arable or mixed farming towards an emphasis on livestock that is, for example, seen to characterise parts of the West Midlands is less obvious in east Kent.[13] There are still indications, however, that certain enterprising individuals in Kent were capitalising on the expanding domestic market and that some were also supplying the garrison town of Calais.[14] Moreover, butchers from the Weald are known to have operated in the Romney Marshes, and London's hinterland extended into north Kent, whose ports perhaps supplied livestock as well as grain.[15] At Hythe many of the town's butchers probably focused on the local trade, as they lived in Market Ward where they had easy access to the market place. Some are known to have had shops nearby, although whether these were lock-ups or part of their main dwelling is not always clear. Either way, they operated from permanent premises rather than stalls, retailing meat, as well as

10. EKA, H1058, fo. 16v.

11. Centre for Kentish Studies (hereafter CKS), Maidstone, PRC 32/2, fo. 251.

12. Maryanne Kowaleski provides a detailed account of the meat trade in Exeter, and even though it was a far larger urban centre than Hythe there are similarities, not least the presence of butcher–graziers: M. Kowaleski, *Local markets and regional trade in medieval Exeter* (Cambridge, 1995), pp. 293–307. Chester's meat trade seems to have involved distinct groups: the butchers purchased livestock from drovers who acted as middlemen between the butchers and farmers in the surrounding countryside; having bought the livestock at the city's cattle market, the butchers kept them in the Crofts, either slaughtering them there or at their shops: J. Laughton, *Life in a late medieval city: Chester 1275–1520* (Oxford, 2008), p. 135.

13. Men such as Roger Heritage of Burton Dassett, Warwickshire, who employed a considerable number of agricultural servants, geared his substantial agrarian enterprise to the market, invested in his large farm and bequeathed the same to his son: C. Dyer, 'Were there any capitalists in fifteenth-century England?' in J. Kermode (ed.), *Enterprise and individuals in fifteenth-century England* (Stroud, 1991), pp. 1–24. Andrew Bate of Lydd, Kent, may fit this criterion: S. Dimmock, 'English small towns and the emergence of capitalist relations, c.1450–1550', *Urban History*, 28 (2001), pp. 16–20. Perhaps a better candidate, however, would be Stephen Thorneherst, whose accumulated land, property holdings and commercial dealings provided his three sons with substantial agrarian assets in the 1560s: G. Draper, 'The farmers of Canterbury Cathedral priory and All Souls College on Romney Marsh c. 1443–1545', in J. Eddison, M. Gardiner and A. Long (eds), *Romney Marsh: environmental change and human occupation in a coastal lowland* (Oxford, 1998), pp. 120–4.

14. M.E. Mate, *Trade and economic developments 1450–1550: the experience of Kent, Surrey, and Sussex* (Woodbridge, 2006), pp. 43–4.

15. D. Keene, 'Small towns and the metropolis: the experience of medieval England', in J.M. Duvosquel and E. Thoen (eds), *Peasants and townsmen in medieval Europe: studia in honorem Adriaan Verhulst* (Ghent, 1995), pp. 230, 232–3.

selling hides and skins and supplying the tallow chandlers: these latter commodities were valuable by-products of the butchery trade. After about 1480, however, the butchers apparently opted for Middle Ward as their preferred residential area, perhaps indicating a desire to keep a reasonable distance between their homes and their commercial operation, but some may also have been engaged in the cross-Channel livestock business.[16]

In terms of longevity within the meat trade at Hythe between the mid-1440s and mid-1480s, there seems to have been only a small number of butchers, including the 'foreign butchers' (as outsiders, these men were listed separately at the end of the account), who operated for just a few years (although presumably those in the early lists and those who appear in the records at the beginning and end may have been in business for some time). There were, however, three men who were active for most of the time, while Robert Hooker was followed in the 1460s by John Hooker, perhaps his son, who continued the business for the next twenty years and probably until his death in 1497. At that time his shop in the market place was inherited by his wife but his measuring weights passed to his son and another man, possibly his partner.[17] At first John Hooker appears to have worked independently, but during the early 1480s and possibly thereafter he operated in partnership with Matthew Down as one of several joint enterprises recorded in the taxation returns.[18]

In addition to Robert and John Hooker, the other well-established butchers were Stephen Brombard and the brothers John and Thomas Honywode, the latter, like the Hookers, following in the footsteps of their early fifteenth-century predecessors.[19] Together Brombard and the Honywode brothers accounted for most of the business and, indeed, for a few years in the early 1460s they monopolised the trade. In terms of the meat trade, Brombard and the Hooker family seem to have concentrated solely on butchery, because none of their wills suggests that they held more than a small acreage, perhaps used merely to graze animals before slaughter.[20] Yet they were prepared to expand their commercial

---

16. In 1480–1, for example, Nicholas Aulisforde, John Fraryk and Nicholas John all undertook several voyages carrying cattle in their ships across the sea, and three years later John was also involved in the transport of horses and mares: EKA, H1058, fos. 221v, 224v, 225v, 263. John also seems to have been willing to transport a wide variety of cargo, when he was not fishing, because his earlier voyages in 1479–80 had involved the separate carriage of pilgrims and firewood: EKA, H1058, fo. 211.

17. CKS, PRC 32/4, fo. 156.

18. Robert Hooker generally traded independently but in 1445–6 he was joined by Richard Boteler, a butcher who had become a freeman three years earlier: EKA, H1055, fos. 22, 65.

19. John and Robert Honywode, the father and uncle of John and Thomas, were listed as butcher–graziers in the maletote records for 1418–20. John Hooker also had a butchery business at this time and a Stephen Brombard, perhaps the father of the later Hythe butcher, was recorded among the foreign butchers: EKA, H1059; H1054.

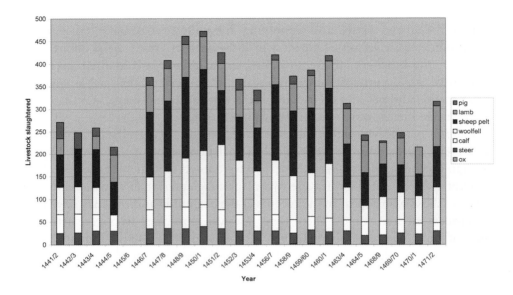

Fig. 6.2 Annual sales of slaughtered livestock by John Honywode, 1441–70, and his widow, 1470–72. Source: EKA, H1055; H1019; H1058.

interests in other ways because Brombard, or more probably his wife, brewed ale occasionally: 20 brewnods (a Cinque Port measurement) in 1447–8, for example, 19 the following year and 40 in 1464–5.[21]

In contrast, the Honywode brothers jointly held land in Hythe as well as in the neighbouring areas of Saltwood, West Hythe and Postling, and their agricultural property included a barn, several stables and a mill.[22] Each may also have held lands separately because Thomas is known to have had lands at Cheriton and in Romney Marsh, and both men bequeathed 6s 8d for church works to each of the parish churches of Dymchurch and Boroughmarsh (as well as to Saltwood and Postling), while Thomas left the same sum to Newington parish church.[23] Moreover, their

---

20. The second John Hooker may have had been the exception because he seemingly had slightly more land as he also owned a barn and he sometimes sold livestock (about 150 sheep and up to 50 cattle) rather than every beast going for slaughter: CKS, PRC 32/4, fo. 156. At his death Stephen Brombard had a messuage in Hythe, a stable he had bought and further lands, although his son Thomas (who was his successor) made little reference to land or property in his own will except for the family house in Brode Street: CKS, PRC 32/2, fo. 575; PRC 30/4, fo. 154.

21. EKA, H1055, fos. 104v, 120; H1019, fo. 149v.

22. As freemen of Hythe they were exempt from royal taxation but as landholders outside the liberty they were not. For example, John and Thomas were assessed jointly under the Folkestone hundred in 1447–8 at 20d: The National Archives (hereafter TNA), Kew, E179/229/147.

23. John Honywode: CKS, PRC 32/2, fo. 202. Thomas Honywode: CKS, PRC 32/2, fo. 262.

maletote returns always included livestock sales in addition to animals killed, which would seem to confirm their dual activities as livestock fatteners and butchers.

The Honywodes were by far the largest of the butcher partnerships and, in terms of individual levels of production, John Honywode was the most important in Hythe, closely followed by his brother.[24] The total number of animals that passed through their hands suggests that it is possible that the mid-fifteenth-century depression did not have much effect on their enterprises (Fig. 6.2). Rather, it was the early/mid-1440s that may have been a more difficult period, although there is no way of knowing how successful the brothers had been in the 1430s and it seems unlikely that their position as jurats would have hampered their commercial activities.[25] Unfortunately the butchery profiles of Stephen Brombard and Robert Hooker are less clear, but they too seem to have slaughtered fewer animals until the later 1440s. In both of their cases, however, it was not until the later 1450s that their businesses witnessed a significant upturn, although whether this was due to local or wider factors is difficult to assess. In contrast, during the 1450s and 1460s the Honywode brothers were increasingly active as livestock sellers and butchers, and it was only towards the end of the 1460s that they reduced their butchery trade to more moderate levels. The expansion in livestock sales at this time may have been a compensatory strategy, perhaps reflecting their personal circumstances rather than a downturn in the overall market, as both men must have been elderly: John died in 1470 and his brother four years later. Moreover, their widows continued the business for at least a year, John's widow with her brother-in-law at first and the following year with Walter Cowle (Coly), her son-in-law.[26]

From about the mid-century the number of butchers operating in Hythe seems to have risen, particularly from the mid-1460s. Furthermore, after the deaths of the Honywode brothers several others took their place, albeit individually at a lower level. Another of John Honywode's daughters had also married a butcher, William Jenkyn, although they seem to have lived outside Hythe because he was classed as a 'foreign butcher' in 1469–70 and John's testamentary gifts to the pair included a messuage, barn and stable at Saltwood.[27] The year after John's death Jenkyn appears to have worked in some form of partnership with his wife's uncle but thereafter he acted alone.[28] Lands in Hythe, Saltwood and Folkestone are recorded in a will of a

---

24. As well as their father and uncle, their grandfather Alan Honywode, who died in 1401, may have been a butcher–grazier too: CKS, PRC 32/1, fo. 12.

25. For example, one or both brothers were jurats for most of the 1440s: EKA, H1055.

26. EKA, H1058, fos. 54, 74v.

27. *Ibid.*, fo. 38.

28. *Ibid.*, fo. 74.

William Jenkyn of Hythe, probably his son, which survives from 1523.[29] Among William junior's other holdings were a messuage and barn at Saltwood, the house where he lived and a slaughter house. This seems to suggest that William senior was emulating his father-in-law by engaging in livestock production in addition to his butchery business, and others of his generation in and around Hythe, such as John Hooker, seemingly saw the advantages of this approach.[30] Perhaps also indicative of the buoyancy of the livestock sector in mid and later fifteenth-century Hythe is John and Thomas Honywode's extremely limited involvement in other commercial activities apart from the sale of hides, skins and tallow as by-products of the meat trade, although that in itself was a considerable undertaking.[31] The sale of a few horses appears to have been the main venture that either man undertook, but Thomas did sell wool and wine occasionally. John's activities extended to renting out land within the liberty and in some years he was taxed for retailing wine.[32] His widow continued the latter activity. She appears to have been selling wine at a tavern, although this may have been Walter Cowle's premises because there is no specific mention of it in John's will, unless it was part of his principal messuage. Alternatively, Walter and his mother-in-law may have used the shop that Walter and his wife Alice had inherited from her father John Honywode.[33] Nearby was John's butchery shop, which he jointly owned with his brother; after John's death it was inherited by his namesake and nephew, who subsequently received the other half at his own father's death.

As John Honywode was the largest operator in the livestock and butchery trades at Hythe it seems worthwhile to investigate his activities in more detail, focusing on the three main species of livestock. In terms of unit price, beef was presumably valued most highly. This was reflected in the maletote level and was due to greater production costs occasioned by stocking rates and the need for supplementary feed and possibly winter housing. Thus, looking first at John's cattle business (Fig. 6.3), live sales as a proportion of total cattle numbers accounted for a far smaller share during the early 1440s (the lowest level was 18 per cent in 1443–4), than in 1451–2, when they exceeded 50 per cent; thereafter they never fell below 60 per cent, peaking at over 70 per cent in 1456–7. Steers predominated, but very occasionally John sold calves (exceptionally, in 1456–7, calves outnumbered steers) and oxen.

29. CKS, PRC 32/13, fo. 141.

30. See note 20.

31. In terms of the numbers of woolfells, hides and pelts, John's business was at its height during the fifteen-year period between 1446 and 1461, producing over 300 each year.

32. Both brothers, for example, were taxed for selling at retail a pipe of wine each in 1442–3: EKA, H1055, fo. 23v. In later life this part of his business may have expanded because he sold a pipe each of red and white, and a third of sweet wine, in 1468–9: EKA, H1058, fo. 16.

33. CKS, PRC 32/2, fo. 202.

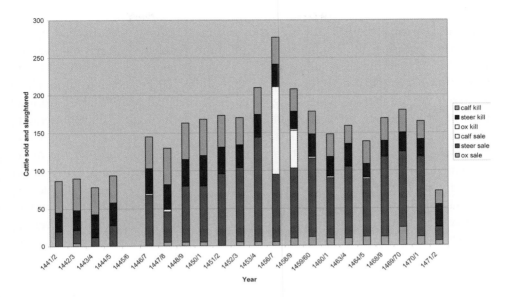

Fig. 6.3 Annual sales of live and slaughtered cattle by John Honywode, 1441–70, and his widow, 1470–2. Source: EKA, H1055; H1019; H1058.

Regarding these adult cattle, John did have a minor but growing interest in the live trade, especially from the early 1450s. Nonetheless, although the number rose to a peak of 25 in 1469–70, it was only in this year that it amounted to as much as a fifth of his live cattle sales. This general pattern seems to reflect Albarella's recent findings concerning consumer preference in late medieval towns compared to the countryside, the two distinguishing features being the preference for juvenile animals and the popularity of beef over mutton and pork.[34] Whether John's cattle were destined for the cross-Channel market at Calais with its garrison or local Kentish cattle markets is unknown, but either may help to explain his involvement in the live oxen trade. There is some evidence from the early 1480s regarding the transport of horses and cattle, and, indeed, by the early sixteenth century ships from Hythe were frequently carrying live animals across the Channel.[35] Alternatively, John's oxen and other cattle could have been transported via Dover, as in 1440 the port had gained the privilege of shipping all animals to Calais.[36]

The townspeople of late fifteenth-century Hythe would have fitted Albarella's

34. U. Albarella, 'Meat production and consumption in town and country', in K. Giles and C. Dyer (eds), *Town and country in the middle ages: contrasts, contacts and interconnections, 1100–1500* (Leeds, 2005), pp. 133–6.

35. See note 16. For the sixteenth-century trade: Mate, *Trade*, p. 99.

36. Mate, *Trade*, p. 98.

hypothesis because there is little indication of a meat trade in oxen. Instead, apart from very occasionally slaughtering an ox, John butchered steers and calves. Furthermore, calf numbers almost always exceeded steers and in terms of total cattle numbers ranged between over 15 and almost 50 per cent. Additionally, although the number of calves slaughtered each year had nearly halved from a peak of 48 in the late 1440s to 30 in 1469–70, the latter figure still represented almost 20 per cent of his total cattle. Obviously in terms of weight steers provided far more, but veal as a luxury item commanded a premium and so the high percentage of calves seems to indicate that there was a significant prosperous minority in Hythe and surrounding parishes who were willing and able to purchase such meat: a nucleus of local consumers who were able to sustain their relatively high standard of living throughout the third quarter of the fifteenth century, and perhaps beyond. The testamentary evidence substantiates this assessment. For example, several female members of the Stace family bequeathed silver spoons and other silver items, such bequests being fairly common among Hythe will-makers (a very small proportion of the town's total population), and at least two people owned gold rings when they died, the one inherited by Agnes Down having a diamond set in it.[37]

Nonetheless, sheep outnumbered cattle in John's transactions (Fig. 6.4). Again, his commercial interests covered animals both on the hoof and on the hook, although this hardly ever extended to the sale of lambs, presumably because, as with calves, he rarely had a surplus after his own butchery requirements had been met. The almost total absence of any wool sales would suggest that he was a livestock fattener rather than producer, but there were others who sold wool to the town's weavers, who as well as weaving woollen cloth also wove linen.[38] Dennis Fraunceys, for example, produced 600 cloths of each fabric in 1451–2.[39] Lower wool prices in the fifteenth century may have been a contributory factor regarding John Honywode's decision to use the rich grazing lands of the Downs at West Hythe, Saltwood and Postling, and the marsh pastures at Boroughmarsh, to fatten his cattle and sheep, rather than concentrate on wool production.[40]

Like the composition of the beef trade, the urban market for mutton was biased towards juvenile animals. John's trade fits this pattern at Hythe and possibly also elsewhere if his live sheep sales represent animals sold to other

37. Christine Stace (1475): CKS, PRC 32/2, fo. 309; Katherine Stace (1475): CKS, PRC 32/2, fo. 297; Alice Stevyn (1488): CKS, PRC 32/3, fo. 174.

38. One rare occasion occurred in 1464 when he was taxed on the sale of 15s worth of wool: EKA, H1019, fo. 121v.

39. EKA, H1055, fo. 154.

40. B.M.S. Campbell, *English seigniorial agriculture 1250–1450* (Cambridge, 2000), pp. 154, 160, 164.

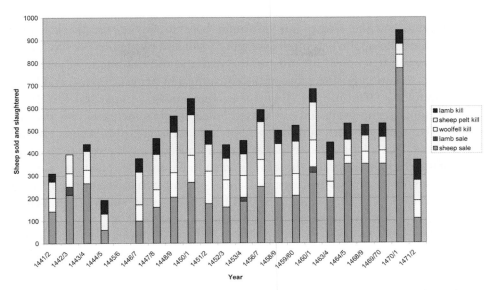

Fig. 6.4 Annual sales of live and slaughtered sheep by John Honywode, 1441–70, and his widow, 1470–2. Source: EKA, H1055; H1019; H1058.

butchers, possibly including those engaged in the Calais market. In numerical terms live sales at their lowest comprised a third of his total transactions relating to sheep, but as a proportion this doubled over the recorded period. The resulting pattern, being broadly comparable to that of his cattle, is interesting because it also represents an actual rise in the number of sheep (and steers). However, the reasons behind such a development are probably impossible to uncover from the available evidence, although it may have been due to John's widow's involvement in the family business in 1470–71 following his death.

Turning to the local meat market, John butchered all three types of sheep: lambs, shearlings ('pyltys') and woolfells ('wollefells'), but the ratio among them varied over time. As a group the shearlings were the most important numerically, and as a proportion of the slaughtered sheep they frequently comprised at least 40 per cent, although this declined to about 30 per cent during John's last years. The older woolfells comprised a slightly smaller percentage (and number), but whether their presumably greater weight was sufficient to compensate in financial terms is unknown. Although mutton was the main sheep meat offered by John, his customers were also able to purchase lamb because he annually slaughtered at least 30, frequently 60 and (in 1463–4) 78. Consequently, as a proportion, lambs almost always accounted for at least 20 per cent of his slaughtered sheep and in 1464–5 they represented 40 per cent. As a delicacy, his lamb was presumably the most expensive per pound of meat, and those Hythe people who purchased veal could, similarly, have afforded lamb.

As a guide to the size of his customer base in Hythe, for these luxury commodities alone John was often averaging a calf and two lambs per week if he was able to sell fresh meat for most of the year and did not sell any during the prohibited seasons.[41] Furthermore, if the consumption patterns of veal and lamb by the monks at Westminster Abbey is an appropriate comparison for Hythe elite consumers, the availability of these choice animals for particular periods (lamb in late spring to early summer, veal perhaps for longer until August) would have risen.[42] This might indicate that at certain times during the year John could offer one and a half calves and three lambs each week; and if it is further assumed that each of his customers headed a household of five, each eating one portion of veal and one of lamb that week, he would have had almost twenty customers – almost three a day for this sector of his business alone.[43]

The Honywode brothers, therefore, jointly had a large number of customers at their shop near the market place, and a more modest number who, in addition, purchased veal and lamb, perhaps relatively frequently. By comparison, however, their activity as pork butchers in Hythe was exceedingly limited.[44] Although this may also reflect the likelihood that at least some of their customers would have kept a pig for home consumption, John's lack of interest in the pig meat trade became more apparent over time, for whereas in the early 1440s he was annually slaughtering 36 pigs, almost 30 years later the number had fallen to a dozen animals.

The scale of the brothers' commercial operation and the family's longevity in Hythe and its hinterland meant that John and Thomas were leading participants in the government of the town. As a mark of their prosperity and status they were frequently active on the town's behalf, their trade not being seen as a bar to such works.[45] For example, John provided two horses for a civic journey to Gravesend and four for the shorter ride to Dover in 1450–51, and in the difficult years that followed the town was often financially beholden to him.[46] Moreover, both men were expected to serve as senior civic officers, their election as jurats being a

---

41. Among the civic regulations at Canterbury was one that stated 'that no bochers stoppe calves nor lambys in sommer, upon payne of forfetoure and make fine to the kyng', but whether such rules were applied elsewhere is unclear: *Historical Manuscripts Commission*, 9th Report and Appendix 1 (London, 1883), p. 172.

42. B. Harvey, *Living and dying in England 1100–1540: the monastic experience* (Oxford, 1993), p. 52.

43. This calculation has used the figures produced by Harvey for matters such as carcass weights and the percentage of edible substance per carcass: *Ibid.*, pp. 53–6.

44. Albarella, 'Meat production', p. 133.

45. Heather Swanson has commented that such craftsmen might be disliked, especially when they bought their way into public office, but in small towns where the pool of sufficiently prosperous freemen was limited men like the Honywode brothers were valued personnel: *Medieval British towns* (Basingstoke, 1999), p. 115.

46. EKA, H1055, fos. 148v, 177v.

formality from the 1440s. Further elevation followed, and in John's case he received in 1451–2 an allowance of £13 6s because he had spent 133 days attending Parliament on the town's behalf.[47] The early 1450s were a tense time politically, and the leading men of the Cinque Ports were keen to establish alliances with the local gentry as well as national figures like the archbishop. John Honywode seems to have been viewed by his peers as a suitable advocate for the town in such meetings. For example, in 1452 he visited Sir John Fogge, an important Kentish gentleman, and six years later he was a member of the delegation that went to London to negotiate on the ports' behalf.[48] His stature does not appear to have diminished in later life, which meant that he was again called upon to act for the town in its discussions with Sir John Scott and Sir William Haute in 1468–9, and in the following year it was John who paid the wages of the town's men (soldiers) who rode north with the earl of Warwick and the duke of Clarence.[49]

John Honywode not only saw himself, but was also seen by others, as a man of consequence in both the political and religious lives of the town. As a senior baron of Hythe he would have been present each year at the annual election of the jurats in St Leonard's church, a civic appropriation of sacred space that he may have felt was especially appropriate for one of the ancient Cinque Ports.[50] Unlike other towns that, by the later Middle Ages, had constructed halls for the holding of civic elections and courts, the Cinque Ports, even after they had a purpose-built hall, continued to use their churches especially for elections.[51] At Hythe the election probably took place in St Edmund's chapel (where the bailiff and jurats had held their courts before transferring to the Common Hall), and it was there that John wished to be buried, although he was also joining his grandfather and perhaps other family members.[52] His will indicates that he intended this association with St Edmund's chapel should be strengthened still further because he bequeathed the sum of 16s 4d to the parish priest and one other who were to celebrate exequies and requiem masses for his soul from the day of his death until his month's mind in the same chapel, and a further 40 marks (£26 13s 4d) for a single priest to maintain his

47. *Ibid.*, fo. 161.

48. *Ibid.*, fo. 178; H1019, fo. 78v.

49. EKA, H1058, fos. 16, 36.

50. Justin Croft has discussed the importance attached to civic elections and town custumals for the Cinque Ports: J. Croft, 'The custumals of the Cinque Ports, c.1290–c.1500: studies in the cultural production of the written record' (PhD thesis, Kent, 1997), p. 23.

51. S. Sweetinburgh, 'Mayor-making and other ceremonies: shared uses of sacred space among the Kentish Cinque Ports', in P. Trio and M. de Smet (eds), *The use and abuse of sacred places in late medieval towns* (Leuven, 2006), p. 172.

52. Croft, 'Hythe MS. 1061', p. 93. John Honywode: CKS, PRC 32/2, fo. 202: Alan Honywode: CKS, PRC 32/1, fo. 12.

temporary chantry there. Furthermore, it is worth noting that Thomas sought to join him in death as they had been together in life, and, like his brother, he too established a temporary chantry in Hythe church, extending its provision to five priests initially and then to a single priest for two years.[53]

In addition, John was a member of the most prestigious fraternity at the church. Although membership was not confined to the 'better sort', the fraternity of the Assumption of Our Lady appealed to them in particular, and there was a link between the town governors and their chosen saint because the civic elections took place on another of the Virgin Mary's feast days, that of the Purification.[54] The responsibilities of the guild warden and the senior brothers and sisters included the maintenance of the Lady Chapel and altar, as well as ensuring that the feast day on 15 August was celebrated appropriately. This was the high point of their liturgical calendar, the fraternal mass followed by a feast of meat, bread, spices and ale that was held in the large room over the south porch.[55] The fraternity was wealthy enough to employ its own priest, but when it required an additional sum in 1469 John Honywode provided 5s 4d.[56] Such a pious and charitable act presumably further enhanced John's standing in the locality, placing him at the forefront of Hythe society.

Nevertheless, the noisome nature of his commercial operation – the preparation of large numbers of hides and skins, as well as the slaughter process and its waste products – meant that, like many butchers in this period, he found himself before the town courts on various occasions.[57] How far this detracted from his public persona is impossible to ascertain but he was prepared to maintain his business in the town's Market Ward, yet he may have resided elsewhere. Several clauses in his will suggest that he was deeply concerned to try to enhance the status of his married daughters, and an appropriate dwelling house was seen as providing such a marker, with suitable furnishings and other objects having the potential to augment the effect. Consequently, John bequeathed a messuage and land to his daughter Marion Stappe and her husband and also a silver goblet, six silver spoons and a sum of cash on the condition that she was to make a new 'hall house'.[58] His other married daughters similarly received property and the same

53. Thomas Honywode: CKS, PRC 32/2, fo. 262.

54. In 1471 guild membership stood at 102 persons: EKA, Hy/Z4/4; D.C. Forbes, *Hythe Haven: the story of the Cinque Port of Hythe* (Douglas, Isle of Man, 1982), p. 76.

55. Forbes, *Hythe*, p. 76.

56. EKA, H1058, fo. 36.

57. EKA, H1023; H1020.

58. CKS, PRC 32/2, fo. 202.

type of silverware, while his wife, too, was provided with property, cash and suitable goods and the household servants were each given a sum of money.

Although Thomas Honywode had a larger family he appears to have had sufficient resources at his death to provide a similar level of inheritance for his own children. In his will he included the condition that if his wife remarried his sons' inheritance was to be administered by his fellow jurats as custodians until his sons reached adulthood.[59] As well as demonstrating his confidence in his peers, this might be considered as a means of underlining the family's importance in the town and its standing in the locality more broadly.

Because of regional and local differences in terms of land holding and urban structure it is difficult to compare the prosperity and standing of John and Thomas Honywode to that of others elsewhere in England, but it is possible that they resemble men such as Roger Heritage of Warwickshire and Robert Parman of Suffolk rather than some of the extremely wealthy wool merchants and clothiers of East Anglia or Wiltshire.[60] Yet whether it would be appropriate to class John Honywode as a capitalist is not totally clear, although the family was able to rise in society over succeeding generations. As a result, by the mid-sixteenth century one of Thomas' sons, another John Honywode from Newington-next-Hythe, had joined the ranks of the gentry. Like his father and uncle he was at least partly dependent on cattle and sheep for his wealth, but his landed interests comprised, among other properties, the manors of Casebourne, Send and Enbroke, downland in and around Hythe and extensive tracts of marshland in Romney Marsh. He was, therefore, in a strong position to assist his three sons in 1558, providing them with luxury household goods.[61] Such assets and the status they denoted allowed members of the family to climb even further up the social ladder, the fifteenth-century butcher–graziers having provided the springboard for one of the regionally important armigerous families of seventeenth- and eighteenth-century east Kent.[62] Thus, this investigation of the careers of John and Thomas Honywode and their fellow butchers has opened up a fruitful line of enquiry regarding the interconnections between town and countryside and the place of the individual in late medieval society.

59. *Ibid.*, fo. 262.

60. Dyer, 'Were there any capitalists?' pp. 10–20; *idem*, 'A Suffolk farmer in the fifteenth century', *Agricultural History Review*, 55 (2007), pp. 7–22.

61. CKS, PRC 32/27, fo. 26.

62. M. Zell, 'Landholding and the land market in early modern Kent', in M. Zell (ed.), *Early modern Kent 1540–1640* (Woodbridge, 2000), p. 41; Canterbury Cathedral Archives and Library, Canterbury, U11/7.

7. The houses of the Dronfield lead smelters and merchants, 1600–1730

*David Hey**

Few local historians give the study of vernacular buildings the attention that they deserve, while many careful and detailed surveys by architectural historians take little account of the family histories and local connections of the people who built the houses under study, or of the ways by which the wealth that paid for them was accumulated. This division between local historians and scholars of vernacular architecture is an unnecessary and unproductive consequence of increased specialisation.[1] Local historians are often put off the study of vernacular architecture because they do not understand the technical literature, with its use of terms such 'stylobate', 'pulvinated frieze', or 'truncated principal purlin roof'.[2] They can, however, make a real contribution to an understanding of a group of buildings that are similar in style and period even if they do not recognise the finer points of detail. Clearly, the more technical knowledge that local historians have the better they will be informed, but lack of expertise in architectural study should not prevent them from using buildings as prime evidence for the history of their local communities, for the surviving houses of a town or a rural parish do so much to determine the character of a place.

My purpose here is to demonstrate how the social and economic history of a

* I am much indebted to Stanley Jones, who has made detailed surveys of Holmesfield Hall and Dronfield Woodhouse Hall, and from whom I have learned a great deal during our visits to houses in and around Dronfield.

1. There are, of course, notable exceptions to this generalisation. See the excellent article by A. Longcroft, 'Local history and vernacular architecture studies', *The Local Historian*, 39 (May 2009), which explores this division.

2. Stylobate is the term for a stone footing upon which a timber post, e.g. a cruck blade, rests; a pulvinated frieze is a feature copied from classical architecture and takes the form of a pillow-shaped roll above a door or a window; a truncated principal purlin roof can be seen, for instance, at the Merchant Adventurer's Hall at York.

particular district and the family and business ties between various householders can illuminate the visual evidence provided by a group of distinctive houses. The ancient parish of Dronfield, which covered 15,580 acres of wood pasture and moorland between Sheffield to the north and Chesterfield to the south, contained seven townships with many scattered settlements at the heart of the Derbyshire lead smelting district (Fig. 7.1).[3] The parish has an impressive collection of substantial stone houses that date from the seventeenth and early eighteenth centuries. Who built them and how did their builders obtain their wealth?

During the second half of the sixteenth century Derbyshire became the leading supplier of lead in Europe. In the early 1540s Derbyshire's lead mines produced only 3000 loads of ore a year, but by 1600 annual output had reached 34,000 loads and by the 1640s 120,000 loads. Smelters and merchants enjoyed substantial profits. During the 1570s and 1580s the old bole hills on windy escarpments, some of them still commemorated by minor place-names, were replaced by a new smelting technology that was introduced from the Mendips into Derbyshire in 1571 by George, sixth earl of Shrewsbury, whereby coppiced wood that had been dried into white coal was fired to a high temperature by a water-powered bellows in a smelting mill alongside a fast-flowing stream in order to produce a pig of lead. This technology was used until the middle decades of the eighteenth century, when it was gradually replaced by the coal-powered cupola.[4] After the earl's death in 1590 aristocratic families, including the Cavendishes of Chatsworth and the Manners family of Haddon Hall, and numerous gentry of lower rank invested in the new smelting technology. They included gentlemen such as the Eyres of Hassop and the Gells of Hopton, who built fine halls out of their profits, and minor gentry and rising yeomen in north-east Derbyshire, including the large parish of Dronfield, who became smelters and lead merchants. These rising men built the substantial stone houses that help to give Dronfield parish, particularly the central village, a sense of identity to this day. The wealth generated by the trade explains why so many outstanding vernacular buildings were erected in this district in the seventeenth and early eighteenth centuries.

Lead was mined in the carboniferous limestone district in what has become known as the White Peak, further west, but the smelting mills were sited in the wooded valleys to the east of the river Derwent. No Derbyshire smelting mills remain standing and none has been excavated, but Crossley and Kiernan have

3. J.M. Wilson, *The imperial gazetteer of England and Wales*, 2 (Edinburgh, 1870), p. 599. The townships comprised Dronfield, Holmesfield, Dore, Totley, Coal Aston, Unstone and Little Barlow.

4. D. Kiernan, *The Derbyshire lead industry in the sixteenth century*, Derbyshire Record Society, 14 (Chesterfield, 1989).

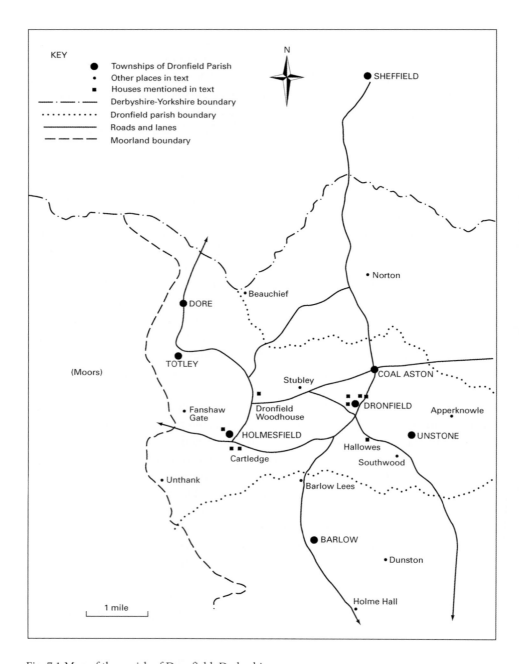

Fig. 7.1 Map of the parish of Dronfield, Derbyshire.

identified 59 sites in and around the Peak District. They have shown that smelting mills required neither extensive buildings nor the large ponds associated with the iron industry, so they were often sited in the upper reaches of streams adjacent to the coppice woods that provided their fuel. Scores of circular hollows about twelve to fifteen feet in diameter and two to four feet deep, which mark the sites of the pits or kilns where coppiced wood was converted into white coal for the smelters, survive in all the ancient deciduous woods between Sheffield and Chesterfield. There the wood was stripped of its bark and dried, using wood, and later coal, as fuel. Crossley and Kiernan estimate that some 18,000 acres of carefully managed coppice were required to maintain the Derbyshire lead industry in the late seventeenth century.[5] The mills were sited conveniently halfway between the mining district and the inland ports, notably Bawtry on the Yorkshire–Nottinghamshire boundary, from where the finished pigs of lead were exported. Several of these mills lay in the townships of Dore, Totley and Holmesfield, within the parish of Dronfield.[6]

Who were these smelters and merchants and what were their family backgrounds? The large gabled hall with stringcourses, mullioned windows and projecting wings at Hallowes was built in local sandstone in a typical mid seventeenth-century style by Andrew Morewood, a lead merchant, who carved his and his wife's initials and the date 1657 over the door (Plate 1). In the Middle Ages the Morewoods were peasant farmers just a few miles to the north in Hallamshire, where they took their name from an isolated farm. They were resident at another farm, the Oaks, two miles north of their ancestral home, for over three centuries. Rowland Morewood, who died in 1619, was the first of the family to be described as a gentleman. We do not know how he rose in the social ranks, but his unusual Christian name might link him with Rowland Eyre, the prominent lead smelter of Hassop Hall, to whom he was related through marriage.[7] Certainly, during the seventeenth century the Morewoods owed their prosperity to the smelting and trading of lead. Rowland Morewood's eldest son inherited the Oaks, two other sons moved across the county boundary into north Derbyshire, and the last became a London merchant. In 1625 the Morewoods shipped 1874 fothers of lead,

5. D. Crossley and D. Kiernan, 'The lead smelting mills of Derbyshire', *Derbyshire Archaeological Journal*, 112 (1992), pp. 6–47; D. Hey, 'Barlow: the landscape history of a Peak District township', in R.W. Hoyle (ed.), *People, landscape and alternative agriculture: essays for Joan Thirsk*, British Agricultural History Society (Exeter, 2004), pp. 1–29.

6. J.V. Beckett and J.P. Polak (eds), 'The Scarsdale surveys of 1652–62', in *A seventeenth-century Scarsdale miscellany*, Derbyshire Record Society, 20 (Chesterfield, 1993), pp. 3–72.

7. D. Hey, *Historic Hallamshire* (Ashbourne, 2002), pp. 60–62; J.W. Clay (ed.), J. Hunter, *Familiae minorum gentium*, 4 vols, Publications of the Harleian Society, 37–40 (London, 1894–6), 3, pp. 1062–7.

292 firkins of red lead and 128 firkins of lead shot to his London warehouse; this amounted to 61 per cent of the total Derbyshire trade in that year.[8] In the next generation three other sons set up in business in London and another was killed in Barbados. These London and overseas connections form a recurrent theme in the history of some of the minor gentry and substantial yeomen of north Derbyshire and south Yorkshire; setting up as a merchant in the capital while retaining family links back home was the way that younger sons made their fortunes. By the time of the hearth tax returns of the early 1670s the Morewoods had ten branches in north Derbyshire and south Yorkshire. Anthony Morewood paid tax on ten hearths at Hallowes[9] and was described as a gentleman on his tombstone in the chancel of Dronfield church in 1700. Two members of the Morewood family served as High Sheriff of Derbyshire.[10]

Another early building erected by lead smelters is Cartledge Hall in the township of Holmesfield (Plate 2). The John Burton who lived at Dronfield in the mid-sixteenth century was descended from a Leicestershire family, one of whose senior members, incidentally, was William Burton, the antiquarian who wrote the *Description of Leicester Shire* in 1622. John's son, Thomas Burton, yeoman, moved to Cartledge in 1566 upon his marriage to Alice Wolstenholme, whose ancestors had arrived there from Lancashire about 1450.[11] Although Thomas was apparently unable to sign his name, he became a substantial farmer and lead smelter. In 1581 he was operating a foot blast at a smelting site in Holmesfield, but he soon switched to the new technology. Between 1580 and 1584 he was one of the many alleged infringers of the patent for water-powered smelting granted to William Humfrey and Christopher Schütz. When he died in 1585 he left 'stock at making of lead' at Stoke smelting mill valued at £47 15s 10d.[12] As the rooms that were listed in his probate inventory consisted only of a house, parlour, kitchen and buttery, with chambers above, it is likely that it was not he but his son Thomas who built the present Cartledge Hall, which from the outside looks

8. D. Kiernan (ed.), 'Lawrence Oxley's accounts, 1672–81', in J.V. Beckett and J.P. Polak (eds), *A seventeenth-century Scarsdale miscellany*, Derbyshire Record Society, 20 (Chesterfield, 1993), p. 13. In Derbyshire a fother was 22.5 or 21.5 hundredweights, or 1145 or 1095kg (Crossley and Kiernan, 'Lead smelting mills', p. 8).

9. D.G. Edwards, *Derbyshire hearth tax assessments, 1662–70*, Derbyshire Record Society, 7 (Chesterfield, 1982).

10. His wife's tombstone in Dronfield parish church records that they had seven daughters, but no sons are mentioned. A list of the High Sheriffs of Derbyshire is provided by Gladwyn Turbutt, *A history of Derbyshire* (Cardiff, 1999), 2, pp. 903–9.

11. Clay (ed.), *Familiae minorum gentium*, 1, pp. 337–43.

12. Lichfield Joint Record Office, probate inventory of Thomas Burton (1585); Kiernan, *The Derbyshire lead industry*, pp. 186–9, 213–14. His livestock, crops, wool and agricultural implements were valued at about £140 and his household goods at £21 4s 2d, and he was owed £92 4s 6d.

much as it did in late Elizabethan or Jacobean times. Alongside it stands another substantial seventeenth-century house, known as Cartledge Grange (Plate 3), a taller building with a projecting wing and mullioned and transomed windows, but with no datestones and no documentation. As it shares the same site as the hall in this small hamlet, it is likely that it was erected either by the Burtons or by the Wolstenholmes (who were still at Cartledge in 1670, when the two houses were taxed on eight hearths apiece).

Thomas Burton I founded a dynasty of prosperous lead smelters and merchants. His eldest son and namesake, Thomas Burton II of Cartledge, leased the Linacre Over lead smelting mill from 1596, and in 1623 he was among a small group of north Derbyshire men who testified that he had sold lead at the inland port of Bawtry for many years.[13] He became so prosperous that he was granted a coat of arms and was appointed High Sheriff of Derbyshire in 1628. He died without issue in 1645. Meanwhile, his brother Michael Burton (1567–1656) had set up home at Holmesfield Hall, half a mile away from Cartledge. The outbuildings of Holmesfield Hall conceal a timber-framed manor house which has been dated by dendrochronology to the 1450s.[14] This was succeeded about 1613, according to an internal datestone in an upstairs room, by a new stone structure, probably built by Michael Burton. The front of the hall at Holmesfield was re-styled in good-quality ashlar stone about 1730, judging by the Burton coat of arms in the broken pediment above the door. The building was probably given its new hipped roof at the same time, although the Welsh blue slates are Victorian. The side walls show that the 1613 house was built of coursed rubble; at the back, the mullioned windows have been filled in. Despite the alterations we can recognise the original design, with an off-centre entry and the usual three-unit plan: one room for sleeping, one for eating and relaxing, one for preparing food, with chambers above for servants' and children's bedrooms, and storage.

Thomas II and Michael were provided with lead ore from the parish of Eyam

13. Kiernan, *Lead industry*, p. 235.

14. Stanley Jones (personal communication and detailed survey report to the Hunter Archaeological Society, 1996); Nottingham University, Survey by the Royal Commission on Historical Monuments of England (1991–2), list 49, 7a, 7b; D. Hey, 'A manorial landscape at Holmesfield', in P. Riden and D.G. Edwards (eds), *Essays in Derbyshire history presented to Gladwyn Turbutt*, Derbyshire Record Society, 30 (Chesterfield, 2006), pp. 3–22. Three small brass plaques in the chancel of Dronfield parish church commemorate Michael Burton (d. 1656), William Burton gent (d. 1657) and Mrs Ann Burton, wife of Francis Burton of Dronfield, esquire (d. 1668).

15. Kiernan, *Lead industry*, pp. 194 and 214, notes that Francis Burton of Foolow, who died in 1612, had 'One Grove in Croslow Rake, within the parishe of Eyam'. However, this Francis does not seem to have been a younger brother of Thomas and Michael, for they are the only sons mentioned in their mother's will in 1624 (Lichfield Joint Record Office, will and inventory of Alice Christophers).

by another member of their family, Francis Burton of Foolow,[15] and Michael Burton soon had a thriving business. In 1632 he built two smelting mills and a forge at Mousehole, to the north of Sheffield, and in 1653 he bought the manor of Totley, including two smelting mills: the Upper Mill and Hall's House. He prospered so much that, in 1654, when he was described as Michael Burton of Holmesfield, esquire, he was able to buy several messuages, farms and cottages in Dronfield (including Woodhouse and Stubley) for the large sum of £4,063.[16] He also owned the manor of Dore from 1658 to 1671 and had two smelting mills there: Burton House Smelting Mill (or Nether Mill) and the Wash Mill.[17] Like his elder brother, Thomas, he served as High Sheriff of Derbyshire. Thomas and Michael both died childless, in 1645 and 1656 respectively. Michael was succeeded at Holmesfield Hall by his cousin, William, whose son, Thomas Burton (1645–1702), was taxed on twelve hearths there in 1670.

Stanley Jones has shown that the hall at Dronfield Woodhouse, less than a mile away from Cartledge and Holmesfield, originated as a late medieval cruck structure of at least four bays, with a two-bay open hall (Plate 4). This became the home of a junior branch of the Eyres, a leading north Derbyshire catholic family. The Eyres had established themselves a little further south at Holme Hall and Dunston, in the parish of Brampton, where as early as 1505 Robert Eyre and his brother John Eyre constructed two boles with smelting ovens. John's grandson, Thomas Eyre (1592–1646), moved to Dronfield Woodhouse upon his marriage to Elizabeth, the daughter of Robert Outram and the heiress of at least four generations of Outrams who had lived there and whose surname originated in this locality.[18] Elizabeth's mother was the sister of Michael and Thomas Burton of Holmesfield. Thomas Eyre, or perhaps his son and namesake, built most of the present house, retaining one pair of cruck blades behind the gabled stone exterior. This elder Thomas was a captain of horse in the royalist army and died a prisoner at Derby in 1645. His son, also Thomas, was taxed on five hearths at Dronfield Woodhouse in 1670. Jones has demonstrated that the probate inventory of the younger Thomas Eyre, gentleman, taken in 1684, takes us through rooms that can each be related to the present building; all the rooms in the inventory with hearth implements can be accounted for. The house had not yet received its south-facing parlour, which must have been built by Thomas's

---

16. Nottinghamshire Archives, 157/DD/P/70/43.

17. C. Ball, D. Crossley and N. Flavell (eds), *Water power on the Sheffield rivers*, South Yorkshire Industrial History Society, 2nd edn (Sheffield, 2006), pp. 152–3; Crossley and Kiernan, 'Lead smelting mills', pp. 23–5.

18. Stanley Jones (personal communication). These Outrams may have had a family connection with the Edward Outram who owned a smelting mill at Bradway in 1613, and with Christopher Owtram of Dronfield, who smelted lead at Francis Burton's mill at Dore in 1637; Clay (ed.), *Familiae minorum gentium*, 2, pp. 555–7.

son, Vincent Eyre of Dronfield Woodhouse (1671–1758). This Vincent had three sons, two of whom used their catholic connections to rise in the service of the duke of Norfolk, lord of the manor of Sheffield, while the middle one became a silk merchant in London.[19]

Two of the three witnesses to Thomas Eyre the younger's will in 1684 were lead smelters: Robert Greenwood (who will feature later) and John Dand. Dand, who in 1670 was taxed on eight hearths at Southwood in Unstone township, not far from Hallowes, was a lead smelter who died unmarried in 1703, aged 64. His younger brother, Thomas Dand (1641–1716), who was taxed on three hearths at Dronfield, was described in 1669 as a lead merchant. Both brothers were referred to as gentlemen upon their burials in the chancel of Dronfield church, alongside their father, Thomas Dand, a clergyman with a reputation as a scholar, who was born into a gentry family in Mansfield (Nottinghamshire) and who died in 1669, aged 71.[20] The younger Thomas Dand had three daughters and a son named Thomas, who died in 1724, when the male line failed. The Dands are commemorated by three small brass plaques in the chancel of Dronfield parish church.

The third phase of major development at Dronfield Woodhouse Hall seems to have occurred in the 1690s, or shortly afterwards, when Vincent Eyre, the new owner, rebuilt the western bay as a high-ceiled parlour above a cellar, with a parlour chamber, attic and a new stair. The dating evidence is provided by what Pevsner called cross windows, which were, as we will see, very fashionable in the other houses that were built by Dronfield lead smelters and merchants at this time. Cross windows formed from a single mullion and a transom were in use from the 1680s and 1690s in many parts of England, before they were replaced by sashes in the early eighteenth century. Those at the Customs' House at King's Lynn, for instance, date from 1683 and those at Hellaby Hall in south Yorkshire date from 1690. In north Derbyshire cross windows provide reliable dating evidence from about 1690 to 1720.[21] They were installed enthusiastically by the Dronfield lead smelters and merchants.

Meanwhile, Francis Burton, the brother of Thomas Burton of Holmesfield, seems to have inherited the lead ore business at Foolow in the parish of Eyam

19. *Ibid.*, pp. 555–7.

20. *Ibid.*, 3, pp. 1003–6; Nottinghamshire Archives, 157/DD/P/70/48 (power of attorney granted to Thomas Eyre of Dronfield Woodhouse and John Dand of Unstone); Kiernan (ed.), 'Lawrence Oxley's accounts', p. 163 (in 1675 John Dand was trading with London through the lead merchant, Lawrence Oxley). John Dand's will and inventory show that he was occupying just a parlour and a chamber at Southwood at the time of his death; he left a nephew 'Forty of my biggest Lawe bookes' and his sister 'my best gold Ring with the Ruby in it'. He also left lands in the manor of Mansfield to two other nephews.

21. For example, the Elder Yard Unitarian Chapel in Chesterfield has a 1694 datestone.

which had once been run by his namesake and relative. Residence in a lead-mining district in the White Peak explains why his brother-in-law, Mr John Wright of Eyam, and Thomas Statham of the adjoining parish of Tideswell, were chosen as the executors of his will in 1687, and why three of his daughters – Jane, Elizabeth and Ellen, each described as 'of Dronfield, gentlewoman' – chose to marry at Eyam church between 1689 and 1697. Francis' brother Thomas was made overseer of the will and guardian and trustee for the children.[22] Francis Burton had bought the manor of Dronfield in 1658 and was described as 'esquire' four years later when he was granted a royal charter to hold a weekly market and annual fairs at a road junction in the village just down the High Street below the manor house,[23] and again when he was taxed on nine hearths in Dronfield in 1670. His account book from 1660 to his death in 1685 records the many chief rents that he received as lord of the manor, and from 1681 onwards it mentions his smelting mills in Dore and Totley, two of them leased to others and one 'in my owne hand'.[24] He and his second wife Ellen had two sons and six daughters, each of whom was left at least £300 when he died in 1688, with all his 'messuages, lands, tenements, mills, woods and hereditaments' going to his eldest son, Ralph, who was still a minor.[25]

Within a decade or so of his father's death Ralph Burton built a strikingly different house from the gabled halls that had been fashionable a generation or two before. This large new manor house was designed as a symmetrical structure two storeys high, four bays deep and seven bays long, with a projecting central porch and a hipped roof (Plate 5). When it was converted into the public library in modern times it was re-roofed and the interior was gutted, but the exterior retains both its overall shape and much of its external character, as revealed by a drawing in a plan of the estate of c.1710.[26] It has lost its chimney stacks and dormer windows, and the windows at the front have been replaced with sashes, but the original cross windows can still be seen at the rear. Another sure piece of dating evidence from the same period as the cross windows is the pulvinated frieze above the archway of the front door. Some of the outbuildings survive to the rear, but the formal gardens have been replaced by a car park. Ralph Burton died in 1714 without male heirs. Meanwhile, a junior branch of the family,

---

22. Sheffield Archives, CeR 39 (will of Francis Burton); J.G. Clifford and F. Clifford (eds), *Eyam parish register, 1630–1700*, Derbyshire Record Society, 21 (1993), pp. 158–9, 176. Their marriage partners came from distant parishes. John Wright of Eyam, gent, was buried on 2 January 1694 (p. 168).

23. Nottinghamshire Archives, 157/DD/P/70/45.

24. Sheffield Archives, MD 184.

25. *Ibid.*, CeR 39.

26. *Ibid.*, Cecil-Rotherham, CeR 1: 'A survey of the manor house, Dronfield, 1710'. The property included the bowling alley that was mentioned in his father's account book from 1670 onwards (*ibid.*, MD 184).

descended from John Burton, the younger brother of Thomas Burton I, flourished into the first half of the eighteenth century in various parts of Dronfield parish, including Apperknowle, Cartledge, Fanshaw Gate and, especially, Holmesfield. Nevertheless, this prolific family had died out in the male line by about 1740.

Down the street from the Manor House a substantial contemporary building known as the Hall was erected by John Rotherham, a lead smelter, maltster, farmer and lessee of millstone quarries, notably the major one at Millstone Edge overlooking Hathersage. The hewing of millstones and their export via the river port at Bawtry was another industry for which Derbyshire had a national reputation at this time.[27] The first Rotherham to appear in Dronfield records was John Rotherham, originally a mercer, who in 1643 married Helen Drabble, the daughter of a local yeoman. He was taxed on only three hearths in 1670. When he died at Churchdale Farm, Dronfield in 1696, however, he was described as a lead merchant and his inventory included a pig of lead at the mill worth £129. This may have been the Cliff smelting mill at Dore, which he is known to have held in the early 1670s.[28] A brass memorial in the central aisle of the nave of Dronfield church names Mr John Rotherham of Dronfield and Helen his wife, who died two years later, both aged 80. They left four sons: John the younger (1645–1706), who was taxed on five hearths in 1670; Aeneas (1648–1685), a chandler and lead smelter at Totley; Anthony (1652–1734), a Dronfield yeoman; and Joseph, a Dronfield grocer.[29]

John Rotherham the younger, as he was usually known in contemporary documents, featured regularly in Francis Burton's account book from the late 1660s onwards, first of all as someone who rented a malthouse and who dried malt and oats for Burton. By 1675 this younger John Rotherham was also renting the Hall meadow and other land in Dronfield.[30] He seems to have been a man with a keen eye for business opportunities wherever they occurred, but upon his death he was described as a lead merchant by the appraisers of his probate inventory. He built Dronfield Hall in the 1690s or early 1700s (Plate 6), the cross windows on all sides of the house and the pulvinated friezes in the interior suggesting the date. The Hall rivalled the Manor House as the most up-to-date building in the village – or small market town – when it was erected. It was designed as a tall, double-pile structure with a symmetrical appearance instead of old-fashioned gables. Parapets

---

27. Hey, *Historic Hallamshire*, chapter 7: 'Millstones on the moors', pp. 112–25.

28. Ball *et al.* (eds), *Water power*, p. 149.

29. J.W. Walker (ed.), J. Hunter, *Familiae minorum gentium*, Publications of the Harleian Society, 88 (London, 1936), 5, pp. 126–7. The surnames Rotherham and Drabble each originated within ten miles from Dronfield.

30. Sheffield Archives, MD 184. The malt house was still in the Rotherham family's possession in 1714.

adorn the top storey at the front and the rear of the house to mask the lead roofs. The interior is also arranged symmetrically on either side of a passage that goes straight through the house, and the original structure of the rooms, as revealed by his probate inventory, is preserved. Sturdy, re-used timbers support both the cellars and the attic storey, where some were arranged as upper crucks or used as crude purlins, partly hidden behind plaster.[31] John was succeeded by his son Samuel (1680–1743) and his grandson John (1717–71), who continued to prosper through lead smelting and the trade in millstones. This third John became an esquire, JP for Derby and High Sheriff of Derbyshire. In 1755 he added the Manor House to his properties after the male line of the Burtons had failed, and he gradually acquired other properties in and around Dronfield.[32]

There are two more large houses in Dronfield to consider. They stand together on the hillside across the valley of the river Drone, to the east of the main settlement. The first is known as Chiverton House, although it was originally Dam Flatt House.[33] This large building, with cross windows and a flat symmetrical front with a small central gable and a rather strange tower at each end, is substantially unaltered both internally and externally (Plate 7). It was built for Richard Hall (1648–1709), the third of that family to live at Barlow Lees, on the southern edge of Dronfield parish. His widowed mother, Mary, was taxed on seven hearths there in 1670, and his father, Richard Hall of Barlow Lees, gentleman, was tenant of the Calver smelting mill from 1656 to 1667 and the lessee of a farm at Coal Aston in Dronfield parish from 1664.[34] Mr Richard Hall the younger paid rent to Francis Burton, lord of Dronfield manor, from 1682 onwards 'for the howses at smilting house dam', so it seems that he too was involved in the lead smelting business.[35] A plan of Richard Hall's estate in Dronfield in 1692 shows a timber-framed house and the rooms in his probate inventory taken shortly after his death in 1709 tally very well with those of the present building, so Chiverton House was obviously erected

31. Lichfield Joint Record Office, probate inventory of John Rotherham the younger of Dronfield, lead merchant, 22 January 1706/7, lists the following rooms: hall, great parlour, little parlour and closet, hall chamber and closet, little parlour chamber and closet, kitchen chamber and closet, great parlour chamber and closet, garret at stairhead, best garret, men's garret and store chamber, pantry, kitchen, hall closet, cellars, brewhouse, corn chamber, stable and stable chamber.

32. Sheffield Archives, Cecil-Rotherham, CeR/2, CeR/196, CeR/301a (will of John Rotherham, 1766, including his 'chaise and pair', library and 'silver tea kettle, lamp and coffee pot').

33. In the 1890s the Rhodes family changed the name to Chiverton because of their links to a house of that name in Cornwall (Mrs Ann Brown, archivist of the Old Dronfield Society, personal communication). Dam Flatt was enclosed by Chesterfield Road and Snape Hill (Sheffield Archives, Fairbank, Dro 3S).

34. Clay (ed.), *Familiae minorum gentium*, 2, pp. 567–8; Crossley and Kiernan, 'Lead smelting mills', p. 13; Nottinghamshire Archives, 157/DD/P/71/16.

35. Sheffield Archives, MD 184.

between those two dates, as we would expect from its style.[36] A tombstone north-west of the church tower in Dronfield churchyard depicts Richard Hall's coat of arms and informs us that he was buried on 14 February 1708/9 and that he had been married twice to daughters of local gentlemen. His widow Dorothy was buried alongside him in September 1711. He died childless and bequeathed his property to his brother, Charles Hall of Kettlethorpe in Lincolnshire, who seems to have sold it after Dorothy's death.[37] A datestone of 1712 over the door on the right tower at Chiverton House bears the initials of John Browne of Heston, Middlesex, and his wife, Anne. Their tombstone in the chancel of Dronfield Church describes Browne as a gentleman and displays his coat of arms, but little is known about him.[38]

We are on firmer ground when we move next door to Rose Hill, a house that is similar in style to Chiverton House, although a little smaller (Plate 8). It has tiny gables, a short central parapet on the top storey and stringcourses that rise over the windows. A 1612 datestone appears on an internal wall, but the house was substantially rebuilt in the second decade of the eighteenth century. Datestones from 1717, 1719 and 1720 confirm that the house as we see it was erected in the years following its purchase in 1716 from the Morewood family by Robert Greenwood, a lead merchant. Robert did not live long to enjoy his house, for he died three years later. The first reference to the Greenwood family's involvement in the lead trade is a deed of 1669, which refers to Thomas Greenwood of Dronfield, lead merchant, who had previously been an ironmonger with a messuage, shop and yard in Dronfield. The 1669 deed also mentions his son, Edward Greenwood of Dronfield, yeoman, and Thomas Dand of Dronfield, lead merchant. In the hearth tax returns for Dronfield in 1670 Edward Greenwood paid for five hearths, Thomas Greenwood for three and Robert Greenwood for three. As we have seen, Robert Greenwood was a witness to the will of Thomas Eyre of Dronfield Woodhouse in 1684. Although Edward Greenwood was described as a yeoman at that time, in 1674 he was shipping lead. In 1693, in a deed in which he was involved with John Rotherham the younger, lead merchant,

36. Old Dronfield Society archives, Peel Centre, Dronfield, 'A copy of part of a survey of the estate of Mr Richard Hall made by Joseph Parker in 1692'; Lichfield Joint Record Office, will and inventory of Richard Hall, 1709. Hall's rooms and outbuildings consisted of hall, parlour, kitchen, pantry, cellar, parlour chamber, hall chamber, little garret, great garret, brewhouse, brewhouse chamber, Mr Hall clossit, corn chamber, nether clossit, barn, stable and ass house.

37. His second marriage in 1694 was to Dorothy Pegge of Beauchief Hall, just beyond Dronfield parish; they both left bequests for a preacher at Beauchief Chapel and for sermons at Dronfield Church, where Richard Hall had been churchwarden in 1690. They also left a house in Soper Lane, Dronfield, and a small property in Coal Aston.

38. His son and three daughters were baptised at Dronfield between 1713 and 1721. Browne was also described as a gentleman in 1713, when he took a 21-year lease of the nearby field called Dam Flatt (Nottinghamshire Archives, 157/DD/F3/7/16/4).

he was described as a gentleman, in recognition of his rising prosperity. His eldest son, Edward, moved to the neighbouring parish of Norton.[39]

Dronfield parish has several other houses that date from the seventeenth century, at least in part. Unthank Hall in the township of Holmesfield may have been built from profits acquired through the lead trade, for Thomas Wright of Unthank was joint-owner of the Calver smelting mill when the Eyre estates were sequestered during the civil war.[40] The central streets of Dronfield have four more seventeenth-century houses, immediately recognisable by their gables and mullioned windows, and old photographs show two large inns (now demolished) in a mid or late seventeenth-century style.[41] Opposite Dronfield Hall are a group of three terraced houses three storeys high above their cellars but only one room wide. They are dated by the pulvinated friezes over their doors to c.1690–1720, and may have been built for men who helped to run the Rotherhams' lead and millstones business. We have no evidence to prove this suggestion, but the lead smelters and merchants did not have rooms in their own houses designated as offices in their probate inventories.

The new style of building by the leading Dronfield lead smelters and merchants went out of fashion in the 1720s. In 1731, according to a Latin inscription above the door, the inhabitants of Dronfield arranged a voluntary subscription to pay for a house for the Usher, or Assistant Master, of the nearby Elizabethan Grammar School. It was very different from the houses of the lead smelters and merchants, for it was built in the Georgian style, with small hand-made bricks and with new-style sash windows arranged symmetrically; it was given new iron windows in the early nineteenth century. This was the first brick house in Dronfield and it was such a sensation that it acquired the name The Red House. It is quite common on the coal-measure sandstones of Derbyshire and Yorkshire to find that the first brick house in a locality was given this nickname. The Old Vicarage, another brick building next door, must have been built soon afterwards, with bay windows whose joints show that they were contemporary with the main structure. A new era of building had begun, but the grand houses of the lead smelters and merchants sufficed for later generations of their families and their successors. They stand as a lasting memorial to the prosperity of the Derbyshire lead trade in the late seventeenth and early eighteenth centuries.

39. Sheffield Archives, Cecil-Rotherham, CeR/33/1–2 and CeR/180/1–2; Bagshaw Collection, 2868; Kiernan (ed.), 'Lawrence Oxley's accounts', p. 135.

40. Crossley and Kiernan, 'Lead smelting mills', p. 13. He was taxed on eight hearths at Unthank in 1670.

41. R. Redfearn, *Dronfield and district: Britain in old photographs* (Stroud, 1999). The ancient parish of Dronfield also has some earlier timber-framed houses and a fine medieval church.

8. A community approaching crisis: Skye in the eighteenth century

Edgar Miller

While walking in his native Skye in 1854, the Scottish geologist Sir Archibald Geikie described hearing a 'strange wailing sound'.[1] Eventually he could see that this came from a procession of people leaving the settlement of Suishnish in the Strath parish. This consisted of

> at least three generations of crofters. There were old men and women, too feeble to walk, who were placed in carts; the younger members of the community on foot were carrying their bundles of clothes and household effects, while the children, with looks of alarm, walked alongside.

After mentioning that the group paused to say goodbye to the minister and his family at Kilbride, the passage continues:

> Everyone was in tears, each wished to clasp the hands of those who had so often befriended them, and it seemed as if they could not tear themselves away. When they set forth once more, a cry of grief went up to heaven, the long plaintive wail, like a funeral cronach [a dirge], was resumed, and after the last of the emigrants had disappeared behind the hill, the sound seemed to echo through the whole wide valley of Strath in one prolonged note of desolation.[2]

1. A. Geikie, *Scottish reminiscences* (Glasgow, 1906), pp. 224–7.
2. *Ibid.*, pp. 225–7.

This particular instance arose from one of the last of the Highland Clearances, which had started in the last decade of the eighteenth century. Nevertheless, the picture of misery that is described was one that must have occurred many times across the Highlands as a result of people being turned out of their homes and denied their usual livelihoods.

Popular accounts of the Highland Clearances as well as some of those intended to be more sophisticated have tended to contrast the suffering produced by the Clearances with the supposedly attractive existence which the Highlanders had hitherto previously enjoyed. The Clearances were assumed to have brutally ended a way of life that had considerable benefits. Many of the earlier analyses resulted in statements about the people of the Highlands prior to the Clearances such as: 'a more happy and contented race never existed',[3] or the people lived 'under the best possible system that has ever been or will be devised'.[4] One of the most influential and lasting proponents of this benign view was Hugh Miller who wrote in 1851:

In truth the golden age of the Highlands was comprised in that period which extended shortly after the suppression of the rebellion of 1745, and the abolition of the hereditary jurisdictions, down to the commencement of the clearance system. It is to this period that Mrs Grant's description of Celtic habits and Celtic character belong, and which give the idea of so contented, and, in the main, so comfortable a people, that, save for our own early recollections when we lived among the Highlanders, we would be disposed to suspect that the good lady had drawn on her imagination for the colouring of the picture.[5]

With exceptions such as Prebble,[6] who has written what is still the most widely available book on the Clearances, identifying the rapaciousness of the landlords as the main cause and linking this to the after effects of Culloden, more recent accounts have indicated that life for the ordinary people in the Highlands prior to the Clearances was nothing like as idyllic as has been portrayed.[7] Change was

3. D. Stewart as quoted by E. Richards, *The highland clearances* (Edinburgh, 2002), p. 35.

4. J.S. Blackie, *Highland depopulation and land law reform* (Edinburgh, 1880), p. 35.

5. H. Miller, 'The highlanders', in H. Miller (ed.), *Essays, historical and biographical, political and social, literary and scientific* (Edinburgh, 1862), pp. 127–41.

6. J. Prebble, *The highland clearances* (London, 1963).

7. R.A. Dodgshon, *From chiefs to landlords* (Edinburgh, 1998); Richards, *The highland clearances*; R. Mathieson, *The survival of the unfittest: the highland clearances and the end of isolation* (Edinburgh, 2000).

already under way and there were several influences that acted to threaten the traditional Highland way of life. One of these was social in nature: landlords who, as the old clan chiefs, had maintained a relationship of more or less mutual interdependence with their clansmen were now viewing this relationship in purely commercial terms, as that between landlord and tenant, and using it to support a more luxurious lifestyle.[8] In addition, agricultural improvers increasingly regarded practices in the Highlands as primitive and in need of change, while increasing pressures were brought to bear as a result of the considerable growth in population over most of the eighteenth century.[9]

This essay aims to carry out a further critical examination of the period leading up to the Clearances and, in doing so, build on or extend the work of more recent authorities such as Dodgshon and Richards.[10] The aim is to explore in more detail the impact of one of the pressures for change mentioned above: that of population change. In doing so, one source employed is of a kind unique to Scotland. On three occasions the Church of Scotland required reports from each of its parishes describing not only ecclesiastical practices but also more secular features such as local agriculture and population. These are known as the 'Statistical Accounts', of which the first, the 'Old Statistical Account', covers the early 1790s. Here 'statistical' involves an earlier meaning of the term as 'state of'; in consequence, the reports are in narrative form rather than largely numerical, as would be expected were the term employed in its current sense.

It is stressed that it is not the intention to deny in any way the very real suffering brought to ordinary people by the actions of landlords in expelling them from their traditional areas during the Clearances. What is being argued, based largely on evidence from the Isle of Skye, is that, even if the Clearances had not occurred, the traditional ways of life were coming under increasing pressure which would necessarily have led to change of some sort. A significant part of this pressure was produced by population increase and this was probably a sufficient cause in itself to disrupt the old way of life. Had the Clearances not occurred as they did, some other major changes would have been inevitable because the old way of life was ceasing to be sustainable. Whether the undoubted misery inflicted on the Highlanders by the Clearances was an appropriate or necessary response to the situation is a separate issue.

8. Dodgshon, *From chiefs to landlords*; S. Nenadic, *Lairds and luxury: the highland gentry in eighteenth-century Scotland* (Edinburgh, 2007).

9. R.A. Dodgshon, 'Farming practice in the western highlands and islands before crofting: a study in rural inertia or opportunity costs', *Rural History*, 3 (1992), p. 173.

10. Dodgshon, *From chiefs to landlords*; Richards, *The highland clearances*.

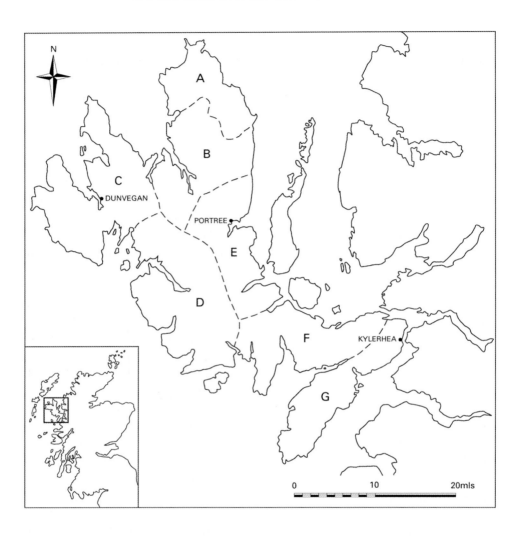

Fig. 8.1 Map of Skye showing parishes and the adjacent mainland.
Key: A. Kilmuir; B. Snizort; C. Duirinish; D. Bracadale; E. Portree; F. Strath; G. Sleat.

Population change

The specific thesis advanced here is that population growth presented an appreciable threat and, even if it acted alone, would have led to a crisis sufficient to disrupt the traditional way of life. In turn, this assertion depends upon the validity of two arguments. The first is that appreciable population growth did occur during the eighteenth century. Population growth *per se* need not necessarily have had a great impact. Where it does lead to considerable difficulty is when it arises in a setting in which it is not possible to mount an adequate response to that growth. The second issue, therefore, relates to the ability of the community to adapt to that population growth. While the evidence considered in discussing these points relates most directly to the Isle of Skye, the general picture is probably typical of much of the Highlands. In this context, 'Skye' is taken to include also the very much smaller inhabited island of Raasay, since this formed part of Portree parish (Fig. 8.1).

There is no real doubt that there was population growth in the eighteenth century. The difficulty with regard to Skye, as for many other parts of the Highlands, is in determining its extent. Comments in the reports regarding the seven parishes on Skye in the Old Statistical Account (OSA) of the 1790s suggest that the parish in question had no proper documents and so the usual parish records of baptisms, funerals and so on that could be used to indicate population numbers and rate of change are thus not available.[11] Rentals, which in England might provide some indication of the population living on an estate, are of little value for this purpose in the Highlands and this is very much the case for Skye. Rentals are of little use because the local system of tenancy involved large sections of land, often known as 'fermtouns', typically being let to a 'tacksman' (a 'tack' is a Scots term for a lease). The tacksman may or may not have himself farmed part of the land associated with his lease but typically sublet large parts of that land on an informal basis to a number of other individuals, who could be removed from their holdings at any time. These sub-tenants, as well as cottars who had no land of their own, did not appear on rentals because only the tacksman and/or the particular fermtoun or 'township' was of direct concern. This was simply because the tacksman was the only person who paid rent directly to the landlord. (It should be noted that, in this context, the term 'town' or its derivatives such as 'toun' or 'township' were used to refer to quite small settlements which might consist of no more than ten dwellings.)

---

11. The first of these, 'The Old Statistical Account', produced reports dated between 1790 and 1795 for the seven Skye parishes. The most readily available source for these is: D.J. Withrington and I.R. Grant, *The statistical account of Scotland, vol. XX, the Western Isles* (Wakeford, 1983), pp. 153–229.

The rentals relating to the estates of the MacDonalds of Sleat and the MacLeods of Dunvegan are typical in listing just the particular townships and the rental paid by the tacksman of each.[12] Up until mid century part of this rental was paid in kind, although this practice was very much on the decline. In 1740 about 5 per cent of the value of rents from the Trotternish section of the MacDonald estates (substantially the parishes of Kilmuir and Snizort) was in kind.[13] Another limitation of rentals is that they are sparse for the eighteenth century and often refer to just one part of a large estate; for the purposes of comparison, a series of rentals for the same part at different times would be needed, and such are extremely difficult to find. A rare exception to these general rules regarding rentals is a rental-like document drawn up for Alexander Murray of Stanhope in 1727 which gives the numbers of men, women and children in each township for his Ardnamurchan estate (situated on the mainland to the south of Skye).[14] Unfortunately, there appears to be no further comparable analysis for this estate, which means that it is not possible to determine population *change*.

Despite the lack of documentary evidence, including the very limited number of surviving Poll Tax returns, the authors of all the OSA reports relating to the seven parishes on Skye attempted to give an estimation of the then population of the parish at the time that the report was written (these vary between 1790 and 1795). Since they also give the figures for Webster's population survey of Scotland of 1755, they enable an estimate of the population increase between 1755 and the 1790s to be calculated. These data are given in Table 8.1. According to these estimates, the population of Skye grew from 11,372 in 1755 to around 14,470 in the 1790s, an increase of approximately 27 per cent. In itself, this is a substantial increase in the number of people to be provided for by an agricultural system that was already considerably stretched to meet the needs of the existing population. However, this estimate does not allow for the emigration that took place between the 1750s and the 1790s. Contrary to what has sometimes been believed, emigration from the Highlands started several decades before the Clearances. An indication of this is provided by Dr Johnson, who, in describing his arrival in Portree by boat from Raasay in 1773, noted that 'a ship lay waiting to dispeople Sky [*sic*], by carrying the natives away to America'.[15] According to the OSA report for the parish of Duirinish,

---

12. MacDonald Lands Trust (hereafter MLT), Armadale, Skye, mss GD 108, GD221; MacLeod of MacLeod, *The book of Dunvegan: being documents from the muniment room of the MacLeods of MacLeod at Dunvegan Castle, Isle of Skye* (Aberdeen, 1939), p. 80.

13. MLT, ms GD 221.

14. Reproduced in R.A. Dodgshon, *The age of the clans: the highlands from Somerled to the clearances* (Edinburgh, 2002), p. 60.

Table 8.1 Population estimates by parish for Skye in the 1750s and 1790s

Parish	1755	1790–5	Increase
Bracadale	1,907	2,250	18%
Diurnish	2,568	3,000	17%
Kilmuir	1,572	2,065	31%
Portree	1,248	1,980	58%
Sleat	1,250	1,788	43%
Snizort	1,627	1,808	11%
Strath	1,200	1,579	31%
Totals	11,372	14,470	27%

Source: D.J. Withrington and I.R. Grant, *The statistical account of Scotland*, vol. XX, *the Western Isles* (Wakeford, 1983), pp. 153–229.

emigration amounted to about 2400 persons for the whole of the island in the decades immediately prior to the writing of the reports.[16] Factoring this into the calculations indicates a total population increase of around 48 per cent in a period of a little less than half a century.

Clearly the data provided in Table 8.1 need to be treated with some caution since they are merely estimates provided by one individual in each parish and are presumably based on little more than general impressions. On the other hand, the authors of the various reports, most commonly the minister, would be in as good a position as any to make such an estimate. The figure of approximately 14,500 for the total population based on the OSA reports, coupled with an allowance for a few years of further expansion at a similar rate, is also not markedly out of line with the 1801 census estimate of around 16,000 for the island. Comparable information from other parts of Scotland is extremely difficult to find, but estimates based on a small number of parishes in the Highland region suggest that the estimates of population increase on Skye may not be unreasonable.[17] Furthermore, Wrigley and Schofield's estimated growth in the population of England over a comparable period is about 42 per cent, which is not very different from the Skye figure of 48 per cent estimated here.[18] Even if the Skye estimates

15. S. Johnson, *A journey to the Western Islands of Scotland* (1775, London, 1984), p. 80.

16. Withrington and Grant, *Statistical account*, p. 161.

17. A. Flynn, J. Gillespie, N. Hill, A. Maxwell, R. Mitcheson and C. Smout, *Scottish population history: from the 17th century to the 1930s* (Cambridge, 1977), p. 245.

18. E.A. Wrigley and R.F. Schofield, *The population history of England 1541–1871: a reconstruction* (Cambridge, 1989), pp. 208–9.

have poor levels of reliability and overestimate the extent of the increase, it seems highly likely that the authors of the various OSA parish reports were reflecting an actual rise in population that was far from trivial in degree.

It can be noted in passing that the OSA figures for the different parishes given in Table 8.1 provide very different estimates of the percentage increases, with a range from 11 per cent to 58 per cent. Factors which might contribute to this variation are that the population figures are rough and ready estimates; there is also the statistical phenomenon that estimates based on the much smaller numbers in each parish are likely to be less reliable (i.e. show more variation) than those based on the larger numbers for the island as a whole. In addition, with the OSA figures not taking into account emigration, it may well be that different parishes experienced emigration to different degrees.

Potential to accommodate

Potentially there are several varied ways in which an increasing population could be accommodated. One is permanent emigration. This has already been mentioned and certainly took place to a significant extent, with the usual destination at this time being North America. However, during the eighteenth century this was not of sufficient degree to prevent an appreciable increase in the resident population, which went up by more than a quarter in less than half a century. A second possibility is seasonal emigration, whereby members of the population might go elsewhere to gain employment for part of the year and use their earnings to help support the family at home.

Mathieson makes the general claim that young Highlanders went to find work in southern Scotland and returned home in the winter with their savings. However, he was writing about the Highlands as a whole and does not indicate how extensive the practice was or whether it was more common in some parts of the Highlands than others.[19] That some islanders, especially young men, went south early in the year in order to earn higher wages and returned in autumn is mentioned in a couple of the OSA reports for Skye. Nevertheless, the impression given is that this did not happen to any marked degree and eighteenth-century visitors to Skye such as Dr Johnson and Thomas Pennant did not appear to be aware of the practice.[20] This suggests that seasonal emigration was not very common and that the money brought back in this way was not such as to have any major effect on the island's economy.

---

19. Mathieson, *The survival of the unfittest*, p. 3.

20. Withrington and Grant, *Statistical account*, pp. 170, 197; Johnson, *Western Islands*; T. Pennant, *A tour in Scotland and voyage to the Hebrides, 1772* (1974, Edinburgh, 1998), pp. 281–314.

This leaves two further possibilities for coping with population growth, increasing food production and the sale of produce, which will be considered below in greater detail.

Increasing food production

The major items in the diet were meal obtained from oats and bere (a form of barley), dairy products, fish, particularly herring, and potatoes. Meat was not a common part of the diet for the ordinary population. Potatoes were grown on the island only from around mid-century onwards, as is indicated by Dr Johnson's comment in 1773 that 'they have not known them long'.[21] Allan MacDonald, husband of the famous Flora MacDonald, a tacksman and then factor of the MacDonald estates on the Trotternish peninsula, is credited with being a pioneer in the introduction of potatoes to the island.[22] A major virtue of this crop is that it enabled some increase in the number of mouths that could be fed.

Apart from any land set aside for growing potatoes, and prior to the latter's introduction, the usual cropping cycle consisted of two years of oats and one year of bere. However, the overall amounts of grain actually produced from oats and bere were very similar.[23] Bere produced about double the yield of oats at least partly because it could be sown a month later than oats and harvested a month earlier. Among other things, this reduced its vulnerability to adverse climatic conditions.

There were several limitations to expanding production or introducing new crops. Apart from a few more favoured places in the Highlands, such as the Black Isle, which lies on the east coast of the mainland between the Moray and Cromarty Firths, the terrain of the Highlands is hilly and mountainous. This applies very much to Skye. Even in the few relatively level areas on the island, mostly in valleys and adjacent to the sea, the soil is poor and rock is close to or breaks through the surface. Furthermore, much of the more level land is boggy, with patches remaining waterlogged even through a relatively dry summer. While the typical fermtoun or township would have had access to a large tract of land, only small areas could be used to grow crops. Dodgshon used very early nineteenth-century rentals at a time shortly prior to any clearances on Skye itself to estimate the proportion of ground that could be used for arable production. This amounted to just 7 per cent of the area in the MacDonald estates.[24] There is

---

21. Johnson, *Western Islands*, p. 91.

22. H. Douglas, *Flora MacDonald: the most loyal rebel* (Stroud, 1999), p. 108.

23. R.A. Dodgshon, 'Coping with risk: subsistence crises in the Scottish highlands and islands 1600–1800', *Rural History*, 15 (2004), p. 9.

24. Dodgshon, 'Farming practice', p. 174.

little reason to suspect that this figure would have been atypical in relation to other parts of the island or, indeed, much of the Highlands.

The effective area that could be devoted to arable could be further reduced by the way in which the 'rigs' (after 'ridges') or strips for planting were constructed. Channels were cut on the sides of rigs, for two purposes: firstly, they provided drainage, as can be deduced from the fact that, where traces of rigs appear on sloping ground or hillsides, the channels always run from top to bottom and never across the hillsides; secondly, the soil resulting from cutting these channels was piled on top of the rigs to increase the depth for the crops. Where the layer of soil was originally rather thin, the channels would be cut wider to provide additional soil to be placed on the rigs. The effect of this was to reduce the effective area available for planting. The need to maximise the use of any land adaptable for arable production is indicated by the fact that it is still possible to see the outlines of rigs on the sides of relatively steep hills. Using the steeper parts of hillsides for arable production was only possible in a few places because the majority of hillsides are covered in rock. It is also the case that crops on the hillside would be more exposed to adverse weather conditions and so be less productive.

This discussion leads to climate, another significant limitation to arable production. High rainfall, coupled with the nature of the soil and the terrain, meant that drainage was always a major problem. In addition, spring comes late and autumn early, providing only a relatively short growing season with even poorer yields if spring was unusually delayed or autumn set in too soon. Poor harvests produced considerable distress from time to time, with especially difficult situations arising in 1744–5, 1771–2, 1778–9 and 1782–3, to cite but some examples from the later eighteenth century.[25] The frequent high, mainly westerly, winds were not conducive to arable production and were a further major factor in reducing the range of crops that could be grown. For example, wheat was not a viable crop partly due to the strong winds.

Yet a further restriction lay in the technology that could be applied, so making production very labour intensive. Even in the late eighteenth century there were not many ploughs on Skye. The ground was often cultivated by hand using a special kind of wooden spade called the 'caschrom'.[26] The continuing use of this and other 'primitive' methods bolstered arguments that agriculture on the island, as well as the Highlands in general, was highly inefficient and, to many eyes, needed drastic improvement. On the other hand, as Dodgshon (among others) has argued, allowance has also to be made for local circumstances. Very rocky and

25. Dodgshon, 'Coping with risk', p. 3; Withrington and Grant, *Statistical account*, p. 171.
26. I.F. Grant, *Highland folk ways* (London, 1961), p. 103.

irregularly shaped areas of arable land were ill-suited to the use of the plough, if it could be used at all. Even in those places where ploughs could be used, they were small but nevertheless required as many as four men and six horses to operate. At any one time, two horses had to be held resting and in reserve.[27]

As regards the other end of the production cycle, there were few places where mills could be established. In many places the grains of cereals were separated from the straw and chaff by a process known as 'gradanning'. This was described by Martin Martin [sic] after his 1695 visit to the Western Isles in the following way:

> A woman sitting down takes a handful of corn, holding it by the stalks in her left hand, and then sets fire to the ears, which are presently in a flame. She has a stick in her right hand which she manages very dexterously, beating off the grain at the very instant when the husk is quite burnt.[28]

The grain was then often ground using a hand quern, although some communities had access to a mill. Where this was the case, landlords banned the use of querns and those found to be using querns would have them broken.[29]

The main fertiliser in those parishes with access to the coast, such as those on Skye, was seaweed, which was spread over the rigs.[30] However, the taking of seaweed for this purpose was limited in some tacks because of landlords' interests in the kelp industry (see below). Some manure from animals and old thatch from roofs were also used as fertilisers; the latter was readily available, as it often had to be replaced every year.[31] The thatch was steeped in soot because many dwellings did not have proper chimneys and smoke from the fire found its way out through the thatch.

Perhaps unsurprisingly, crop yields were generally poor. Estimates suggested that oats yielded around three times as much as was sown, of which around a third had to be held back for sowing the next year.[32] In comparison, at a similar time places in Britain with a more congenial climate and land more suited to arable production could achieve a yield for oats that was at least two and even three times that of Skye.[33]

---

27. Dodgshon 'Farming practice', p. 177.

28. M. Martin, *A description of the Western Isles of Scotland, circa 1695* (1698, Edinburgh, 1999), p. 127.

29. Grant, *Highland folk ways*, p.112.

30. Dodgshon, 'Farming practice', p. 178.

31. Grant, *Highland folk ways*, p. 160.

32. Johnson, *Western Islands*, p. 90.

33. M. Overton, *Agricultural production in England: the transformation of the agrarian economy* (Cambridge, 1996), pp. 63–132.

The general conclusion with regard to arable production has to be that only small patches of land permitted the growth of crops and that considerable labour had to go into creating what were rather low yields. As Dodgshon has suggested, communities 'had extended their bounds of cultivation to their absolute limits'.[34] Finally, there were no agricultural improvements in the offing that might change this situation.

Dairy produce provided an important item of diet. Very little beef was eaten, with the main value of cattle lying in the making of dairy products and especially as a means of generating income. The rearing of cattle as a commercial enterprise, together with the limitations of this activity, will be considered below. Transhumance was practised, with the cattle being taken to higher ground from spring to autumn, both to extend the available grazing and to keep cattle away from the growing crops. Where traces of shielings still exist, these can be found not very far in horizontal distance from the townships that they served, which is testimony to the very hilly nature of the terrain.

Fishing was another source of food, with the main species caught being herring, ling, cod, haddock and mackerel. The contribution of fish to the diet was limited by a number of factors. Fish movements, especially those of herring and mackerel, tend to be seasonal. The common occurrence of bad weather, especially high winds and heavy seas, can make fishing from small boats hazardous and even impossible. In addition, comments for the parish of Portree and Snizort in the OSA indicate that an inability to secure an adequate supply of salt made it impossible to preserve larger catches of herring in the summer season, when they were plentiful, for later use during the winter.[35] When situations were extreme, islanders would even eat limpets taken from the sea shore.

A number of animals other than cattle were reared, including sheep and horses. The value of horses lay not only in their ability to draw a plough, where the use of the plough was possible, but also as a beast of burden, carrying cut peats back to the township and transporting seaweed for use as fertiliser, for example. The primary sources consulted give no indication of any wheeled vehicles that could be pulled by horses and this is to be expected given the lack of roads on the island, as was testified by Dr Johnson; transport between different places on the island was mainly by boat.[36] Very little is said about sheep in primary sources but there was considerable domestic production of cloth and so wool would have been important.

---

34. Dodgshon, 'Farming practice' p. 176.

35. Withrington and Grant, *Statistical account*, pp. 192, 221.

36. Johnson, *Western Islands*, p. 70.

Sale of produce

One possible way of supporting a growing population would be to produce for sale and use the proceeds to buy food and other essentials. Again, this was a limited option given the level of isolation and the need to transport goods between the island and significant centres on the mainland, such as Inverness and Fort William, which required travel over long distances using boats and poor roads and tracks.

Despite these problems, there were two major lines of production for external sale: kelp and black cattle. Islanders, like many others in the Highlands, raised 'black cattle' (black-coated Highland cattle) which were sold to drovers during the summer. The drovers then took the cattle south, selling them at the annual cattle trysts at Crieff or Falkirk, from where they were typically taken much further south. Such cattle could even end up on dinner tables in London after being fattened near to the metropolis. From the islanders' perspective, cattle were not raised for meat. Their local food value was almost entirely confined to dairy produce. The sale of cattle was the only consistent source of cash for the ordinary islander, however, and this cash was needed to pay rent to the tacksmen as well as to purchase those necessities which could not be produced by the islanders themselves.

Expanding the number of cattle raised was not a viable option, at least to any appreciable degree. The poor summer grazing resulted in the need for souming (stinting) and another major limitation arose from the need to overwinter cattle. It was hard to produce adequate fodder for the winter period and during that season the condition of the cattle typically deteriorated. Martin Martin, describing the situation in the last few years of the seventeenth century, noted that 'cows are likewise exposed to the rigour of the coldest seasons, and become mere skeletons in the spring, many of them not being able to rise from the ground without help'.[37] While Martin was sometimes prone to what might seem to be improbable exaggeration, his comments on this point echo those of others: it was not easy to ensure that cattle would survive the winter in this environment.

Another source of income was kelp. This industry, which got under way in the middle of the eighteenth century and then went into decline after the Napoleonic wars, involved collecting seaweed, drying it onshore and then burning it in specially constructed kilns. This yielded a residue that was rich in soda ash (sodium carbonate) and mainly used in the manufacture of soap and glass. The industry was fairly widespread over much of the western seaboard of the Highlands, although the major location for kelp was the Outer Hebrides, especially North and South Uist.[38] Kelp could be a rather erratic source of

---

37. Martin, *Western Isles*, p. 100.

income, however; the Spanish equivalent, barilla, was considered to be of better quality and so the fluctuating availability of this import affected the prices that could be obtained for kelp.[39] It is therefore not surprising that the peak decade for Highland kelp production was the 1790s, when Britain was at war with Spain.

It seems that, unlike the situation on the Uists, kelp production was never a major source of income for ordinary people on Skye and was, of course, an activity not possible in Highland parishes without any access to the coastline. Around the height of the kelp industry, in the last decade of the eighteenth century, the overall production of kelp per head of population on Skye was less than a tenth of that on the Uists,[40] where the kelp industry was a significant contributor to the ability of ordinary people to pay rents. The various reports for Skye in the OSA also suggest that there was quite appreciable variation in the amount produced in the different parishes on the island. Gray has discussed the economics of the kelp industry, which are relatively complex. The people doing the actual work, mainly tacksmen's sub-tenants and cottars, who cut, dried and burned the kelp, received little financial reward for their labour, partly because landlords controlled the seashore and could control the price paid for harvesting the seaweed. In addition, the workers had no formal leases, meaning that they were forced to operate under terms dictated to them by landlords and tacksmen.[41]

Other than the above sources of income, at least one Skye parish, Duirnish, exported some herring.[42] This was certainly not a major item of trade for that parish and the export of fish is not mentioned in the OSA accounts of any other parish. In contrast, the report for Bracadale specifically states that very little fishing occurred in that parish, implying that it was highly unlikely that any fish caught in this parish would be offered for sale.[43]

As far as the possibility of developing any other forms of commercial activity was concerned, the isolation of the island, as of many other places in the Highlands, would have made things difficult. The two closest significant centres of population to Skye were Inverness and Fort William, both of which are of the order of a hundred miles away by land. Fort William was potentially accessible by boat but, even so, the need to pass round the Ardnamurchan peninsula meant that this centre was no nearer by boat than it was by foot. Access to the outside

38. M. Gray, 'The kelp industry in the Highlands and Islands', *Economic History Review*, 4 (1951), pp. 197–209.

39. Grant, *Highland folk ways*, p. 55.

40. Gray, 'The kelp industry', p. 205.

41. *Ibid.*

42. Withrington and Grant, *Statistical account*, p. 159.

43. *Ibid.*, p. 153.

world was not helped by the poor road system in the Highlands, the lack of roads on the island and the need to convey everything to and from the mainland by boat. Cattle, which were made to swim the half-mile between Kylerhea on Skye and Glenelg on the mainland, were the only exception to this. Although this is the shortest crossing its use is complicated by the very strong currents running between the island and the mainland at this point.

The isolation would have cut two ways, therefore. It made it difficult to market anything that islanders might possibly have had for sale, such as eggs, wool and dairy produce; it is of significance that the only appreciable source of income from export to the outside world from Skye was cattle, and the drovers actually came to the island to purchase these. Similarly, buyers came to take away kelp when and where this was produced. But it also meant that the islanders' ability to obtain necessities from outside was poor, although some externally produced goods did reach the island. One consequence that follows was that many necessities that might have been purchased from outside the island, such as cloth, shoes and, to some extent, even tools, had to be produced locally. In addition, such things as cutting peat and the often annual necessity to replace thatch on houses[44] would ensure that islanders had little time to devote to producing things for sale to outside markets even if they had enjoyed better access to these.

Conclusion

It can be argued with justification that the Clearances put the final nail in the coffin of a traditional way of life and organisation of society, both on Skye and in the rest of the Highlands. To stretch this metaphor a little further, the thesis being advanced here is that the body that went into this coffin was not, as has often been supposed, the outcome of a sudden death. Rather, there had been a slow decline into a near-terminal state.

A prime reason for this state of affairs was the growth in population, which was substantial in the eighteenth century despite the effects of increasing emigration. It has to be acknowledged, however, that there were other pressures which also acted to curtail the continuance of the traditional way of life, such as changes in the relationships between landlord and tenant and the contemporary concern with agricultural reform. However, these latter influences remain outside the concerns of this particular chapter, which has only been able to consider what was probably the most significant of the many factors: the large growth in population. A significant net increase in population occurred in a context in which it was not possible to expand food production to anything like

---

44. Grant, *Highland folk ways*, p. 160.

the degree required to feed the increased numbers, and this despite the introduction of potatoes. Any land that could be used for arable production was already in use. Similarly, limitations in grazing and the problem of overwintering cattle curtailed any expansion in the pastoral aspects of farming. Additionally, the isolation of Highland communities such as Skye acted to limit the available options to adapt to a changing situation.

The conclusion has to be that, even if the Clearances had not occurred, some radical restructuring of life on Skye, together with much of the rest of the Highlands, would have been unavoidable. It is difficult to see how this could have happened in the context of the times without increased emigration, either to places abroad or to the more industrialised areas of Britain.

9. 'By her labour': working wives in a Victorian provincial city

Jane Howells

Women were central to the character and success of the economy of Victorian Salisbury.[1] Retail trades, hospitality and other service industries typical of the increasingly diversified economic structure of the city were exactly the location of women's contributions as producers and suppliers. The opportunities that the changing commercial character of Salisbury presented to women for using their skills to earn a living were exploited by married women as well as by single women and widows, working on their own or in family enterprises. One-third of the women in the city in 1851 were recorded with an occupation, so it was likely that in practice many more were active in the local economy.[2] Men continued to dominate some parts of that economy, such as manufacturing, transport and construction, but there were exceptions to this general picture, with women heading bricklaying, chimney-sweeping, painting and glazing businesses, while both men and women were involved in shopkeeping and in the food and drink trades. Within each sector of the economy there were enterprises of varying size, from single individuals to family groups and employers with a dozen or more workers, although none was large by standards elsewhere.

Salisbury had been a major centre for the manufacture of woollen cloth in earlier centuries, but from the later decades of the eighteenth century the local economy had been gradually diversifying and the city had developed into a

---

1. This paper is based on part of J.E. Howells, 'Independent women in public life in Salisbury in the second half of the nineteenth century' (PhD thesis, London, 2007), chapter 3.

2. Unless otherwise specified, data in this paper comes from 1851 census enumerators' books for Salisbury parishes in The National Archives (hereafter TNA), HO 107/1847.

regional service centre for a widespread agricultural hinterland.[3] This chapter looks at the main categories of commercial activity for wives who worked, both in aggregate terms and by identifying some individuals. This is possible only for a few, but the occasional chances to link work and home throw light on their diverse experiences both in the domestic sphere and in the public economy. While Victorian Salisbury had a special identity created by its unique combination of history, location and culture, it shared many characteristics with other communities. The larger research programme which is the basis of this chapter demonstrates the wealth of information that can be used, and other researchers could pursue the same line of inquiry. The sources, such as census enumerators' books, local newspapers, directories and ephemera, are widely available and generally accessible. Women in smaller provincial towns and cities have been largely neglected by historians; an accumulation of similar studies elsewhere would contribute to a broader and deeper understanding of their lives.

The Victorian ideal required that men of all social classes should support their wives (and children).[4] Marriage was considered the only acceptable objective in life for women, and their education and training, such as it was, prepared them for little else. Married women would then care for their husbands (and children) in the confines of the home, taking responsibility for the organisation of the household and the maintenance of high standards of physical and moral health. As Bessie Rayner Parkes, an advocate of 'more meaningful lives for middle class women, and more tolerable and varied working conditions for working women', put it in 1859:[5]

> All good fathers wish to provide for their daughters; all good husbands think it their bounden duty to keep their wives. All our laws are framed strictly in accordance with this hypothesis; and all our social customs adhere to it more strictly still. We make no room in our social framework for any other idea ...

But for many this was an impossible ideal, as Harriet Martineau confirmed in the same year: the supposition 'that every women is supported ... by her father,

---

3. The total population of Salisbury was 7,600 in 1801, 9,500 in 1851 and 17,000 in 1901.

4. For a concise summary of the use of 'the pervasive rhetoric of "separate spheres"' see K. Gleadle, *British women in the nineteenth century* (Basingstoke 2001), pp. 1–2, and further discussion in R. Beachy, B. Craig and A. Owens (eds), *Women, business and finance in nineteenth-century Europe* (Oxford, 2006), pp. 1–11.

5. B.R. Parkes, 'The market for educated female labour', *The English Woman's Journal* (1859), reprinted in C.A. Lacey (ed.), *Barbara Leigh Bodichon and the Langham Place group* (London, 1986), p. 142. Cited description of Parkes' position from Joanne Shattock, 'Elizabeth Rayner Parkes (1829–1925), campaigner for women's rights and journalist', *ODNB*.

Table 9.1 Social classification of occupations in Salisbury, 1851. Percentage of men and women (recorded with an occupation) in each class

Class	Women	Men
1 (professional)	–	3
2 (intermediate)	4	4
3 (skilled)	47	63
4 (semi-skilled)	46	16
5 (unskilled)	3	13

her brother or her husband ... has now become false, and ought to be practically admitted to be false'.[6]

Many women worked for an income, as well as working unpaid inside the home (Table 9.1).[7] For most it was financial need that put them in the former situation. Women who were married to men whose job or business generated low or erratic remuneration contributed to the family by earning money themselves, but this was feasible only when there were appropriate local employment openings for women. An alternative strategy for them was to set up a small independent business, a route often taken by women from families with traditions in commerce.

Evidence that financial need was one factor pushing married women into work (provided that there were employment opportunities available to them) can be found by comparing the socio-economic group of a section of Salisbury's working married women to that of their husbands (Table 9.2). Classification schemes have been widely debated, with different systems being developed in varied contexts, some based on contemporary and some on modern categorisations; see, for example, the discussion and references in Drake and Finnegan's book *Sources and methods: a handbook*.[8] Armstrong's method has been selected for this study. His example of York had similarities with Salisbury at this time, and the few individual occupations that do not appear in Armstrong's list[9] can be allocated through a

---

6. H. Martineau, 'Female industry', *The Edinburgh Review*, 222 (1859), p. 297.

7. I have argued, contrary to the position first set out by L. Davidoff and C. Hall, *Family fortunes: men and women of the English middle class 1780–1850* (London, 1987), that there was a reduction in the presence of married women in the public economy by the middle of the nineteenth century, that evidence for Salisbury shows 'women continued to earn incomes, to support themselves and their families, and to hold positions of authority in business', and that a significant number of these were middle- and lower-middle-class married women: Howells, 'Independent women in public life in Salisbury', chapters 1 and 3.

8. M. Drake and R. Finnegan, *Sources and methods: a handbook* (Cambridge, 1994), chapter 3.

9. Drake and Finnegan, *Sources and methods*, pp. 48–9.

Table 9.2 Social classification of occupations of married couples* with working wives, Salisbury, 1851

	Husband's social classification				
Wife's social classification	1	2	3	4	5
1	—	—	—	—	—
2	2	2	6	2	—
3	—	1	97	18	16
4	—	—	18	18	21
5	—	—	3	1	8

(* couple omitted if husband absent or occupation not known, pauper or pensioner)

process of sensible guesswork. Its major disadvantage is the size of Class 3, which captures some diverse occupations. This happens partly because the defining boundaries are vague, partly because the occupational labels given to individuals do not always specify the necessary variables (existence of employees indicating scale of business, for example), and partly because the level of skill in women's occupations is less clearly identified than for men's. The inevitable consequence is the clustering of both men and women in Class 3.

Wives *were* earning to contribute to the family income where their husbands had lower status and presumably less remunerative jobs. As Table 9.2 shows, 34 women with Class 3 occupations were married to husbands with jobs in Class 4 or 5 and more than four-fifths of wives had husbands in occupations of equal or lower status. The evidence suggests that, overall, wives were more likely to have husbands in lower-status jobs than themselves (17 per cent) than husbands were to have lower-status working wives (12 per cent).

Economic need can also be examined by considering the *types* of occupations undertaken by the husbands of working wives. These were preponderantly low-paid, low-status jobs, some of which would also be liable to irregular, perhaps seasonal, employment, such as casual work as labourers and porters. Shoemaking also stands out. Moreover, in many cases both husband and wife were employed in the same industry (such as horsehair manufacturing), and so *both* breadwinners would be vulnerable to its market fluctuations.

The picture, however, was more complex than simple financial need, because there were men in the same occupations whose wives were apparently *not* working. Firstly, as is well-established, some of this difference can be explained by under-recording in census enumerators' books of married women's occupations; more wives probably were earning from casual, part-time work that was not considered

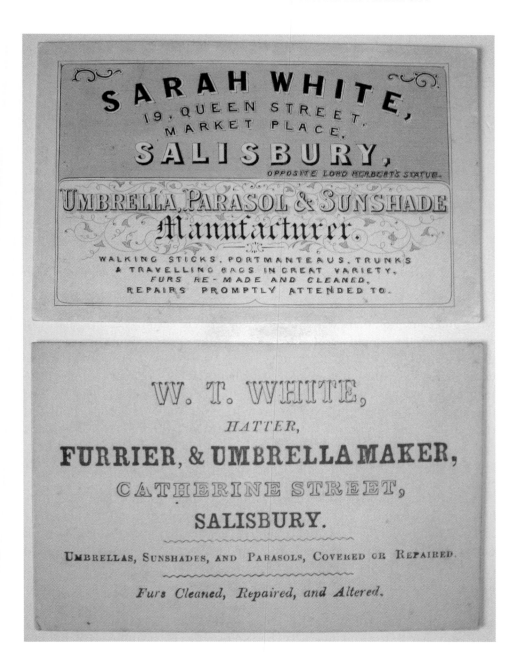

Fig. 9.1 Trade cards for Mr and Mrs White.

sufficiently significant for inclusion or was not happening on the date of the census.[10] The case of Mrs White provides an example of this, as well as demonstrating the value of corroboration between different sources.

Sarah White was given no occupation in the 1861 census return, but on her personal trade cards she advertised herself as an 'Umbrella, Parasol and Sunshade Manufacturer'. Her husband was a hatter and furrier in both the census and contemporary directories, and in 1867 Sarah too was thus described. At one time they ran separate establishments at different addresses, but the overlap of their activities was shown on their cards (Fig. 9.1): Sarah's had in small print 'furs re-made and cleaned', beneath 'walking sticks, portmanteaus, trunks and travelling bags in great variety'. Her husband, William Thomas White, added 'umbrellas, sunshades and parasols covered or repaired' to his card. It can be imagined that they catered for the varied needs of their customers to combat the weather. After being widowed, Sarah, together with her daughter Catherine, were both umbrella-makers in 1871, demonstrating a common continuity.

Secondly, *within* these occupations where some men are found with working wives and some not, there was a hierarchy of levels of earnings and regularity of employment that could result in a range of prosperity. Some wives might therefore need to work, and others not. Taking 'shoemaker' as an example, at one end of a possible continuum was Mr Sydenham, 'ladies shoemaker employing 6 men and 6 women', living in the High Street with his wife, four sons, one daughter and a servant girl. Not far away were Mr and Mrs Forder, 'boot and shoe maker' and 'boot and shoe maker's assistant'; Mr and Mrs Wapshare, shoemaker and shoebinder; Mr and Mrs Rambridge, bootmaker and laundress; and the Fricker and Salisbury families, both headed by shoemakers whose wives were not recorded with any occupation.

A third factor to be considered was family size and structure: who else in the household was earning, and how many dependents made demands on the family income? Employed older children could free their mother from the need to work outside the home, while small children could prevent her doing so, and indeed restrict her opportunities for working at home. On the other hand, many mouths to feed would increase the need for an additional income, especially if older children could mind younger ones while their mother worked for cash. For example, in White's Buildings, New Street, in 1851 Mr Fricker and Mr Salisbury were both shoemakers and their wives had no recorded occupations, as mentioned above. The Salisburys had three young children and the Frickers two young sons plus a 14-year-old daughter employed as a nursemaid. At number 7, Mrs

---

10. E. Higgs, *A clearer sense of the census* (London, 1996), pp. 97–8.

Plate 1 Hallowes Hall, Derbyshire.

Plate 2 Cartledge Hall, Holmesfield, Derbyshire.

Plate 3 Cartledge Grange, Holmesfield, Derbyshire.

Plate 4 Dronfield Woodhouse Hall, Derbyshire.

Plate 5 Dronfield Manor House, Derbyshire, now the public library.

Plate 6 Dronfield Hall, Derbyshire.

Plate 7 Chiverton House, Derbyshire.

Plate 8 Rose Hill, Derbyshire.

Fig. 9.2 Salisbury High Street in the early 1870s. Louise Rayner watercolour (detail).

Table 9.3 Occupations of married women, St Ann's Street and Exeter Street, Salisbury, 1851

Wives' occupations	Husbands' occupations		
	Wife under 25 years	Wife aged 25–45	Wife over 45 years
Washerwoman (3)	—	Not given	Bricklayer's labourer
	—	—	Not given
Tailoress (2)	Cabinet maker	Bootbinder	—
Dressmaker (3)	—	Rope maker	—
	—	Journeyman blacksmith	—
	—	Linen draper	—
Principal of an establishment for young ladies (1)	—	Baptist minister	—
General servant (1)	—	Not given	—
Governess (1)	—	—	Schoolmaster
Schoolmistress (1)	—	Hackneyman	—
Shoebinder (1)	—	—	Not given
Charwoman (2)	—	Ropemaker	Postboy
Plain needlewoman (1)	—	Not given	
Laundress (3)	—	—	Gardener
	—	—	Bricklayer's labourer
	—	—	Chelsea pensioner
Seamstress (1)	—	Bricklayer's labourer	—
Agricultural labourer (1)	—	—	Shepherd

Rambridge probably did her work as a laundress at home so that she could care for her two sons at the same time. The Forders, who were both employed, had two daughters, one apprenticed to a milliner (so costing her parents for her training), and the younger engaged in 'netting', so unlikely to be earning very much.[11] There were six children in the household of another neighbour, Mr Andress, a

11. Netting was the process of creating a netted fabric of loops secured by knots, the product ranging from coarse fishing nets to delicate ornamental snoods.

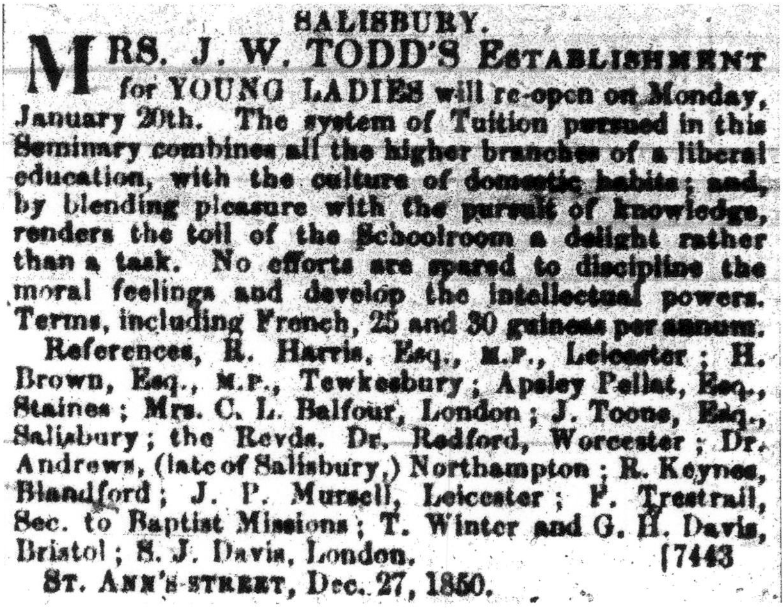

SALISBURY.

MRS. J. W. TODD'S ESTABLISHMENT for YOUNG LADIES will re-open on Monday, January 20th. The system of Tuition pursued in this Seminary combines all the higher branches of a liberal education, with the culture of domestic habits; and, by blending pleasure with the pursuit of knowledge, renders the toil of the Schoolroom a delight rather than a task. No efforts are spared to discipline the moral feelings and develop the intellectual powers. Terms, including French, 25 and 30 guineas per annum.

References, R. Harris, Esq., M.P., Leicester; H. Brown, Esq., M.P., Tewkesbury; Apsley Pellat, Esq., Staines; Mrs. C. L. Balfour, London; J. Toone, Esq., Salisbury; the Revds. Dr. Redford, Worcester; Dr. Andrews, (late of Salisbury,) Northampton; R. Keynes, Blandford; J. P. Mursell, Leicester; F. Trestrail, Sec. to Baptist Missions; T. Winter and G. H. Davis, Bristol; S. J. Davis, London.   [7443
ST. ANN'S-STREET, Dec. 27, 1850.

Fig. 9.3 Mrs Todd's advertisement, *Salisbury and Winchester Journal*, 11 January 1851, p. 2.

whitesmith who worked with his eldest son, while two other sons, aged 13 and 11, were employed elsewhere. His wife had no listed occupation, and presumably she looked after the three younger children at home as well as being housekeeper to the four workers in the family. The Forwards also had six children (the eldest aged 10) perhaps indicating why the income earned by James Forward in his white-collar job as 'clerk to wine merchants' needed supplementing. Ellen Forward worked as a 'dealer in fishing tackle', equipment in great demand for the trout-filled chalk streams around Salisbury.

The combinations of specific jobs followed by married couples can be examined by looking at just two census enumeration districts in more detail. In 1851 these areas had almost identical rates of married women working (23.9 per cent and 23.8 per cent) but were otherwise different. The High Street is a central artery of the city, running from St Thomas's church to the main gate into the Cathedral Close (Fig. 9.2). It contained an important hostelry and major retail sites, and had a resident population of 757, including 443 females. St Ann's Street and Exeter Street are on the southern outskirts of the city and contained more mixed properties, including both elegant eighteenth-century townhouses and cottages on Bugmore.

Table 9.4 Occupations of married women, High Street, Salisbury, 1851

Wives' occupations	Husbands' occupations		
	Wife under 25 years	Wife aged 25–45	Wife over 45 years
Schoolmistress (3)	Ivory and wood turner	Schoolmaster	Accountant
Dealer in Berlin fancy goods (1)	—	—	Master cabinet maker
Dressmaker (3)	—	Hairdresser & perfumer	—
	—	Tailor	—
	—	Not given	—
Shopkeeper (1)	—	Railway fitter	—
Milliner (2)	—	Cabinet maker	—
	—	Law stationer*	—
Boot and shoemaker's assistant (1)	—	—	Boot and shoemaker
Milliner's apprentice (1)	Not given	—	—
Shoebinder (1)	—	Bootmaker	—
Staymaker (1)	—	—	Not given
Tailoress (2)	Bricklayer	Cabinet maker	—
Office keeper (1)	—	Carpenter	—
Milliner and dressmaker (1)	—	Not given	—

* wife: 'milliner and mantua maker, mistress employing 3 adult assistants and 5 apprentices'; husband: 'law stationer and writer, accountant and general commission agent'

Taking the latter area first (Table 9.3), with few exceptions the couples demonstrated the need for two incomes for each household. Combinations of wife and husband with occupations such as washerwoman and bricklayer's labourer, dressmaker and rope maker, laundress and gardener, charwoman and postboy all suggest workers in relatively low-status and low-income jobs. Their better-off neighbours were likely to provide the employment by requiring personal services such as laundering or gardening. The wives' occupations, in particular, had the additional characteristic of flexibility – extra washing or sewing would supplement erratic earnings by their husbands and fit in with domestic responsibilities. The main exception to this pattern is the Baptist minister and his wife, who was 'principal of an establishment for ladies' (Fig. 9.3). A non-conformist minister's wife might well need to supplement the family income to maintain a suitable household, and she might be able to provide the combination of commercial, educational and social skills necessary for running a school.

A similar examination of the High Street in 1851 (Table 9.4) revealed working married couples of higher levels of skill and social status, and a larger proportion of people who could be described as small business proprietors rather than employees. These included combinations of wife and husband occupations such as schoolmistress and accountant, fancy goods dealer and master cabinet maker, shopkeeper and railway fitter. There was one clear example of a husband and wife working together – Mr and Mrs Forder the boot and shoemaker, and boot and shoemaker's assistant – although this may also have been the case with some others, particularly the shoebinder and bootmaker.

The Dawkins' household (indicated by * in Table 9.4) in the High Street was given a particularly full description by the census enumerator and can serve to develop a more detailed examination of working married women. It also provides another example that reinforces the importance of seeking additional information: trade directories were compiled to alert potential customers and suppliers to businesses in a specific locality, and newspapers carried advertisements for new products, special offers, changes of address and vacancies for employees. As both these means of communication were of particular value to enterprises such as retail businesses, they were used to explore further the activities of women in commerce.

Mr and Mrs Dawkins had two 'assistants in wife's business' and three apprentices resident at the time of the 1851 census, while an assistant and two apprentices either regularly lived out or happened to be away on census night. Ann Dawkins was evidently a woman of initiative and ambition: she exhibited at Salisbury's Exhibition in 1852 and in 1860 she made the most of an opportunity when she took over and sold on the stock-in-trade of a failing fellow milliner. She advertised specific products from time to time, placing the emphasis on different parts of her stock range, such as children's clothing and baby linen in 1860.[12] The principals were away from home at the time of the 1861 census, but Mr Dawkins' sister Arabella was there as 'housekeeper', thus underlining Mrs Dawkins' superior position in the establishment: she was a businesswoman rather than a housewife.

Mr and Mrs Wood, or James Wood & Company (Fig. 9.4), occupied Norman House, on a substantial corner plot in a central location. In the 1861 census Emma Wood was recorded with no occupation, although within the past year she had been advertising for outdoor apprentices and improvers and announcing to 'the

---

12. *Salisbury & Winchester Journal* (hereafter *SWJ*), 14 April 1860, p. 5.

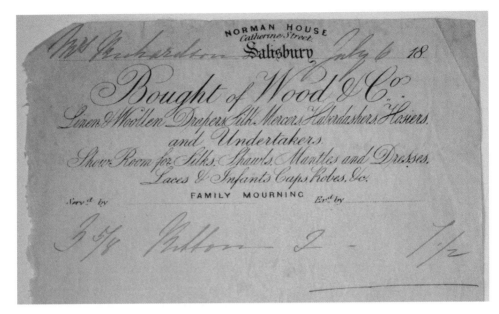

Fig. 9.4 Wood bill-head.

ladies of Salisbury and its neighbourhood that her Show Room is now complete. An early inspection is solicited.'[13] The Woods had one son in 1851 but he was no longer in the household in 1861 when they had a six-year-old boy and two girls of two years and four months respectively. Also resident were a female assistant and two female apprentices, along with two female domestic servants. Emma Wood was in an economic position to employ staff in both her business and her home, either to free her from domestic responsibilities or permit her time with her young children, or perhaps to divide her time between these two areas.

Mr and Mrs Stodart (silk mercer and dressmaker), whose business was located in the New Canal, announced in April 1860 that they were 'in Paris selecting silks, muslins and other French goods together with the fashions in millinery, dressmaking, etc'.[14] Aged 40 in 1861, Louisa Stodart was seven years older than her husband. They had a six-year-old son and employed four resident assistants and an apprentice. The establishment probably had an even larger staff, however, as in March 1860 Mrs Stodart advertised vacancies in her 'Millinery and Dressmaking Establishment' for two outdoor apprentices and improvers.[15] It was

---

13. *Ibid.*, 2 June 1860, p. 5.

14. *Ibid.*, 7 April 1860, p. 5.

15. *Ibid.*, 17 March 1860, p. 5.

common for Salisbury fashion businesses to seek seasonal supplies and ideas in London; going abroad was less usual and indicated a determination and awareness of competitive pressures.

Not everyone could afford to patronise an establishment that bought its stock in Paris or to engage the services of a dressmaker, and manufactured ready-made clothing did not dominate the trade until the early twentieth century.[16] An alternative strategy for the less well-off was to buy second-hand clothing from specialised dealers. Mr and Mrs Dennis, 'Purchasers of Ladies' and Gentlemen's Left-Off Wearing Apparel', as advertised in 1897, ran a business that had been established for 40 years, and they were well aware that discretion was an important, indeed essential, quality in this business: 'Ladies and Gentlemen punctually and privately waited on at their own residence'.[17]

Women's responsibility for food and clothing in the household transferred almost without question to their public roles. The enterprises concerned with the production, sale and care of clothing among the examples discussed so far were typical of women's businesses in the nineteenth century. Dressmakers, milliners, bonnet-makers, mantua-makers, stay-makers and others provided a personal service to other women; they selected, advised and fitted; they had intimate knowledge of their customers' physical characteristics and financial constraints. Mrs Williams offered 'bonnets cleaned and altered in the newest style' and 'ladies own materials made up' to customers who were unable to buy new.[18]

There was a similar degree of intimacy between a laundress and her customers. Taking in other people's dirty washing and returning it clean, starched and ironed was a significant source of income for individual wives and mothers at home, requiring little equipment they did not have anyway and therefore no capital outlay, and being very flexible in terms of hours worked, which could vary with need and with other commitments. It has been argued that laundresses' work was 'unusual in that it could be carried on over a lifetime, was dominated by married or widowed women, and could be adapted to domestic responsibilities more readily than most other occupations'.[19] In Salisbury in 1851 the marital status of women working in this industry was almost equally divided between married, unmarried and widowed, but a much clearer characteristic was the dominance of older women: over 60 per cent were

---

16. S. Nenadic, 'The social shaping of business behaviour in the nineteenth-century women's garment trades', *Journal of Social History*, 31 (1998), pp. 625–45.

17. *Langmead and Evans' Directory* (Salisbury, 1897), p. xxv.

18. *SWJ*, 7 April 1860.

19. P. Malcolmson, *English laundresses: a social history 1850–1930* (Chicago, 1989), p. xiii.

aged 40 and over, nearly 40 per cent were 50 and over, and the latter group included seven individuals over 70.[20]

Apart from those working in the laundries of institutions such as the workhouse, the infirmary or the House of Mercy, there were 218 women aged 20 or over classified as 'washerwoman, mangler, laundry-keeper' in 1851, 259 classified as 'laundresses' in 1861, and 220 classified as 'laundry-keeper' in 1871. There was no clear pattern of 'laundress' being used to describe higher-status women (as judged by their husband's occupation), although lower-status couples generally included 'washerwoman' rather than laundress.[21] In the Barnard's and Rolf's Chequer area, for example, the following married couples with occupations were to be found in 1851: washerwoman and general labourer, washerwoman and scavenger, washerwoman and coal porter, washerwoman and carrier's porter, laundress and farm labourer, laundress and cordwainer, laundress and tailor, laundress and confectioner, laundress and policeman. In Culver Street, the Noah family was headed by John, a confectioner. His wife Sarah was described in the 1851 census as a laundress, as were their three eldest daughters, Emily, aged 25, Mary, aged 20, and Ellen, aged 18. John and Sarah also had two younger daughters and three young sons. Mrs Mary Connor in Winchester Street was another laundress. She is an interesting case because of the explicit description of her husband's occupation as 'labourer and keeper of brothel' – a valuable level of detail provided by individual enumerators, based perhaps on their diligence and local knowledge.

'Fancy work' was an area of activity where the private interests of the higher classes coincided with the public interests of commercially astute women. As the popularity of embroidery for decorating both the person and the home using an astonishing variety of materials grew, so did economic opportunities for selling the necessary supplies. And this, like dressmaking and millinery, was a situation with women on both sides of the shop counter. One part of this enthusiasm was for Berlin wool work, embroidery on canvas with coloured wools following a printed chart. Mrs Charlotte Harding ran a Berlin wool establishment (Fig. 9.5); her husband was a saddler and rope and twine maker.

Louisa Potto was just one of the many women involved with the supply of food and drink. Census enumerators' books revealed her career as single woman, wife and widow at the same establishment, the Haunch of Venison near the Poultry Cross. In 1871, as Louisa Bradbeer, she was working as housekeeper for the licensee, Firmin Potto. Over the next decade she married her employer, who then

---

20. Howells, 'Independent women in public life in Salisbury', p. 101.

21. 'Laundress' was always used when there were several women working together.

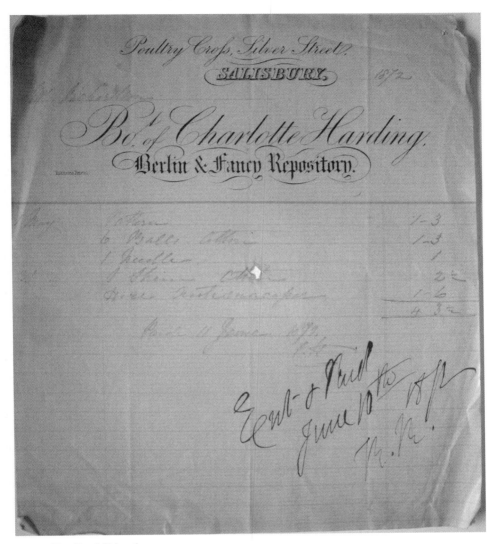

Fig. 9.5 Harding bill-head.

died, leaving her as a widow described in the 1881 census as 'innkeeper', with one of her sisters and a niece as 'barmaid' and a nephew as 'innkeeper's assistant'. Ten years later Louisa was recorded as a 'wine and spirit merchant', with two sisters, two nieces and a nephew all as 'assistant'. Her business cards were headed 'Haunch of Vension Wine Vaults', and the trade included 'Foreign Wines and Spirits. Irish and Scotch Whiskey, Devonshire Cider, London and Dublin Porter,

Aloa Ale, Foreign and British Cigars, etc'. From her secure economic position and enhanced status Louisa was able to provide employment and a home for other members of her family.

Many of these businesses run by married women gave indications of being successful. They operated for a number of years, trained apprentices and employed assistants, their premises were centrally located in the most expensive part of the city, and they advertised high-quality products. Significantly, the women's husbands were either part of the same business with their wives, or were successfully involved in some other enterprise. Mr and Mrs Wood and Mr and Mrs Dawkins were prime examples. This runs counter to the argument discussed above that married women worked owing to financial need. There was no apparent necessity for Emma Wood or Ann Dawkins to work, as their husbands could have provided for them and their families. Of course, profits from the women's businesses generated additional income, but they could also be a source of satisfaction, of self-fulfilment, of achievement. Personal testimony might support this speculation, but the voices of the women themselves are silent.

Local history and women's history have developed in parallel, each building on and appreciating the approach of the other. The richness of a 'micro-history' view that removes barriers 'between public and private lives, between economic and non-economic behaviour, between production and consumption'[22] is fruitful for identifying and celebrating the roles of women in communities in the past. Events organised by local history societies and those held, for example, under the auspices of the Women's History Network are equally likely to contain contributions that focus on the detail of women's lives in particular places. And in her unique essay Joan Thirsk has written that women *as local historians* are likely to have insights that are 'original and influential'.[23]

---

22. P. Hudson, 'Industrialization in Britain: the challenge of micro-history', *Family and Community History*, 2:1 (1999), p. 12.

23. J. Thirsk, 'Women local and family historians', in D. Hey (ed.), *The Oxford companion to local and family history* (Oxford, 1996), p. 498.

10. Religious cultures in conflict: a Salisbury parish during the English Reformation

Claire Cross

Previously a bastion of the late medieval Catholic Church, within two generations in the sixteenth century England had become an at least nominally Protestant nation and, as on the continent, towns had been at the forefront of this change. Historians have frequently commented upon the apparent readiness of the country at large to comply with the diametrically opposed legislation of the reigns of Henry VIII, Edward VI, Mary and Elizabeth, while at the same time recognising that this outward show of obedience must have cloaked a clash of competing religious cultures. As communities understandably went to some pains to conceal their ideological differences from central government, such conflicts have normally remained hidden. This, however, is far from being the case in Salisbury, where the chance survival of a rare combination of national and local records makes it possible to trace in detail the disputes which polarised the clergy and laity in the parish of St Thomas during the Reformation period.[1]

Salisbury, or New Sarum as it was originally called, dates only from the early thirteenth century, when the bishop decided to move his cathedral from the heights of Salisbury Plain to the fertile valley below. The inhabitants of the new town planted to the north of the cathedral quickly achieved many of the attributes of a self-governing corporation. They had their own mayor by 1261 and little more than a century later the mayor and an inner group of councillors

---

1. E. Duffy, *The stripping of the altars: traditional religion in England 1400–1580* (New Haven and London, 1992), pp. 377–593; P. Collinson and J. Craig (eds), *The Reformation and English towns 1540–1640* (Basingstoke, 1998), pp. 1–19; P. Marshall and A. Ryrie (eds), *The beginnings of English protestantism* (Cambridge, 2002), pp. 1–13: among much else these volumes provide a valuable introduction to recent writings on the Reformation in England.

known as the twenty-four were holding regular assemblies; in 1406 they acquired from the crown the right to hold lands in mortmain, but they never obtained their own court independent of that of the bishop. The commonalty first petitioned for a royal charter of incorporation in 1452 and made a second attempt in 1465, only for Edward IV to re-confirm the bishop's authority outright. After Henry VII's accession they brought up the matter of incorporation yet again, but made no better progress, with the result that throughout the Tudor period the city was still technically an episcopal borough with the mayor obliged to swear his oath every year before the bishop's officer and the inhabitants to sue in the bishop's court.[2]

The town was also at a disadvantage in its religious provision compared with the more ancient cathedral cities of London, Winchester, Norwich, Lincoln and York, which all possessed a great multiplicity of small parishes. Salisbury, in contrast, until well into Victoria's reign had a mere three: St Martin's, which took in the much older hamlet on the eastern periphery of the new settlement; St Thomas's, the central and most important parish; and St Edmund's, carved out of the northern part of St Thomas's parish by Bishop Walter de la Wyle on his creation of the college of St Edmund of Abingdon in 1269. The city prospered in the later Middle Ages largely on account of its thriving cloth industry and by the early sixteenth century both St Thomas's and St Edmund's had over 1000 communicants.[3]

Founded in the early part of the thirteenth century, the church of St Thomas of Canterbury underwent a very considerable restoration and extension on the collapse of the chancel roof in 1447, when the wealthy merchant, William Swayne, assumed the sole responsibility for the reconstruction of the south chancel aisle and other leading parishioners made substantial contributions to the rebuilding work. The laity also seem to have undertaken the refurbishment of the church's interior at this time on a very grand scale. The stained glass included a Tree of Jesse and the Assumption of the Virgin and the wall paintings scenes from the Annunciation, the Visitation and the Adoration of the Shepherds, in addition to the spectacular new Last Judgement over the chancel arch. The city's two chief guilds, the Taylors' Guild and St George's Guild, the latter representing

2. F. Street, 'The relations of the bishops and citizens of Salisbury (New Sarum) between 1225 and 1612', *Wiltshire Archaeological and Natural History Magazine* (hereafter *WAM*), 39 (1916), pp. 185–257, 319–67; E. Crittall (ed.), *A history of Wiltshire, vol. VI [The boroughs of Wilton and Old Salisbury, the city of New Salisbury, the hundred of Underditch]: Victoria History of the Counties of England* (London, 1962), pp. 94–7, 101–3 (hereafter *VCH Wiltshire 6*). Spelling in all quotations has been modernised.

3. *VCH Wiltshire 6*, pp. 69, 385; A.D. Brown, *Popular piety in late medieval England: the diocese of Salisbury, 1250–1550* (Oxford, 1995), p. 74.

the mayor and commonalty in their religious guise, both maintained altars and priests in the church. By the end of the Middle Ages St Thomas's had quite literally become a monument to the aspirations of the civic community.[4]

The bishop of Salisbury had retained the advowson of St Thomas's until 1399, when he granted it to the dean and chapter, who from then onwards received the greater tithes from the parish, valued at the sizeable sum of £30 in 1535. The dean and chapter never instituted a vicarage but merely appointed a chaplain, leaving the congregation to supply his salary, which, in the century between the Reformation and the Civil War, a time of acute inflation, increased from only £10 a year to a barely adequate £13 6s 8d. The absence of a formal endowment, however, seems to have had little effect upon the actual number of clergy. No fewer than 26 chaplains and 11 unbeneficed clergy were officiating in the church in 1380, and even as late as 1530 a testator, the merchant Thomas Marten, could casually refer to there being 18 priests in the parish.[5]

This very substantial clerical establishment had emerged almost entirely through lay initiatives. During the course of the Middle Ages parishioners founded at least four perpetual chantries, each with its individual priest. As well as providing his priest with a higher stipend than that of the parish chaplain, William Swayne furnished his chantry with precious vessels and ornaments, a parchment missal and five sets of damask and velvet vestments of black, green, white and blue. Not to be outdone, the tailors equipped their guild chantry with a chalice and other vessels, a mass book, various frontals, a hanging of painted canvas, a blue worsted vestment ornamented with swans, a green vestment worked with red velvet and numerous other vestments. The priests of the less influential craft guilds celebrated at different altars in the church, while at least ten fraternities, of which that at the Jesus altar was by far the most popular, had come into existence by the beginning of the sixteenth century. All these chantry, guild and fraternity priests enjoyed some security of tenure; in addition, the church also offered some sporadic employment for humbler members of the clerical proletariat willing to serve temporary chantries or to earn a pittance by performing requiem masses.[6]

The parishioners' appetite for such masses continued unabated in the early Tudor period and in the thirty years between 1505 and 1536 as many as 19 testators

---

4. *VCH Wiltshire* 6, p. 149; C. Haskins, *The ancient trade guilds and companies of Salisbury* (Salisbury, 1912), pp. 134–9; A. Hollaender, 'The doom painting of St Thomas of Canterbury, Salisbury', *WAM*, 50 (1944), pp. 351–70.

5. *VCH Wiltshire* 6, pp. 147–8; The National Archives (hereafter TNA), PROB 11/27 (Thomas Marten).

6. H. Hatcher, *Old and New Sarum or Salisbury* (London, 1834), part of C. Hoare, *History of modern Wiltshire*, 6 vols (London, 1822–44), 4, pp. 264–5; Haskins, *Ancient trade guilds*, pp. 146, 163; Brown, *Popular piety*, pp. 137, 139.

paid for a priest to celebrate for their souls and the souls of family members for periods varying from 12 months to 20 years at an annual salary of around £6. In 1523, for example, the mercer, Thomas Coke, left the sizeable sum of 200 marks (£133 6s 8d) to hire an honest secular chaplain for 20 years to say mass daily for his soul and the souls of his mother and father, brothers, sisters, friends and all the faithful departed, and as late as 1535 another mercer, John Stone, arranged for an honest priest to sing, serve and pray for him and for all those for whom he was bound to pray for 12 years at an annual wage of £6 13s 4d. Most of the laity set up their temporary chantries for shorter periods: in 1526 Thomas Brodgate, merchant, instructed his executors to employ an honest priest for 7 years to sing for his soul and the souls of his father and mother, his three wives, Joan, Joan and Katherine, and for all Christian souls. In addition to establishing a chantry for 5 years in 1523, William Kellow *alias* Webbe, a mercer, paid for 6 priests together with the parish priest to sing requiem mass daily by note in the church in the month after his death. Some testators, such as William Coke and Thomas Marten, stated explicitly that as well as praying for their souls and the souls of members of their families they expected their priests to assist in the parish liturgy every day, keeping 'the choir there, reading and singing as the most honest doth'.[7]

Only the most affluent parishioners had the means to make post-mortem preparations on this scale, but many more, such as John Godfrey, could afford an annual charge of 13s 4d to set up an obit, a permanent commemoration performed on the anniversary of the donor's death. It cost even less, generally a single sum of between 6s 8d and 40s, to add a name to the bede roll, the roster of deceased parishioners for whose souls the priest bade the congregation to pray Sunday by Sunday. Alan Colett chose to pay in kind in 1505, bequeathing a mass book to St Thomas's for the privilege of being buried under an inscribed marble stone in Our Lady's aisle, and for himself, Agnes and Maud, his wives, his father and mother, Thomas and Agnes, and all their children to be prayed for everlastingly in the bede roll. The two parish fraternities of St John the Baptist and the Name of Jesus also remembered the souls of their dead by name and several members left them money for this purpose. Testators particularly valued the prayers of the poor at their burial, month's mind and twelve-month day. In 1535 John Stone calculated he needed £13 6s 8d to give a penny to each of the 3000 poor people he expected would attend at his funeral, and then as an

---

7. TNA, PROB 11/15 (Aleyne Colett), 11/15 (Richard Bartilmewe), 11/16 (William Godfrey), 11/16 (William Coke), 11/17 (Peter Burges als. Malter), 11/17 (Nicholas Martyn), 11/18 (William Clyfflod), 11/18 (John Godfraye), 11/19 (John Newman), 11/21 (William Kellowe als. Webbe), 11/21 (Thomas Coke), 11/22 (Thomas Brodgate), 11/23 (John Aben), 11/24 (Katherine Beche), 11/24 (William Lobbe), 11/25 (John Stone), 11/25 (Anne Stone), 11/27 (Thomas Marten), 11/27 (Joan Peerse).

afterthought he went on to instruct his executors that 'if that is not enough, to put more in to serve.' A year later his widow, Anne Stone, made an identical benefaction.[8]

Testators frequently revealed their predilection for new devotions and for the elaborate polyphony (or pricksong) being provided in the more prosperous parish churches as well as in cathedral and collegiate churches by the end of the Middle Ages. In 1526 Thomas Brodgate donated certain lands and tenements in Salisbury to trustees for the maintenance of the Lady mass in St Thomas's for ever more, while the beer brewer William Lobbe gave £10 to augment the funds of the same foundation in 1532. The immensely popular Jesus Fraternity, responsible for the celebration of the Jesus mass, attracted regular bequests. Having chosen to be buried behind the high altar, Joan Perse, the widow of a former mayor, gave £10 in 1536 towards the gilding and painting of the images of Our Lady and St Anne, for curtains and for mending the glass window, ceiling and walls about their altar, and a further £10 for vestments for the 'good choir man' hired to sing for her soul at their altar for 10 years. Then, looking to the particular needs of the parish, she made a contribution towards a new mass book, left a fine diaper cloth to the high altar, provided the huge sum of £45 13s 4d for vestments in the choir, paid for a salve to be sung in pricksong before the rood every Friday for a year, and finally laid on a breakfast for all the priests and clerks of the church 'and the twenty-four masters of the city' and their wives, her 'brothers and sisters', at the completion of her month's mind.[9]

The burning of relapsed lollards, chiefly from Berkshire, which occurred almost annually in Salisbury between 1502 and 1520 during the episcopate of the rigidly orthodox Edmund Audley, seems only to have reinforced the late medieval piety of the civic elite. On Audley's death in 1524 the crown offered the bishopric to the papal diplomat Lorenzo Campeggio in order to gain a sympathetic advocate at the Holy See. Since Campeggio never subsequently resided in England, and indeed visited the country only once after his consecration to investigate the legality of Henry VIII's marriage to Katherine of Aragon in 1528, this had the effect of leaving the diocese leaderless at the very time that revolutionary religious ideas were beginning to penetrate the country from the continent. The king's failure to persuade the pope to annul his marriage

8. TNA, PROB 11/15 (Aleyne Colett), 11/22 (Thomas Brodgate), 11/25 (John Stone), 11/25 (Anne Stone), 11/16 (William Godfrey), 11/18 (John Godfraye).

9. C. Burgess and A. Wathey, 'Mapping the soundscape: church music in English towns, 1450–1550', *Early Music History*, 19 (2000), pp. 1–46; L. Colton, 'Choral music in York', in P.S. Barnwell, C. Cross and A. Rycraft (eds), *Mass and parish in late medieval York: the use of York* (Reading, 2005), pp. 41–56; TNA, PROB 11/22 (Thomas Brodgate), 11/24 (William Lobbe); 11/27 (Joan Peerse).

eventually resulted in the break with Rome and parliament's declaration of the royal supremacy over the English church. Finding it politically unacceptable in the altered circumstances to have a papal representative in possession of an English see, the king deprived Campeggio of his bishopric by act of parliament in 1534 and replaced him early in the following year with Nicholas Shaxton, an advanced evangelical, who had first come into contact with Luther's teachings in the previous decade when a student at Gonville Hall in Cambridge and who had recently been appointed almoner to Anne Boleyn. Never a man to do things by halves, on his arrival in the diocese accompanied by his Scottish chaplain, the former Dominican prior John MacDowell, Shaxton immediately began promoting the new learning and the reading of the bible in English.[10]

The bishop's frontal attack upon traditional practices revealed the extent of the local antipathy to the new religious culture. Matters came to a head early in 1537 on the council's failure to punish townspeople who had torn down the king's licence permitting the eating of white meats in Lent. Alluding to the incident in a sermon on Passion Sunday, MacDowell publicly questioned the support of Salisbury's better sort for the royal supremacy. He went much further in a private letter to Shaxton, charging the citizens with ignoring the king's commissions and dispensations, retaining the bishop of Rome's name in their mass books and continuing to display papal pardons. The councillors responded by imprisoning MacDowell on the grounds that he had used himself uncharitably and slanderously against them.[11]

Each side now began abusing the other, the bishop and his chaplain branding the townspeople crypto-papists while the mayor, commonalty and their allies denounced Shaxton and MacDowell as dangerous sacramentaries, who, contrary to royal injunctions, had denied the miracle of the mass. Yet, while they undoubtedly sympathised with the old religion, the councillors realised that the crown's onslaught upon the ancient privileges of the church presented them with a unique opportunity to make a fresh attempt to procure their emancipation from episcopal control, and they went on to petition Thomas Cromwell, Henry VIII's chief minister, to 'qualify' the fifteenth-century charter which had confirmed the bishop's lordship over the city. In a parallel letter Shaxton retaliated by complaining that Thomas Chaffyn, a member of the twenty-four

10. J. Hughes, 'Audley, Edmund (c.1439–1524), bishop of Salisbury', *ODNB*; T.F. Mayer, 'Campeggi (Campeggio), Lorenzo (1471/2–1539), diplomat and bishop of Salisbury', *ODNB*; S. Wabuda, 'Shaxton, Nicholas (c.1485–1556), bishop of Salisbury', *ODNB*; J. Durkan, 'MacDowell (Maydland, Madwell, Maydwell), John (b. c.1500, d. in or after 1566), Dominican friar and evangelical reformer', *ODNB*; Street, 'Relations of the bishops and citizens', pp. 322–8.
11. *Letters and papers of Henry VIII* (hereafter *LP Hen VIII*), 12, pt. 1, nos 746, 755, 756, 824, 838.

and a leading parishioner of St Thomas's, had encroached upon his liberties by freeing persons arrested by his under-bailiff and against all legal warrant had been asserting that

the city is the king's city, the mayor is the king's mayor and the king's lieutenant', with other great words, whereas by plain and manifest words in the grant of King Edward IV the city is the bishop's city, the citizens the bishop's citizens and the mayor the bishop's mayor, with no authority in the city but that of the clerkship of the market, by composition, and now justice of the peace by the king's authority.

To add insult to injury, and taking their lead from their councillors, the populace had then gone about shouting 'the city is the king's etc., the bishop is an heretic, and we trust to see him hanged'.[12]

Further evidence of religious conservatism surfaced a year later, when the bishop's under-bailiff protested about 'the privy practices of certain priests in Sarum who in confession forbid white meats in Lent, the reading of the New Testament in English and the company of those of the new learning'. He over-reached himself, however, during Easter 1539 when he stopped the people from kissing an image which, unbeknown to him, contained a consecrated host, and had hurriedly to explain to Cromwell that, in obedience to the king's injunctions and proclamations, he had acted against the abuse of the practice and not against the blessed sacrament itself. At the height of the controversy and with the constitutional stalemate between the bishop and the city still unresolved, the tide nationally began to turn against the evangelicals. On the passing of the Act of Six Articles, which subverted so many of their beliefs, Shaxton took the unprecedented step of resigning his see in July 1539. His much less belligerent successor, John Capon, had the good sense to let sleeping dogs lie and the quarrel died down for at least a generation.[13]

Despite these accusations of foot-dragging, the parishioners of St Thomas's nevertheless outwardly conformed to all the Henrician religious legislation, not least in the matter of their church's dedication. Once he had embarked upon his contest with the papacy, the king developed a particular hatred for Thomas Becket, the defender *par excellence* of the independence of the medieval church, and in 1538 he ordered the destruction of all images of the saint and the erasure

---

12. *LP Hen VIII*, 12, pt. 2, nos 52, 1114.
13. *LP Hen VIII*, 13, pt. 2, nos 141, 606; 14 pt.1, nos 777, 778; 15, no. 498 (57); A.J. Louisa, 'Capon (Salcot), John (d. 1557), bishop of Salisbury', *ODNB*.

of his name in all service books. The parish complied by changing their patron saint to the biblical, and ideologically unobjectionable, St Thomas the Apostle. Yet, not withstanding the state's renunciation of papal authority, prohibition of the worship of the saints and undermining of the doctrine of purgatory, the churchwardens' accounts, which survive intermittently from 1545, give the impression that in the last years of Henry VIII's reign services were continuing in the church very much as they had done before the calling of the Reformation Parliament. The wives, the young people and the servants were still raising funds for the parish at Hocktide and on the Friday in Whitsun week as they had always done, and contributions were still coming in to maintain the font taper on Holy Thursday, Easter Eve and Easter Day. The church had kept its vestments and banners, and in the last year of the reign the wardens bought seven yards of cloth to make a new lenten veil and spent 4s on repairing a silver cross.[14]

Such a state of affairs did not long outlast the old king's death in January 1547, and the parish received a rude awakening within months of the accession of Edward VI when Thomas Hancock decided to propagate the gospel in the city. An Oxford graduate who, after the passing of the Act of Six Articles, had been suspended from his curacy at Amport near Andover for teaching that Christ had suffered once only for the sins of the whole world, Hancock had speedily regained his preaching licence in the altered religious climate of the new reign. Now, in a set-piece sermon in St Thomas's church before the chancellors of the bishops of Salisbury and Winchester and other important members of the clergy and laity, he took as his text the verse from Matthew XV. 13: 'Every plant which my heavenly Father planted not, shall be rooted up'. This provided him with the opportunity to inveigh 'against the superstitious ceremonies as holy bread, holy water, images, copes, vestments etc. and at the last against the idol of the altar, proving it to be an idol, and no God, by the first of St John's gospel, ["No man hath seen God at any time." John I. 18.]'. To drive his point home he then observed to the congregation 'but that the priest holdeth over his head you do see, you kneel before it, you honour it and make an idol of it, and you yourselves are most horrible idolaters'.[15]

Deeply offended by this attack upon the doctrine of transubstantiation, the doctors and other clergy walked out of the church and, after the service had ended, a leading parishioner, Thomas Chaffyn, in his capacity as the city's mayor, charged Hancock with infringing a recent royal proclamation against reviling the sacrament of the altar. To this Hancock retorted 'that it was no sacrament, but an

14. H.J.F. Swayne (ed.), *Churchwardens' accounts of S. Edmund and S. Thomas, Sarum, 1443–1702* (Salisbury, 1896), pp. 273–4.
15. J.G. Nichols (ed.), *Narratives of the days of the Reformation*, Camden Society, old ser., 77 (Westminster, 1859), pp. 72–3.

idol, as they do use it'. Most of those who had heard the sermon sided with the mayor and thought Hancock should be thrown in gaol. He avoided this fate, however, on 'six honest men' offering to stand as his sureties, and at his subsequent appearance at the assizes the lord chief justice bound him over for a second time. Having heard that the judge had set his bond at £100, Harry Dymock, a woollen draper and a member of the parish, allegedly claimed that a hundred would be bound for him in £100, while another bystander went even further, boasting a thousand would be bound for him in a £1000. In the event a hundred pounds sufficed, £10 put up by the parishioners and £90 by Hancock himself, who then rode off to London to seek his discharge from the duke of Somerset. On his return to obtain his release from his bond, the lord chief justice, who by this time had moved on to Hampshire, ordered him not to teach such doctrines in Southampton or he would cause the same dissension there as he had done in Salisbury.[16]

Although Hancock almost certainly inflated the number of his supporters, the conservatives in the parish found themselves powerless to obstruct Protestant innovations as the reign progressed. In response to an episcopal visitation in 1547 the churchwardens raised 36s from the sale of two hundredweight of memorial brasses with their unacceptable invocations of prayers for the dead, and pulled down the statues of St George and other saints, although two images still remained to be defaced in the following year. Having surrendered the greater part of their valuable liturgical vessels and vestments, which the state now deemed superfluous to the needs of a reformed church, in 1549 they acquired two copies of the first *Book of Common Prayer*, one for the priest and one for the choir, and several psalm books, carted off their redundant Catholic service books to the Cathedral Close, and no longer referred to the sacrament of the altar as the mass but the communion service. With the laity now expected to communicate in both kinds, in 1551 the wardens invested in a tin bottle 'to fetch wine in for the church'.[17]

Yet old practices died hard, and some parishioners proved very reluctant to abandon their belief in purgatory. In October 1550, two years after parliament had dissolved the chantries and religious fraternities, Alice Martin could still instruct her son to bestow £16 upon the poor in the expectation that they would 'pray for his father's soul and mine and for all Christian souls', and go on to make arrangements for a dirge and communion with all the customary ceremonies to be offered for the welfare of her soul at her funeral and month's mind, 'if it may be suffered'. In addition to bequeathing his soul in the traditional way to 'Almighty God, our blessed lady, St Mary the Virgin and to all the holy company

---

16. Nichols, *Narratives*, pp. 74–7.
17. Swayne (ed.), *Churchwardens' accounts*, pp. 275–9.

of heaven', as late as 1551 Christopher Chaffyn, a mercer and former mayor, similarly set aside 100s to be given to the city poor on the day of his burial and a further 100s at his month's mind. Attempts such as these to perpetuate Catholic practices under cover of the new service book brought home to Archbishop Cranmer and like-minded theologians the necessity for further liturgical revision and in the autumn of 1552 parliament authorised the replacement of the 1549 prayer book with the unequivocally Protestant second *Book of Common Prayer*.[18]

Within little more than half a year the religious revolution was halted in its tracks by the death of Edward VI on 6 July 1553. Mary Tudor had never attempted to conceal her personal beliefs throughout the reigns of her father and brother and, long before legislation could be introduced into parliament to restore the old religion and reconcile the nation to the papacy, in parts of the country priests and their congregations voluntarily brought back the mass. Certainly in Salisbury some prominent citizens could scarcely wait to rid themselves of the innovations of the previous two decades. In addition to making munificent donations to the city council, the hospitals, the highways and the poor at his burial, his month's mind and his twelve-months' day, William Webbe, a former mayor, in his will of January 1554 bequeathed to St Thomas's 'all such vestments as I lately bought by virtue of a commission sent down for the sale of the same by the late King Edward the Sixth', before going on to grant an annual payment of 20s in perpetuity towards the cost of celebrating the morrow mass and the Jesus mass, and a further 20s a year for 20 years to the clerks and singing men 'for the maintenance of God's service'. At his death 4 years later Hancock's great adversary, Thomas Chaffyn, not only provided an annual stipend of £8 for life for his priest, William Gillett, 'to sing and pray for my soul, my friends' souls and all Christian souls', but also set up a stock for the officers of the Jesus mass so that 'their successors shall be the better willing to be stewards of the same'.[19]

Most of the other substantial testators in the parish followed the example of Webbe and Chaffyn and commissioned masses for their souls at their month's mind and twelve months' day, made contributions to Our Lady's mass and the Jesus mass, and, like the widow Joan Dymocke, committed their souls in time-honoured fashion 'into the hands of Almighty God and to the suffrages of our blessed lady the Virgin and to all the holy company of heaven'. They also re-adopted St Thomas the Martyr as their patron saint. Having re-erected the altars, the rood and the images, the churchwardens recorded in 1557, when their accounts recommence, the purchase of incense, processions with banner bearers

18. TNA, PROB 11/34 (Alice Martyn), 11/34 (Christopher Chafyn).
19. TNA, PROB 11/36 (William Webbe the elder), 11/41 (Thomas Chaffyn the elder).

and cope bearers, collections for the font taper and the gathering of money by the wives, daughters and servants to supplement the church's coffers at Hocktide and the Friday in Whitsun week. To all outward appearances the old religious culture of the parish seemed to have triumphed over the new.[20]

Elizabeth's accession on 17 November 1558 and the passage through parliament of the Acts of Supremacy and Uniformity in the spring of the following year put an end to the Catholic revival once and for all and, on the queen's selection in the summer of 1559 of the former Marian exile and leading anti-Catholic controversialist John Jewel as the new bishop of Salisbury, the city had to come to terms as best it could with a proselytising Protestant regime for the second time in its history. Within weeks of his appointment and before his consecration Jewel participated in the royal visitation of the west country, which to his dismay uncovered the extent of the local clergy and laity's attachment to the old religion. To remove a key focus of devotion the commissioners immediately ordered all images of saints to be taken out of churches and burnt. In compliance with their instructions the churchwardens of St Thomas's dismantled their altars, rood and rood beam and went on to buy an English bible, three psalters and four copies of the *Book of Common Prayer*.[21]

Having remained in London for almost a year to conclude the visitation and prepare his philosophical defence of the national church, Jewel did not take up residence in Salisbury until May 1560, but from then until his death in September 1571 he lived in the city for the greater part of every year and devoted himself to creating a model Protestant diocese. In 1560 St Thomas's churchwardens duly acquired the *Paraphrases* of Erasmus, set up Moses's tables at the high altar and paid a painter and his man 'for writing of scripture in the church'. The next year they erected the queen's arms over the chancel arch, the outward and visible sign of the royal supremacy, and around this time silently changed the church's dedication back to St Thomas the Apostle. Yet, despite Jewel's pastoral oversight and constant preaching, some reminders of the Catholic past lingered on in the parish for more than a decade. The churchwardens converted four albs into surplices only in 1572, and a year later sold off the small bells, cruets and a holy water pot they had not needed since the beginning of the reign. On the other hand, in 1578 they furnished the pulpit with a sounding board, which may

---

20. Wiltshire and Swindon History Centre (hereafter WSHC), Chippenham, D4/3/1 fos. 38v–39r. (Sybil Payne), D4/3/1 fo. 58r. (John Saunders); TNA, PROB 11/37 (Joan Dymocke), 11/39 (Thomas Mody), 11/39 (John Batt), 11/40 (Thomas Woodlocke), 11/41 (John Corriatt), 11/42A (Thomas Chaffyn the younger), 11/42A (Thomas Chaffyn the elder); Swayne (ed.), *Churchwardens' accounts*, p. 279.

21. J. Craig, 'Jewel, John (1522–71), bishop of Salisbury', *ODNB*; H. Robinson (ed.), *The Zurich letters*, Parker Society, 7 (Cambridge, 1842), p. 39; Swayne (ed.), *Churchwardens' accounts*, p. 280.

perhaps indicate a growing appetite for sermons, and began to exhibit an increasing antipathy towards surviving memorials of the old religion, in particular their medieval glass, in 1583 'putting out the picture of [God] the Father in the east window at Mr Subdean's commandment'.[22]

If the preambles of wills accurately reflect the beliefs of testators, some parishioners may have actively sympathised with these purges. Even in the Marian period one merchant, John Whelpeley, had spurned the traditional ceremonies and consigned his soul 'unto Almighty God who hath redeemed me with his most precious blood, by whose merits of death and passion mine assured hope and trust is to be saved'. No testator sought the intercession of the Virgin Mary after the first few weeks of the new reign and as early as April 1562 Dorothy Chaffyn, widow and a member of the previously religiously conservative family, left her soul 'to Almighty God, our heavenly father, and to his only son, our saviour, Jesus Christ'. In 1570 George Wylton, a former mayor, bequeathed £5 'to the maintenance of God's service' in St Thomas's church and a further £5 to Thomas Wylton 'minister'. Less than a year after this John Webbe, a councillor and the son of William Webbe who had preserved the church's vestments, bestowed his soul 'unto Almighty God, my maker and creator, and to his only son, Jesus Christ, my saviour and redeemer, by the merits of whose most bitter death and passion I faithfully trust and steadfastly believe to be saved and to be partaker of his most blessed and glorious kingdom of heaven'. In 1572 Anthony Weekes, beer brewer and another former mayor, similarly committed his soul 'into the hands of Almighty God, trusting and firmly hoping and constantly believing to be saved by the merits, death and passion of our saviour Jesus Christ', while in 1580 John West not only requested a sermon at his funeral but also asked for his body to be laid in St Thomas's churchyard 'there to tarry [until the] general resurrection at which time I hope to rise with an incorrupt body and through the merits of Jesus Christ my saviour to enjoy the kingdom of heaven purchased with his most precious blood for his elect'.[23]

The fact that the bishop still possessed the powers of a secular overlord throughout the sixteenth century undoubtedly complicated the early reception of the Reformation in the city. So long as the mayor had annually to swear his oath of office before an episcopal official and the bishop retained his control over the city's court and continued to levy secular taxes, the citizens automatically looked

---

22. Street, 'Relations of the bishops and citizens', p. 329; Swayne (ed.), *Churchwardens' accounts*, pp. 281, 282, 285–6, 286–7, 287–8, 290–1, 293–4.
23. TNA, PROB 11/37 (John Whelpeley), WSHC, P1/2 Reg/119 (Dorothy Chaffin), TNA, PROB 11/52 (George Wylton), 11/53 (John Webbe), 11/55 (Anthony Weekes), 11/55 (John Weste).

upon his interventions as potential invasions of their liberties. The clash of religious cultures may also have been at least partly a generational one, with the Catholic restoration of the Marian period endorsed most enthusiastically by those who had experienced the medieval liturgy and their children more susceptible to Protestant innovations. Only through the frequent preaching of Protestants of the calibre of Thomas Hancock and John Jewel could inroads be made over time into the traditional beliefs of the civic elite. Perhaps as much as anything else it was the permanence of the Elizabethan church settlement which ensured the victory of the Calvinist faction in St Thomas's parish in Salisbury.

11. The Court of High Commission and religious change in Elizabethan Yorkshire

Emma Watson

The accession of Elizabeth I in 1558 ended the brief Marian resurgence of Catholicism and saw the last of the succession of religious changes imposed upon England by the Tudors. The newly established Church retained many traditional structures and rituals alongside a Protestant theology, but despite the attempt to create a *via media* many people were not inclined to compromise, and it is likely that many local magistrates found that social harmony was more easily achieved by ignoring religious differences than by enforcing uniformity. Nevertheless, the Elizabethan government desired uniformity, and the injunctions accompanying the 1559 settlement of religion required the unswerving loyalty of the English people to the newly created church, to be expressed by regular attendance and thrice-annual receipt of the Holy Communion at their parish church. In Yorkshire, religious change was accompanied by a loss of influence and high office for conservative magnates, alongside increased governmental control through the Council of the North and the consistory, chancery and visitation courts that had long been responsible for meting out ecclesiastical justice.[1] Although occasionally presided over by the archbishop, cases brought before these courts were most often heard by his deputies, the vicar general, chancellor and registrar, and many more were heard instead before the archdeacon's courts.[2] The courts dealt with cases of matrimony, tithe, probate, immorality and defamation as well as religion, and the variety of their jurisdiction, coupled with

---

1. J.T. Cliffe, *The Yorkshire gentry from the Reformation to the Civil War* (London, 1969), p. 169.

2. R. Houlbrooke, *Church courts and people during the English Reformation 1520–1570* (Oxford, 1979), pp. 23–7; R.A. Marchant, *The puritans and the church courts in the diocese of York, 1560–1642* (London, 1960), pp. 8–10.

the extensive records of the York diocesan courts, means that they provide a valuable insight into the religious and social history of the north and the attempts of the government to impose its rule upon the region.

The acute shortage of Protestant manpower in 1559 meant that the government was unable to replace many conservative officials, however, and conservative magnates, gentry and parish officers remained dominant virtually everywhere.[3] Not all the officers of the northern church courts supported the changes they were required to implement and the cooperation they required from sheriffs, JPs, clergy and churchwardens in implementing reform and detecting and punishing offenders was received reluctantly, if at all.[4] In the face of these difficulties the Elizabethan government founded the Ecclesiastical Court of High Commission for the Northern Province in 1561 in order to aid in the implementation of the 1559 settlement of religion. Unlike the consistory, chancery and visitation courts this was not a court Christian, but a secular court dealing primarily with church discipline.[5] Nevertheless, the procedures of the High Commission, which was second only to the Council of the North in terms of its power and the extent of its jurisdiction, were modelled upon those of the existing church courts. A significant difference, however, was its ability to administer fines, bonds and prison sentences as punishments, which increased the impact of the court as spiritual sanctions lost their force in the wake of repeated reversals of religion and widespread hostility towards the church.[6]

It is not my purpose here to provide a study of the mechanics of how the Court of High Commission worked, but rather to examine its role in the enforcement of religious change in Elizabethan Yorkshire. The religious conservatism of the north and the widespread belief that political and religious loyalties were inseparable were causes of concern for the Crown, and the establishment of the High Commission can be taken as an indication of this concern in terms of both the long-standing problem of governing the north and the new challenge of enforcing a reformed religion upon a largely unwilling populace. Initially

---

3. S. Taylor, 'The crown and the north of England, 1559–70: a study of the Rebellion of the Northern Earls, 1569–70, and its causes' (PhD thesis, Manchester, 1981), pp. 17, 19, 39–40; W.R. Trimble, *The Catholic laity in Elizabethan England, 1558–1603* (Cambridge, Massachusetts, 1964), p. 17; P. Tyler, 'The significance of the Ecclesiastical Commission at York', *Northern History*, 2 (1967), pp. 36–7.

4. Houlbrooke, *Church courts and people*, pp. 7, 15, 38; C. Haigh, *Reformation and resistance in Tudor Lancashire* (Cambridge, 1975), pp. 231–2.

5. R.A. Marchant, *The church under the law: justice, administration and discipline in the diocese of York, 1560–1640* (Cambridge, 1969), p. 4.

6. M. Ingram, *Church courts, sex and marriage in England, 1570–1640* (Cambridge, 1990), p. 4; Houlbrooke, *Church courts and people*, p. 1.

intended to strengthen the power of Archbishop Thomas Young in his efforts to enforce religious change, the key period of the High Commission's work in fact came during the archiepiscopate of Young's successor, Edmund Grindal (1570–5).[7] Moreover, in the absence of any surviving records from the Council of the North, those of the High Commission provide a valuable insight into the nature and effect of royal rule in the Northern Province. Royal requirements had to be moulded to meet local circumstances, and nowhere is this more in evidence than in the enforcement of religious change. Catholicism remained widespread in the north long after the Elizabethan settlement of religion, and many of the most important families in Yorkshire were either Catholic themselves or retained close ties with Catholics.[8] As a result, the High Commission was often forced to take the line of least resistance, and refrained from pursuing many of the more important Catholic families unless absolutely necessary. Prior to the northern rebellion of 1569 few steps were taken to investigate the religious affiliations of northern gentry families, and those who were tried by the High Commission were treated comparatively leniently. The paucity of loyal Protestant gentry families meant that, for some years after Elizabeth's accession, Catholic gentlemen had to be relied upon to keep the peace in many parts of the county.[9] The strict enforcement of the religious laws against such gentlemen would have led ultimately to unrest with which the government could ill afford to deal, and as a result many known Catholic gentry families simply do not appear in the early records of the High Commission.

The work of historians such as Houlbrooke, Marchant and Ingram has demonstrated many of the difficulties faced by the church courts as they attempted to impose religious, and indeed moral, discipline.[10] Of these, perhaps the most significant was the balancing act which courts were forced to perform between the desires of the government and the realities of the local situation. The will and intention of the government often bore little relation to what local representatives could, or indeed would, do.[11] In Yorkshire, the very personnel of the Commission could restrict the extent to which they were prepared to act against religious conservatism, particularly once it became clear that the Commission's establishment provided a route through which Catholic gentry could be prosecuted for their nonconformity. The social inferiority of many of

---

7. Tyler, 'The significance of the Ecclesiastical Commission', p. 27.

8. *Ibid.*, pp. 36–8.

9. *Ibid.*, pp. 37–8.

10. Houlbrooke, *Church courts and people*; Marchant, *Puritans and the church courts*; Ingram, *Church courts.*

11. Tyler, 'The significance of the Ecclesiastical Commission', p. 36.

those responsible for taking cases to the lower church courts often shielded nonconformist gentry and nobility from prosecution, and the movement of the upper classes between their estates could be used to create confusion over which locality was responsible for ensuring their conformity. The superior status of the Ecclesiastical High Commission, together with its jurisdiction over the entire Northern Province, successfully circumvented these difficulties and ensured that the gentry and nobility were no longer immune from prosecution. Equally significant was the Commission's role in dealing with those persistent troublemakers who had proved to be impervious to the authority of the lesser church courts.[12] Nevertheless, despite their best efforts, the commissioners did not always succeed in their efforts to implement the settlement of religion, and the following examples will demonstrate some of the difficulties they faced.

Sir Thomas and Lady Edith Metham of North Cave in Howdenshire in the East Riding first appeared before the High Commission in 1564. Lady Edith was charged with failing to receive Holy Communion or to be purified after childbirth; Sir Thomas with employing a Catholic tutor, Philip Sherewood, for his children.[13] The Methams' responses to the initial inquiries against them were deemed unsatisfactory, but their vague and evasive answers were not unusual; many Catholics in their position would subsequently do the same in an attempt to avoid conviction. The failure of the Methams to attend court to answer to the charges against them, or to carry out the penances imposed upon them in their absence, resulted in Sir Thomas forfeiting his bond of £200, while Lady Edith was declared excommunicate. Both subsequently submitted and were absolved, but neither conformed for long and despite repeated examinations and periods of imprisonment and house arrest throughout the 1560s the Methams remained steadfast in their beliefs. Consequently, despite trying everything within their power, in 1570 the High Commission was forced to admit defeat and appealed (albeit unsuccessfully) to the Privy Council to deal with the case. The Methams never conformed, and spent the rest of their lives either imprisoned or under house arrest or heavy bond. Their treatment was far from harsh by the standards of the time, however, and it is likely to have been their influence that caused Howdenshire to become a stronghold of recusancy in the later sixteenth century, despite the general conformity of the East Riding. Howden's position as a jurisdictional peculiar may also have been significant, for other peculiars in the diocese of York,

12. Ingram, *Church courts*, pp. 30–1.

13. Borthwick Institute for Archives (hereafter BI), University of York, HC.CP.1564/1; HC.AB3 fos 63r–v, 164r–v; HC.AB5 fos 232v–233r; Two of Metham's sons were later to continue their education at Louvain, whilst their tutor later became one of the first professors of the new English college at Douai. P. Tyler, *The Ecclesiastical Commission and Catholicism in the North, 1562–1577* (York, 1960), pp. 43, 97.

such as Allertonshire and Ripon, also emerged as strongholds of Catholic survival. Certainly, the Methams were not the only people from Howdenshire to appear before the High Commission: in 1590, for example, Thomas Houldale of Hemingbrough was accused of failing to attend his parish church, of hearing Mass, and of receiving the 'sacrament of Christ's body in popish sort'.[14]

Nevertheless, cases such as these remained uncommon and, despite occasional crackdowns, there was no uniform, organised attempt to enforce religious conformity. Catholics were largely left alone in the hope that the lack of access to priests and services would lead to gradual conformity, and it was only after the rebellion of 1569 that the government came to realise how deeply traditional beliefs remained embedded in the religious culture of the north. Therefore, the High Commission cases of the 1560s can be used to track the changing focus of central authorities in the fight against religious conservatism via their reflection of those issues considered most important at the time. Wealthy and influential, the Metham family were viewed as pillars of their faith within their community and so, in its attempt to curb conservative practice, the High Commission invested considerable time and effort in the case against them, and its ultimate failure must have given some hope to other East Riding Catholics.

Similarly important to the continued survival of Catholicism was the presence of Catholic books in the diocese. Just as they had become crucial tools for Protestant education and propaganda, books and pamphlets were vital to the survival of traditional Catholic teachings and to the dissemination of the reformed doctrines coming out of the Council of Trent. The appearance before the High Commission of William Hussey and Thomas More of Barnburgh revealed that both possessed Catholic books and it may have been this that prompted the 1567 investigation into the affairs of the York stationers.[15] The evidence emerging from these cases suggests that, far from being simply a remnant of the traditional past, Catholicism in Yorkshire was thriving and was well informed about the post-Tridentine reforms taking place in continental Europe. Hussey confessed that he had 'a book called Harding's book, another called Piggin's, another called Cocken's, and another called Acchen's, printed beyond the seas'.[16] The extant records do not reveal the titles of these books, but Hussey's possession of them was considered sufficiently serious that he was imprisoned in York Castle in August 1565 and 'learned men' were appointed to 'confer with him touching his

---

14. BI, HC.CP.1590/2.

15. Hussey – BI, HC.AB2, fos 26v, 31v, 33v, 40r, 41r–v, 45r; Stationers – BI, HC.CP.1567/2; Tyler, *Ecclesiastical Commission*, pp. 26–7, 33. More was a grandson of the former chancellor executed by Henry VIII.

16. BI, HC.AB.2, fo. 26v.

conscience' in order to try to secure his conformity.[17] Certainly the possession of a book by Thomas Harding suggests that Hussey was well informed of the key religious controversies and debates of his day: Harding's texts, particularly his responses to the writings and sermons of John Jewel, bishop of Salisbury and an ardent reformer, were some of the most important polemical works of the 1560s and were considered a significant threat to English religious uniformity.[18]

Whether or not the investigation against them was launched as a result of William Hussey's possession of forbidden books, in 1567 the York booksellers John Schofield, Thomas Richardson, John Goldthwaite and Thomas Wrayth were interrogated about the numbers of Latin primers and missals, along with works by Harding, Allen and others, that they had received into their shops, where they had obtained them, how many they had sold and to whom. Wrayth admitted he had received one old missal from Leeds, which he still had, over a hundred primers in English and several grammars and accidences from London. Richardson claimed that he had received only one unbound porteous (a portable breviary, or Mass book), which remained in his shop, while Schofield denied receiving any forbidden books. Goldthwaite, however, admitted that he had received 17 Latin primers and 2 Latin ABCs from a London stationer named Gerard Dawes, who had also offered him some books by Thomas Dorman, which he declined to take.[19] Goldthwaite claimed he had not yet sold any of these books and (like Wrayth) acknowledged he had also received a large number of English primers, accidences and grammars from London. An inventory of their shops indicates that the stationers were largely truthful in their answers; however, a York Mass book that had not been mentioned was discovered in Wrayth's shop. The stationers appear to have escaped with little more than a warning and the forfeiture of their books, although undoubtedly the penalties would have been much more severe had they been found to possess any writings by the Catholic authors named in their examinations.[20] Nevertheless, that they were still stocking Latin texts suggests that there must have been a market for them, and it is worth noting that both Wrayth and Goldthwaite were later prosecuted as recusants.[21] Furthermore, that these booksellers were interrogated about texts such as those of Harding and Allen suggests that York was suspected to

17. BI, HC.AB.2, fos 40r, 41r.

18. L.E.C. Wooding, 'Harding, Thomas (1516–1572), theologian and religious controversialist', *ODNB*.

19. For more on Dorman see F.A. James III, 'Dorman, Thomas (c.1534–c.1577), religious controversialist', *ODNB*. A protégée of Harding's and based at Louvain, Dorman was also involved in the Catholic response to Jewel.

20. R. Davies, *A memoir of the York Press* (Westminster, 1868), p. 33.

21. H. Aveling, *Catholic recusancy in the city of York, 1558–1791*, Catholic Record Society Publications Monograph Series, 2 (London, 1970), p. 32.

be part of a network of European circulation of Counter-Reformation literature and that the authorities saw these connections as a greater threat than continued adherence to traditional ceremony and ritual. Owning and reading such recent and controversial literature would suggest a greater level of engagement with the Catholic faith, and thus with the political issues surrounding religious dissidence, than would a simple devotion to tradition and consequently was perceived by the government as a threat which must be eliminated.

It was not just privately owned Catholic books that came to the attention of the High Commission. Although the continued presence of images, books and vestments of the old religion within parish churches led to the frequent appearance of parishioners and churchwardens before the church courts, particularly during the course of the regular archdeacon's and archbishop's visitations, comparatively few such cases appeared before the Court of High Commission, suggesting that those which did were treated particularly seriously and that the parties involved had persistently ignored previous injunctions from the lesser courts to comply. Certainly it appears that officials recognised the threat to religious uniformity from parishes that did not replace their traditional service books with those of the Elizabethan church, and books and images were increasingly ordered to be publicly burnt to prevent their continued use, even in a mutilated condition. In 1565 William Thompson and Edward Weeks, both of Boroughbridge, were called to answer charges of 'contempt for keeping books, images and other monuments of superstitious religion'.[22] Thompson admitted the charges, but Weeks claimed the items found in his possession had been in a chest in his house when he came to live there, and that he had not known the contents of that chest.[23] Both were imprisoned in York Castle and subsequently ordered to burn their books and make public declarations of their errors and offences in both York and Boroughbridge, suggesting that regional officials were concerned about levels of conservatism in the deanery and about the potential threat that this might pose.[24] Similarly un-defaced idols, images and Latin books found in Aysgarth parish in Richmondshire in 1567 were ordered to be publicly burnt, and the ten parishioners involved in their concealment were to undertake humiliating public penances in which they made a public declaration of their offence in church during service time while wearing sackcloth.[25] A year earlier a special commission from the bishop of Chester

22. BI, HC.AB.2, fos 22r, 24v.

23. *Ibid.*, fos 27r, 28r.

24. *Ibid.*, fos 30r–v, 35r.

25. BI, HC.AB 3, fos 104r–105v; BI, HC.CP 1567/1. See J.S. Purvis, *Tudor parish documents in the diocese of York* (Cambridge, 1948), pp. 144–6 and 225–7, for transcriptions of documents relating to this case.

had uncovered items including rood images, a pyx, a corporas (an embroidered cloth used during Mass) and a Latin hymnal at Aysgarth, all of which the churchwardens later certified had been destroyed. Clearly they had instead been hidden within the church, and local officials evidently hoped that making an example of the offenders when the items were rediscovered would encourage conformity by creating a pattern that would discourage people from continuing to follow traditional religious beliefs and practices.[26] Although unclear, it is possible that one of the ten men who did penance in Aysgarth, John Deane, had some involvement in the rediscovery of the hidden items. Subsequently nominated to serve as parish clerk, Deane faced considerable opposition from parishioners and his position had to be enforced by the courts.[27] The courts never managed to remove completely all traces of Catholicism from Aysgarth, however, for the church still retains a rood screen and other pieces of carved wood salvaged from Jervaulx abbey at the time of its suppression in 1537.

Despite the best efforts of the High Commission, in the 1560s Catholicism was sufficiently widespread and flourishing to have appeared a credible alternative to the Elizabethan settlement for many northerners, and the belief that Catholicism would one day be restored does not appear to have been uncommon in the decade before 1569.[28] However, the outbreak of rebellion later that year proved to be a turning point.[29] Led by the earls of Northumberland and Westmoreland, the largely politically motivated Rebellion of the Northern Earls used religion as a rallying cry in a region which had seen much destruction of its religious culture but no positive Reformation. Perhaps unsurprisingly, the religious propaganda associated with the rebellion led to Yorkshire providing some of the largest contingents of rebels, and High Commission court records for the early 1570s are full of references to parishes whose Protestant service books were destroyed or where Mass was held during the rebellion.[30] There are six known cases of the celebration of Mass in

26. H. Aveling, *Northern Catholics: the Catholic recusants of the North Riding of Yorkshire 1558–1790* (London, 1966), p. 21.

27. Tyler, *Ecclesiastical Commission*, p. 20.

28. D. Marcombe, 'A rude and heady people: the local community and the Rebellion of the Northern Earls', in D. Marcombe (ed.), *The last principality: politics, religion and society in the Bishopric of Durham, 1494–1660* (Nottingham, 1987), pp. 135–6. Haigh, *Reformation and resistance*, pp. 242–4, has argued similarly for Lancashire.

29. For a comprehensive account of the rebellion see K. Kesselring, *The Northern Rebellion of 1569: faith, politics and protest in Elizabethan England* (New York, 2007).

30. For more on the numbers of rebels from Yorkshire, see, for example, G. Thornton, 'The Rising in the North 1569', *Northern Catholic History*, 17 (1983), pp. 4–6; H.B. McCall, 'The rising in the North: a new light upon one aspect of it', *Yorkshire Archaeological Journal*, 18 (1905), pp. 74–87; and the letters of George Bowes, printed in C. Sharp, *Memorials of the rebellion of 1569* (London, 1840).

Yorkshire.[31] For example, Robert Hewar was charged with hearing Mass during the rebellion at Kirkby Fleetham, although he claimed that he had simply come upon the service by chance, while Christopher Simson, the vicar there, admitted that he had said Mass but claimed he was forced to do so. In Hipswell, a chapelry of Catterick parish, James Bower confessed that he had provided the Latin service book that the curate, William Knight, had used to say Mass during the rebellion and in Ripon around 30 parishioners appeared before the High Commission in 1570 for their involvement in Catholic worship. Moreover, the destruction of Protestant service books was widespread, and in early 1570 a quarter of all Richmondshire parishes were ordered by the High Commission to replace Protestant service books damaged or destroyed during the rebellion with new ones.[32] Some men, such as Thomas Beckwith of Well, were personally charged with replacing these books, and many more were fined for their offences during the rebellion. Others, such as Christopher Hutcheson, clerk, and Robert Ward, both of Richmond, and Christopher Beckwith, clerk, of Burneston, were threatened with imprisonment for their roles in the rebellion, while a number of wealthier men, such as John Gower, Thomas Wray and Robert Heighington, escaped abroad.[33] Gower was later ordained at Douai, although it is unlikely that he ever returned to England, and Wray's arrest alongside one Robert Smelt in 1574 after his return to England led to the discovery of several Catholic books in their possession which had previously belonged to one John Moore, a chantry priest.[34]

Although the northern rebellion collapsed before any concerted efforts were made to crush it, and it never posed any real threat to the Crown, contemporaries took it very seriously.[35] Its failure helped to harden much conservatism into Catholic resistance and began the process of consolidation of the old faith, which was continued by the seminary priests from the 1570s.[36] It also arguably marked the beginning of the radicalisation of positions on either side of the confessional divide. Pamphleteers such as Thomas Norton and John Phillips began to use the

---

31. BI, HC.AB 5, fos 114r, 124v, 144r, 159v, 169v.

32. Protestant books were destroyed in at least 65 Yorkshire parish churches: see BI, HC.AB 5 *passim*, especially fos 33v–52r and 63v–67v.

33. BI, HC.AB 5, fos 62r, 73r, 95v–98v, 233v, 236v, 237r; R. Fieldhouse and B. Jennings, *A History of Richmond and Swaledale* (London, 1978) p. 93. Aveling, *Northern catholics*, p. 56, suggested that Gower may have secretly visited Richmond in 1572, but this is unsubstantiated.

34. Fieldhouse and Jennings, *Richmond and Swaledale*, p. 96.

35. K. Kesselring, '"A cold pye for the papistes": constructing and containing the northern rising of 1569', *Journal of British Studies*, 43 (2004), p. 431.

36. M.B. Rowlands (ed.), *English Catholics of parish and town, 1558–1778*, Catholic Record Society Publications Monograph Series, 5 (London, 1999), p. 11.

terms 'papist' and 'traitor' synonymously, deploying the anti-Catholic vocabulary that shaped the English religious culture of subsequent decades. For Protestant polemicists the rebellion offered proof that papistry and treason were one and the same, and the broad popular attachment to traditional religion demonstrated by the rebels, coupled with the participation of ordinary men and women, was held to represent something extremely sinister.[37] The Crown sought to play down the religious element of the rebellion, but in doing so made its significance clear, and, while the actions of the rebels do not demonstrate the committed Romanism attributed to them by Protestant writers, widespread and deep-seated dissatisfaction with Elizabethan religious reforms clearly existed, which continued and crystallised into more obvious forms as the reign progressed.

The results of the 1569 rebellion were diametrically opposed to those hoped for by the rebels. While there was no obvious loss of Catholic power and seigniorial authority in Yorkshire, such as that caused in Norfolk by the execution of the duke of Norfolk, the rebellion exposed the lack of governmental policy for the north and the extent to which the new regime had failed to take root. As a result the government quickly took steps to strengthen Crown control there and advance Protestantism more aggressively by promoting to influential positions both men of known Protestant credentials and 'new men' who owed their wealth and status directly to the monarch.[38] The failure of the rebellion also provided an opportunity for the Crown and archbishop to gain greater control over the northern clergy. A few livings were immediately vacated by the flight or removal of priests, while the forfeiture of lands by laymen who had supported the earls meant that control of a number of advowsons also passed into Crown hands.[39] A more determined drive against Catholics was begun and the translation of Edmund Grindal to the see of York in 1570, closely followed by the promotion of Henry Hastings, earl of Huntingdon, to president of the Council of the North, clearly signalled the government's intention to firmly establish the Elizabethan regime in the north. Nevertheless, despite stricter tests being applied to surviving Marian clergy, and a fresh wave of deprivations, there were still insufficient Protestant clergy to replace all those who did not fully subscribe to the 1559 settlement and many conservative clergy remained within the

---

37. For more on the literary response to the rebellion see Kesselring, '"A cold pye"', pp. 436–41; J.K. Lowers, *Mirrors for rebels: a study of polemical literature relating to the Northern Rebellion, 1569* (Berkeley, CA, 1953); D. Busse, 'Anti-Catholic polemical writing on the "Rising in the North" (1569) and the Catholic reaction', *Recusant History*, 27 (2004), pp. 11–30.

38. K. Kesselring, 'Mercy and liberality: the aftermath of the 1569 Northern Rebellion', *History*, 90 (2005), pp. 224, 226–7.

39. *Ibid.*, p. 226.

established church. Equally, many of those who were deprived remained active, and exiles often maintained their contacts in northern England.[40] The ability of these men to preserve traditional practices and prevent the spread of Protestantism was crucial in determining the nature of northern conservatism.

It was in the aftermath of the northern rebellion, and most particularly after the arrival of Edmund Grindal, that the Court of High Commission really came into its own and the persecution of conservatives and Catholics in Yorkshire noticeably stepped up a gear. On his arrival in Yorkshire Grindal declared the diocese to be like 'another church', so untouched was it by the Reformation, and within three weeks he had declared the three evils of the inhabitants to be 'great ignorance, much dullness to conceive better instructions, and great stiffness to retain their wonted errors'.[41] Grindal's primary visitation as archbishop marked the initial implementation of the Reformation in many areas of Yorkshire and the first real attempt to rebuild religion after a period of destruction. However, rather than ensuring the establishment of the reformed faith by hastening the disappearance of Catholicism, the increasingly vigorous efforts to enforce conformity hardened the will of many Catholics to resist, and in many ways marked the beginning of a crystallisation of Catholic feelings into recusancy. The northern rebellion, and the government's reaction to it, marks the point at which religious divisions within England began to be more sharply defined: from 1570 it starts to become possible to think in terms of Catholics and Protestants, rather than conservatives and evangelists or traditionalists and reformers. There are difficulties with all confessional labels, not least because they are generally imposed by modern historians, but in Yorkshire at least the arrival of Grindal and Huntingdon appears to mark the beginning of much clearer confessional divisions.

Although little force had been used to impose religious uniformity on the north before 1569, after 1570 the hunt for surviving relics of popery intensified and the persecution of nonconformists through the courts increased.[42] The High Commission records reflect the idea of the 1569 rebellion as a turning point for Catholics and a marker after which many church papists either conformed or became recusants. From the 1570s cases begin to appear in which the defendants are accused of harbouring Catholic seminary priests or of reconciliation to the Catholic faith. John Acrigge, a former chantry priest and later a curate in Richmond, initially conformed to the Elizabethan church but fled abroad after the

---

40. Taylor, 'The crown and the north of England', pp. 46–9.

41. P. Collinson, *Archbishop Grindal 1519–1583* (London, 1979), p. 195; W.H. Frere (ed.), *Visitation articles and injunctions of the period of the Reformation,* 3 vols (London, 1910), vol. 3.

42. Tyler, *Ecclesiastical Commission,* p. 63.

rebellion, later returning as a missionary priest. He was captured and imprisoned, dying in Hull Blockhouse in 1585, but his reconciliation to Catholicism after a short period of conformity suggests that the Catholic rhetoric of the rebellion had a considerable impact upon him.[43] In 1590 William Langdale of South Otterington presented his neighbour, Richard Willy, before the High Commission, accusing him of favouring the Romish religion and others who supported it, of absenting himself from church on Sundays and holy days and of harbouring 'divers and sundry seminaries, popish priests and other disobedient in matters of religion … namely one Kirkman a seminary priest and one Nicholas Vayses alias Richardson, also a seminary priest'.[44] There is no record of seminary priests of these names in the extant lists, nor of any other priests harboured in South Otterington parish, but, as the offence of harbouring priests was punishable by death at this point, it would have been a serious accusation to make with no evidence.[45]

In perhaps the most significant of these cases Thomas Bell, a curate at Thirsk, confessed before the High Commission in 1570 that 'being moved in conscience and persuaded in opinion and belief that the Religion now established in this Realm is not the Catholic Religion and true doctrine … [he] intended to leave his orders and forsake the ministry'. Together with George Malton, a curate at Topcliffe, and one Parkinson of Thirsk, layman, Bell fled south. The group was questioned in London after failing to secure passage abroad, but passed themselves off as Oxford scholars before returning to Topcliffe, where they were arrested. Malton conformed after his arrest and appearance before the High Commission, but Bell admitted his reconciliation to Catholicism, which came as a result of reading Catholic literature loaned from Parkinson, and affirmed his belief that the pope was the head of the church.[46] He was imprisoned in York Castle but escaped in 1576 and went to Douai before taking Catholic orders at the English College in Rome. He returned to England as part of the Catholic mission in 1582, and for the next ten years was one of the most influential seminarists in Yorkshire and Lancashire, playing a key role in setting up a network of safe houses across the north and notoriously celebrating High Mass in York Castle in July 1582. Subsequent disputes between Bell and other Catholic clergy, particularly the Jesuits, over the issue of occasional conformity caused Bell to

---

43. Fieldhouse and Jennings, *Richmond and Swaledale*, pp. 95–6.

44. BI, HC.CP.1590/3.

45. G. Anstruther, *The seminary priests vol. I, Elizabethan 1558–1603* (Durham, 1969); D.A. Bellenger, *English and Welsh priests 1558–1800* (Bath, 1984); R. Challoner, *Memoirs of missionary priests*, 2nd edn, revised and edited by J.H. Pollen (London, 1969).

46. BI, HC.CP.1570/5; BI, HC.AB. 1572–4, 1574–6; Aveling, *Northern Catholics*, pp. 28–9.

surrender himself to the Protestant authorities in 1592 and reveal everything he knew about the Catholic mission in the north. Subsequently he became a zealous evangelical preacher in the region and somewhat ironically delivered sermons to Catholic prisoners in York Castle.[47]

These examples provide merely a snapshot of cases dealt with by the High Commission, yet they serve to demonstrate the changing nature of the issues deemed important at particular times as well as some of the ways in which the High Commission was able to tackle religious nonconformity. Regardless of its success or otherwise, it is clear that the role of this court was significant and that it was an important link between the will of the government and the willingness of the populace to accept that will. The cases dealt with by the Commission in the 1560s and 1570s clearly reflect the changing priorities of the Elizabethan government towards the north before and after the northern rebellion and illustrate the extent to which the government was actively trying to enforce religious conformity and uniformity, as well as hinting at the links between Yorkshire Catholics and the European Counter-Reformation. Religion in this period remained a fluid, unstable entity and levels of commitment, whatever the confessional preference, are notoriously difficult to gauge. The complexity and variation of personal religious choices and experiences, the lack of clear confessional divides and the uncertainty about the future of the church creates further difficulties for the historian, as it must have done for Elizabethan court officials, and conformity and partial conformity should be viewed as positive religious choices alongside Protestantism and Catholicism.[48] Shagan has argued that some finely balanced toleration for Catholicism existed within every community and when it collapsed it did so as a result of changes in public discourse about confessional identities rather than changes in people's beliefs.[49] Many political issues crossed the confessional divide and Catholics, Shagan argued, were just as adept as their Protestant neighbours at the performance of political action in public settings.[50] Conformity

---

47. For more on Bell see A. Walsham, 'Bell, Thomas (b. c.1551, d. in or after 1610), Roman Catholic priest and protestant polemicist', *ODNB*; M.C. Questier, *Conversion, politics and religion in England 1580–1625* (Cambridge, 1996), *passim*; A. Walsham, '"Yielding to the extremity of the time": conformity, orthodoxy and the post-reformation Catholic community', in P. Lake and M. Questier (eds), *Conformity and orthodoxy in the English church c.1550–1660* (Woodbridge, 2000), pp. 211–36.

48. Walsham, '"Yielding to the extremity of the time"', p. 213.

49. R. Manning, *Religion and society in Elizabethan Sussex* (Leicester, 1969) p. 272; E. Shagan, 'Introduction: English Catholic history in context', in E. Shagan (ed.), *Catholics and the Protestant nation: religious politics and identity in England, 1534–1640* (Manchester, 2005), p. 14; See W.J. Sheils, 'Catholics and their neighbours in a rural community: Egton chapelry 1590–1780', *Northern History*, 34 (1998), pp. 109–33, for a good example of social harmony crossing the religious divide.

50. Shagan, 'Introduction: English Catholic history', pp. 14–17.

was far from ideologically coherent and was often generated by social rather than religious concerns, and Questier has suggested that the same must often have been true of nonconformity.[51]

Protestantism had no clear definition in England until the early 1570s, which adds to the difficulties of identifying boundaries, and undoubtedly every parishioner in early Elizabethan Yorkshire had their own ideas about what it constituted. For a few it would have been a set of theological beliefs and ideas to which they adhered; for many it was perhaps simply anything that was not traditional Catholicism. These differing views would undoubtedly have led to different interpretations of 'normal' religious behaviour, thus influencing the nature of nonconformity presentments in the courts and leading to varied interpretations of the severity of different transgressions. Thus, any attempts to create anything approaching true religious uniformity were perhaps inevitably doomed to failure. Nevertheless, the importance of the church court records to our understanding of the implementation of religious change in Yorkshire is clear, as is their wider importance in local and regional religious and social history. While the High Commission might not have been entirely successful in wiping out Catholicism in the north, it can perhaps be credited with the elimination of conservatism. Only the most obstinate Catholics persisted in resisting the efforts of the High Commission officials to enforce them to conform and, in the face of increased persecution through the High Commission courts, those with more moderate religious views were gradually encouraged to conform.

---

51. M. Questier, 'Conformity, Catholicism and the law', in P. Lake and M. Questier (eds), *Conformity and orthodoxy in the English church, c.1550–1660* (Woodbridge, 2000), p. 241.

12. From Philistines to Goths: Nonconformist chapel styles in Victorian England

Edward Royle

Churches and chapels – especially chapels – come in all shapes and sizes, so what determines the architectural style of a Nonconformist place of worship? Why in some places and times does it ape the style of the Established Church, most usually some form of Gothic, and at other times appear deliberately different? The purpose of this chapter is to encourage local historians to use surviving Nonconformist buildings as a resource for local history, setting out some ideas about that shift in taste that took many Nonconformists in England from the classical to the Gothic during the course of the nineteenth century. The factors to be considered include fashion, cost, ideology and liturgy, and the illustrations are drawn mainly from Baptist, Congregational, Methodist and Unitarian chapels in Yorkshire, although similar examples are to be found in all other Protestant denominations except the Quakers, and could be discovered in any part of the country. The period surveyed ranges from the mid-eighteenth to the early twentieth century, but the most important decades were the 1840s to the 1870s, during which the so-called 'battle of the styles' was at its height within Nonconformity.[1]

The architectural style of churches in England until the early seventeenth century was Gothic.[2] A late example – what has been called Gothic survival rather than Gothic revival – is St John's Church in Leeds, built in the 1630s. By the later

1. A still useful, although dated, starting point for reading about chapels is R. Thorne, *Chapels!! Their architecture and distribution: a preliminary bibliography* (Ottery St Mary, 1994). I am grateful to Christopher Stell and Christopher Wakeling for their comments on an earlier draft of this article.

2. Some churches, though, were built in or incorporated the vernacular style; see, for example, Whitby St Mary, the old church at Heptonstall, or Morley Old Chapel, rebuilt in the sixteenth century and referred to below.

seventeenth century, though, the classical style associated with Wren and Hawksmoor was predominant. Holy Trinity church in Leeds (1721–7), a nave-and-apse church with Corinthian columns, is typical of the new age. Another example of the Georgian style is the church at Horbury near Wakefield, built as a gift by the York architect, John Carr, for his natal village in 1793, but by this date fashions were again beginning to change. Although in the early nineteenth century Greek revivalism was to be found in some parish churches, such as the new St Pancras in London (1822), by that date Gothic revivalism was in full flow. 'Commissioners' churches', built to expand the accommodation and coverage of the Church of England after 1818, were invariably in the Early English style with tall lancet windows. Their Gothic was modest and cheap, but declared that these buildings were not to be confused with dissenting meeting houses. By the time of the new Leeds parish church, rebuilt in 1841, though, there was a preference for a more elaborate mixture of Decorated and Perpendicular styles. From then onwards creative, powerful, innovative and expensive Gothic was dominant, with churches such as George Gilbert Scott's St George, Doncaster (1858), or William Burgess's Christ the Consoler, Skelton (1871–2), and St Mary, Studley Royal (1878) – the finest work of the highest of high Victorian Gothic architects.[3]

What had the Nonconformists to do with the likes of this? Their initial buildings had been what they could afford and for the most part unpretentious. If built in the seventeenth century, following the exclusions of 1662 and the Toleration Act of 1689, they were erected when Gothic was out of fashion. In the countryside their meeting houses grew out of barns, cottages and farmhouses; in the towns they developed on the model of the Georgian townhouse. Occasionally a building might be inherited from the Established Church, as at Morley, although that building, with its low roof and mullioned windows, had more of the sixteenth-century vernacular farmhouse about it than the medieval Gothic church. Where there was sufficient gentry patronage to build a grand urban chapel or great meeting house, this typically resulted in a square or near-square structure with box pews and a pulpit between round-headed windows on the rear wall, facing the entrance over which there was often a gallery. In Leeds the meeting house of about 1674, altered in the eighteenth century, was of this kind – a square seven-bayed house later dignified with a pedimented front, to which

---

3. See S. Wrathmell, *Leeds*, Pevsner Architectural Guides (London, 2005), pp. 43–7 (parish church), pp. 48–53 (St John), pp. 94–5 (Holy Trinity); B. Wragg, *The life and works of John Carr of York*, ed. G. Worsley (York, 2000), pp. 83, 158, 160 (Horbury); N. Pevsner and E. Radcliffe, *Yorkshire: the West Riding*, The Buildings of England, revised edition (Harmondsworth, 1967), pp. 181–2 (Doncaster); C.M. Smart, Jr., *Muscular churches: ecclesiastical architecture of the high Victorian period* (London, 1989), pp. 160–65 (Skelton), pp. 166–71 (Studley Royal).

Fig. 12.1 Meltham, St Bartholomew Church of England (J. Jagger, 1786), with tower (J.P. Pritchett, 1835) and chancel (1877).

was then added across the front a squat tower containing the organ loft. An alternative form, favoured by John Wesley, was the octagon, such as those built at Yarm (1763) and Heptonstall (1764), influenced perhaps by the Presbyterians' Octagon Chapel in Norwich, designed by Thomas Ivory in 1754–6 and visited by Wesley in 1757. Less usual was the Greek cross layout chosen by the Presbyterians of York in 1693.[4] But all these designs served the same purpose: that of maximising the number of pews gathered around the pulpit.

Meeting houses were not parish churches and they were meant to look different from buildings of the Established Church, although in the eighteenth century parochial chapels-of-ease came in a variety of styles and were sometimes indistinguishable from Nonconformist meeting houses. So, for example, while St Peter, Sowerby, in Halifax parish, is a magnificent Georgian building worthy of

4. C. Stell, 'Great meeting houses', in *Miscellany I*, The Chapels Society, Occasional Publications, 1 (London, 1998), pp. 35–49; C. Stell, *An inventory of Nonconformist chapels and meeting-houses in the North of England*, Royal Commission on the Historical Monuments of England (London, 1994), p. 292 (Morley), p. 285 (Leeds), p. 225 (Yarm), pp. 272–3 (Heptonstall), pp. 185–6 (York); C. Stell, *An inventory of Nonconformist chapels and meeting-houses in eastern England* (Swindon, 2002), pp. 260–2 (Norwich).

Fig. 12.2 Wakefield, Westgate Unitarian (1751–2).

an urban parish church, Meltham in Almondbury parish (Fig. 12.1) was more typical in that it could have been mistaken for a Nonconformist chapel until a tower and chancel were added in the nineteenth century to make it look more like a 'proper' church.[5] The most that dissenters aspired to in the later eighteenth century and first half of the nineteenth was an embellished but still relatively modest rectangular building often under a hipped or ridge roof, like that built for the Presbyterians of Wakefield in 1751–2 (Fig. 12.2), with its two pedimented doors separated by a Venetian window and with rounded windows above at the level of the west gallery.[6] In many places this, or some variant of it, continued to provide the basic 'chapel' shape right through the nineteenth century, although a later building might acquire a grander pedimented front, with classical pilasters or even pillars, usually of the Ionic or Corinthian order. But in an increasing number of places in the second half of the nineteenth century the plain meeting-house or classical styles were abandoned in favour of Gothic.

So far the concern has been with externals. Internally the rectangular box-

5. Pevsner and Radcliffe, *West Riding*, pp. 492–3 (Sowerby) and p. 363 (Meltham), and site visits.
6. Stell, *North of England*, pp. 327–8 (Wakefield).

shape of the chapel, with two aisles and a central bank of pews directly facing the central pulpit, proclaimed the building as a place where the word of God was preached. This was also the principal purpose of eighteenth-century chapels of ease and nave-and-apse churches within the Church of England, and even some new Commissioners' churches of the early nineteenth century still had central pulpits. Nevertheless, Gothic revival churches were increasingly differentiated from preaching-box chapels by their association with the liturgical revival within the Church of England – the Cambridge movement, led by the Camden Society, was the architectural companion of the Oxford Movement. Two and three-decker pulpits were removed from north walls or from centre aisles and separate pulpits and lecterns were set to the sides at the eastern end of the nave; chancels were built, elevated or extended; and simple tables were replaced by altars with crosses and candle sticks. The Gothic church provided, as Pugin famously demanded in *Contrasts* (1836) and *True principles of pointed or Christian architecture* (1841), a truly Christian architecture for truly Christian worship.

This was not what Nonconformists wanted of their buildings.[7] The preaching box continued to suit their form of worship and, whereas the Church of England moved its organs and singers from the west gallery to the sides of the chancel, even half-hidden behind a screen, in most cases the Nonconformists put their organs and their choirs in a gallery behind the pulpit facing the congregation, as if to emphasise their worship of good singing as well as of good preaching. Whether the externals were Greek or Gothic mattered little. In Sheffield, whereas Carver Street Wesleyan, built in 1805, might have been mistaken for a respectable gentleman's townhouse, with its carefully balanced pedimented gable and five bays of round-arched windows on two floors with a central Venetian window over a pilastered and pedimented entrance, Acorn Street Wesleyan, built in 1823, is an early example of a Gothic front and one which Stell finds 'exceptional for its serious attention to Gothic detail'. It had castellated parapets ending in turrets at the outer corners, five bays of pointed windows with stone tracery heads and a central tower rising to three floors and capped with more turrets. The architect, Joseph Botham, was not committed to Gothic, however, and returned to the more conventional 'chapel' style when he designed the grand Brunswick Wesleyan Chapel in Leeds two years later.[8]

---

7. However, Nonconformists were not untouched by Camden Society influences: see C. Stell, 'Nonconformist architecture and the Cambridge Camden Society', in C. Webster and J. Elliott (eds), *'A church as it should be': the Cambridge Camden Society and its influence* (Stamford, 2000), pp. 317–30. Another influence shaping protestant fashions at mid-century was John Ruskin, whose *The seven lamps of architecture* was published in 1849 (London).

8. Stell, 'Nonconformist architecture', p. 318; Stell, *North of England*, pp. 310–12 (Sheffield), pp. 287–8 (Leeds). An even earlier example of a castellated preaching box was Oldham Street, Manchester (1781): see G.W. Dolbey, *The architectural expression of Methodism. The first hundred years* (London, 1964), pp. 78–9 and photograph on plate page six.

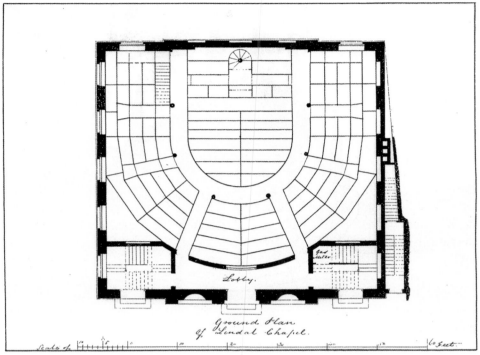

Fig. 12.3 York, Lendal Congregational (J.P. Pritchett, 1816), original arrangement of pews, ground floor, as drawn by the architect.

Botham's versatility with designs for wrapping around preaching boxes illustrates the difference between his approach and that of Pugin. Unlike the latter, but like most of his contemporaries, Botham was prepared to try his hand at whatever style the client wanted. The Congregational architect J.P. Pritchett, when building for his own people in York, began with the classical townhouse of Lendal chapel in 1816 (Fig. 12.3), and by 1839 was in Greek revivalist mode for the temple-like façade of Salem, with its Ionic pillars, but he could also turn his hand (not so successfully) to Gothic when a Church of England client demanded it – as the contrast between the traditional form of Ramsden Street Congregational chapel, Huddersfield (1824), and the perpendicular Gothic of St Peter's parish church (1836) illustrates. As regards the latter, however, his Nonconformist view of the importance of preaching meant that he only reluctantly agreed to provide an acoustically less-efficient central processional aisle rather than the two side aisles of the typical chapel, and he still retained a central pulpit. He could also, when required, turn his hand from the classical tower tacked on to the eighteenth-century Anglican preaching-box chapel at

Fig. 12.4 Leeds, Headingley, Otley Road Wesleyan (J. Simpson, 1844).

Meltham in 1835 (Fig. 12.1) to the full-blown Gothic of nearby St James's, Meltham Mills, only three years later.[9]

One of the more successful examples of early Nonconformist Gothic applied to a chapel was the Wesleyan chapel on Otley Road in Headingley, Leeds (Fig. 12.4), designed by James Simpson in 1844, less than a decade after his standard Georgian Oxford Place chapel in the centre of Leeds and only four years after his Centenary Chapel, York (Fig. 12.5), with its great pedimented portico and four Ionic pillars. Otley Road, with its Gothic lancet windows, nave, aisles, transepts, short chancel and buttressed front with finials and pinnacles, could easily have been mistaken externally for a Commissioners' church.[10]

---

9. W. Ellerby and J.P. Pritchett, *A history of the Nonconformist churches of York*, ed. E. Royle, Borthwick Texts and Calendars, 18 (York, 1993), esp. photograph after p. 118 and architect's drawings on pp. 153–69; R. Willis, *Nonconformist chapels of York*, York Georgian Society Occasional Paper, 8 (York, n.d.); E. Royle, 'Religion in Huddersfield since the mid-eighteenth century', in E.A.H. Haigh (ed.), *Huddersfield. A most handsome town. Aspects of the history and culture of a West Yorkshire town* (Huddersfield, 1992), pp. 101–44, pp. 109, 117–18; Pevsner and Radcliffe, *West Riding*, p. 363 (Meltham). Similarly, R.D. Chantrell could rebuild the tower of Holy Trinity, Leeds in a style reminiscent of Wren (1839) as the same time as he was building the Gothic parish church.

10. Stell, *North of England*, p. 289 (Otley Road), p. 288 (Oxford Place), pp. 188–9 (York).

Fig. 12.5 York, Centenary Wesleyan (J. Simpson, 1840).

The date is significant, for the mid-1840s marked the turning point in the adoption of Gothic as a style acceptable to Nonconformists. This was the decade when the Nonconformists emerged out of the shadow of the Church of England following reforming Whig legislation in the 1830s, which gave them the confidence to take their stand against the Church – the Anti-State Church Association was founded in 1844 and Voluntarism in religious education was at its height. In particular, the Dissenters' Chapels Act of 1844 gave fresh impetus to the Unitarians, who took the lead in adopting the new Gothic style. One of the best examples of this is Gee Cross chapel, Hyde (Fig. 12.6), which has been described as demonstrating 'a full understanding of Gothic construction and a Puginian insistence on separate

Fig. 12.6 Hyde, Gee Cross Congregational (Bowman and Crowther, 1844).

parts: nave, side aisles, eccentric porch, chancel, vestry and west tower with a fine broach spire'.[11] A plaque inside the chapel records how the Dissenters' Chapels Act secured 'to Nonsubscribing Dissenters peaceful Possession Of the Chapels and Endowments of their pious Forefathers'. In other words, following the Trinitarian

11. For Gee Cross, site visit and Stell, *North of England*, pp. 15–16; also C. Wakeling, 'Rolling in the aisles: Nonconformist perspectives on Gothic', in F. Salmon (ed.), *Gothic and Gothic revival: papers from the 26th annual symposium of the Society of Architectural Historians of Great Britain, 1997* (Edinburgh, 1998), pp. 37–44, p. 37, and 'Nonconformity and Victorian architecture', in B. Cherry (ed.), *Dissent and the Gothic revival. Papers from a study day at Union Chapel Islington*, The Chapels Society Occasional Publications, 3 (London, 2007), pp. 44–5.

Fig. 12.7 Leeds, Mill Hill Unitarian (Bowman and Crowther, 1847), interior as modified after 1884.

Dissenters' success in depriving the Presbyterian Unitarians of the endowments of Lady Hewley's bequest, parliament had avoided further litigation by granting to Unitarians possession of the buildings they were currently occupying, irrespective of the theology stated or implied in their original trust deeds.[12] This legal security prompted many Unitarians, as at Gee Cross, to pull down their old buildings and invest in new chapels. In most cases their preferred style was Gothic.

There are several reasons for this. First, fashions were changing. When the Unitarian chapel at Dukinfield in Cheshire was damaged by a storm in 1838 the congregation

12. Lady Sarah Hewley (1627–1710) was a wealthy widow and patron of Nonconformity in York. She left money for, among other charitable causes, the support of small congregations in the north of England and for training Nonconformist ministers. As these congregations and ministers had largely abandoned their Trinitarian beliefs for Unitarianism, orthodox Nonconformists challenged their right to benefit from the bequest and after a long legal battle (1830–42) the Unitarians lost this valuable source of support.

Fig. 12.8 Leeds, Mill Hill Unitarian (Bowman and Crowther, 1847).

had to rebuild and they did so in Gothic even before the legal security of the 1844 Act. Similarly, in 1839, when a congregation of Unitarian seceders from Cross Street, Manchester (a conventional urban and urbane eighteenth-century meeting house), built a new chapel in Upper Brook Street, they chose Charles Barry as architect and he produced a preaching-nave chapel in thirteenth-century Gothic. Any opportunity to build afresh became an invitation to become fashionable in Gothic.[13]

Secondly, some clue might be gained from Mill Hill Chapel, Leeds, rebuilt in Gothic in 1847–8 by Bowman and Crowther (Figs 12.7 and 12.8). Pevsner observes that it was 'no longer essentially different from buildings for the Established Church'. Indeed, that was the point: Mill Hill was a smaller version of the recently rebuilt parish church, minus its tower. Internally and externally, this chapel looked distinctly like a church, built to emulate the newly fashionable Gothic style so strikingly adopted for the parish church.[14] But more than fashion was at stake: the new Mill Hill chapel was also a clear architectural statement of the long-held English Presbyterian belief that the schismatics in 1662 had been the Episcopalians of the Established Church and that the true National Church would be rediscovered only in a reuniting

13. D.C. Doel, *Old Chapel and the Unitarian story* (London, n.d.); Stell, *North of England*, pp. 8–10 (Dukinfield), p. 115 (Manchester).

14. Wrathmell, *Leeds*, pp. 18, 20, 106–8.

Fig. 12.9 Todmorden, Unitarian (J. Gibson, 1869).

of the Protestant body on rational, biblical principles. This aspiration had been dealt a serious blow in 1772 when parliament had rejected the Feathers Tavern Petition for a relaxation of the Thirty-Nine Articles which defined the nature of the Church of England. This rejection marked the beginning of modern Unitarianism in England, when disgruntled Churchmen, notably Theophilus Lindsey, joined the old Socinian Dissenters.[15] Thereafter, the dream of a united National Church gradually faded, as

---

15. So-called after the anti-Trinitarian sect, founded by Laelius and Faustus Socinius in the sixteenth century, whose members rejected the Nicene Creed and believed that Christ's existence dated only from when he was born as a man called Jesus.

Fig. 12.10 Morley, St Marys-in-the-Wood Congregational (Lockwood and Mawson, 1875).

first the Evangelical revival brought new life to Congregationalists and Baptists and created Methodists, and then as the Oxford Movement began to move the Church of England away from its historic Protestant position. The loss of the Lady Hewley Case, which diverted her endowments to the Trinitarian Dissenters, completed the isolation of the Unitarians not only from the Church of England but also from other forms of dissent. Their adoption of Gothic can be seen as their last claim to represent the true, rational, Biblical, Protestant National Church. Where new Unitarian churches were built after this date they were almost invariably in the Gothic style and indistinguishable from 'real' churches.[16]

16. The major exception in Yorkshire was Upper Chapel, Sheffield, enlarged and almost rebuilt in 1847–8 in the classic chapel style: see Stell, *North of England*, pp. 308–9. For the evolution of Unitarianism see C.G. Bolam, J. Goring, H.L. Short and R. Thomas, *The English Presbyterians: from Elizabethan Puritanism to modern Unitarianism* (London, 1968), esp. pp. 175–286. Stell, 'Nonconformist architecture', p. 324, prefers to see this Unitarian enthusiasm not so much as 'an act of defiance' as 'a positive assertion of their newly-acquired religious equality'.

Fig. 12.11 Halifax, Square Chapel, Congregational (T. Bradley, 1772; J. James, 1855–7).

The new Unitarian chapels built at Leeds and Gee Cross are but two examples of this development. To them may be added Huddersfield (1853), Todmorden (1869) (Fig. 12.9), and Halifax Northgate End (1872). By this latter date Gothic was becoming common, although not quite universal, for almost all Nonconformist denominations.[17] The crowning glory of Unitarian Gothic was Todmorden, erected by the sons of John Fielden, whose spinning factories dominated the town. This is a

17. An exception was the Quakers, whose method of worship and plain living kept them true to the traditional meeting-house style. Even so, at Scholes near Leeds (1883) the meeting house took the outward form of a Gothic village chapel. See D.M. Butler, *The Quaker meeting houses of Britain*, 2 vols (London, 1999).

grand church which is, with its central aisle, heavy marble pillars and side pulpit, a church inside as well as out. This was only fitting, as Unitarianism was in effect the established religion in the Fieldens' Todmorden. Their church was an expression of their religious beliefs, their social power and their immense wealth. In Halifax, the Ionic pilasters and pediment of the façade of Northgate End Unitarian chapel, which had been put in place only in 1847, were swept aside in 1872 for a new Gothic chapel with buttresses and pinnacles. Here the motivation may have been rivalry with the Congregational Square Chapel, rebuilt in 1855–7 next to the 1772 original meeting house (Fig. 12.11) and adjacent to the great Piece Hall, the hub of Halifax commerce in the eighteenth century. The new Square Chapel was built in fourteenth-century Gothic with a majestic spire 235 feet high. Overshadowing the Piece Hall, it proclaimed the industrial and economic power of the dissenting manufacturers of the town, especially of the Crossley family, whose ample coffers largely paid for it. Edward Akroyd, former New Connexion Methodist but now Church of England, had already called in George Gilbert Scott to build only a short distance away his All Souls, Haley Hill (1856–9), in Anglo-French Gothic, with a tower 236 feet tall. Gothic had become the language of competition in what was, by the 1850s, a free market in religious provision and practice.[18]

The change in fashion, making the Gothic acceptable, is marked in the literature and the design books of the period. In 1847 the editor of the *Congregational year book*, John Blackburn, published an article of 'Remarks on ecclesiastical architecture as applied to Nonconformist chapels' in which he accepted that Gothic forms might not be incompatible with the needs of Protestant congregational worship and praised the Gothic of the Anglican Highbury Chapel in Bristol, an early work of William Butterfield. This was followed in 1850 by Frederick Jobson's *Chapel and school architecture*. Jobson was secretary to the Wesleyan Model Plan Committee, which commissioned six architects to produce both Gothic and classical designs for use in the Wesleyan Connexion, again accepting that building in Gothic did not commit Protestants to accepting Pugin's assumption of the link between Gothic architecture and 'true' forms of sacerdotal worship. A similar function among Congregationalists was served by another pattern book, George Bidlake's *Sketches of churches designed for the use of Nonconformists* (1865); and for the Primitive Methodists there was G. Hodgson Fowler's *A manual of chapel architecture for the use of Methodist churches* (1873), which came out strongly in favour of the 'simplicity, elegance, and strict economy' of Gothic, even though

---

18. Stell, *North of England*, pp. 436–7 (Todmorden), pp. 256–62 (Halifax); Pevsner and Radcliffe, *West Riding*, pp. 231, 234, 627; Smart, *Muscular churches*, p. 18 (All Souls).

Fig. 12.12 Shipley, Saltaire Congregational (Lockwood and Mawson, 1859).

his reviewer in the *Primitive Methodist Magazine* was not persuaded and continued to prefer the classical.[19]

This battle of the styles was played out on building committees across the country. While, on the one hand, the desire to rival the Church of England led to the adoption of at least some Gothic designs by all the major denominations during the second half of the nineteenth century, on the other hand, the desire to assert their independence of and difference from the Church of England led some Nonconformists to retain their own distinctive styles based on the Georgian meeting house but ever more ornate, with classical touches and Italianate ornamentation. Sir Titus Salt's chapel at Saltaire (Shipley) is a good example (Fig. 12.12). Opened in 1859, and designed by Lockwood and Mawson, it takes the form of a Roman basilica with a semi-circular Corinthian colonnade at the west end surmounted by a domed tower. Nothing could be further from Gothic, although inside the long, thin basilica of a nave required a central aisle – but still with a central

19. Wakeling, 'Nonconformity and Victorian architecture', pp. 46–52; Stell, 'Nonconformist architecture', p. 322; J.H. Anderson, 'Primitive Methodism and the Gothic revival', *The Chapels Society Newsletter*, 41 (May 2009), pp. 11–13. See also J.C.G. Binfield, *The contexting of a chapel architect. James Cubitt 1836–1912*, The Chapels Society Occasional Publications, 2 (London, 2001), pp. 3–4 (Blackburn); and Dolbey, *Architectural expression of Methodism*, pp. 19, 130, 134, 150, 179–80 (Jobson).

Fig. 12.13 Shipley, Saltaire Congregational, interior (Lockwood and Mawson, 1859).

pulpit (Fig. 12.13). Gothic was also shunned at Providence Place, Cleckheaton (1859), again by Lockwood and Mawson; the chapel here was described by Christopher Stell as 'an elaborate Italianate building with a pedimented front and open arcaded loggia of five bays with a giant order of Corinthian columns'. Yet by 1871 the same firm had designed for Crossley and Salt the Congregational chapel at Lightcliffe, Brighouse, in the best fourteenth-century Gothic (Fig. 12.14), followed in 1876 by the replacement for Morley Old Chapel (Fig. 12.10) in the same style.[20]

It is probably safe to say that by the 1870s Nonconformist Gothic had

20. Stell, *North of England*, frontispiece and pp. 312–13 (Saltaire), p. 243 (Cleckheaton), p. 241 (Lightcliffe), pp. 292–4 (Morley).

Fig. 12.14 Brighouse, Lightcliffe Congregational (Lockwood and Mawson, 1871).

triumphed with the Congregationalists as it had previously with the Unitarians but, despite Jobson and Fowler, other denominations were still not quite so sure. The chapel architect John Wills of Derby might assert in the early 1880s that 'it is perfectly possible to construct Chapels in any style with good acoustic properties, not excepting the Gothic', but he still found many clients who firmly stipulated 'not Gothic'. Although Gothic had been promoted initially as cheaper than the equivalent structures in the classical style, by the later nineteenth century the elaborate Gothic preferred by architects could be much more expensive. Nevertheless, fashion was on its side and by the 1870s a Gothic chapel had become for many congregations a necessary statement of social position, made possible by the wealth of the congregation or some influential patron. So the wealthy Congregationalists of Ashton under Lyne, in particular Abel Buckley,

Fig. 12.15 Leeds, Blenheim Baptist (W. Hill, 1858).

could erect the new Albion chapel (1890–5), by the architect John Brooke of Manchester, with no apparent expense spared. In the end over £40,000 was laid out to ensure the expression of those 'ideas of space and grandeur, and ideas and feelings that indicated emotion and sentiment' which were bound up with the Gothic style and were eulogised upon by the minister in a lantern-slide lecture delivered to the congregation on 'The significance of some features of Gothic architecture as seen in our new church'.[21]

---

21. J. Wills, *Hints to trustees of chapel property, and chapel keepers' manual*, 3rd edn (c.1884), reprinted with an introduction by D. Barton (1993), p. 22; J.C.G. Binfield, *The dynamic of grandeur. Albion church, Ashton-under-Lyne*, reprinted from the *Transactions of the Lancashire and Cheshire Antiquarian Society*, 85 (1988), pp. 173–92.

Fig. 12.16 Morley, Wesley Street, Wesleyan (J. Simpson, 1860–61).

The Baptists were generally a less prosperous denomination and, although they were experimenting with Gothic in the 1850s and 1860s with chapels such as Blenheim, Woodhouse Lane, Leeds (William Hill, 1858) (Fig. 12.15), York (William Peachey, 1868) (Fig. 12.24) and Glossop Road, Sheffield (C.J. Innocent, 1869), that at Zion, Bradford (Lockwood and Mawson), retained a classical appearance in 1871 and as late as 1899 the General Baptist chapel at Hebden Bridge (Sutcliffe and Sutcliffe) was a large Italianate structure with an arcaded front.[22] The Baptists' doubts were expressed by C.H. Spurgeon, their greatest preacher of the later nineteenth century, when he stated that Greek was the language of the New Testament, and therefore should also be the true Christian style of architecture for his Metropolitan Tabernacle in London.[23]

The Methodists also sent out mixed messages in the battle of the styles. Half a generation each side of the Morley Congregationalists' St Mary's-in-the-Wood,

22. C.E. Shipley (ed.), *The Baptists of Yorkshire. Being the centenary memorial volume of the Yorkshire Baptist Association* (London, 1912), illustrations following p. 144 (Leeds), p. 169 (York), p. 252 (Sheffield), p. 118 (Bradford); and Stell, *North of England*, pp. 267–8 (Hebden Bridge).

23. As Stell points out, Spurgeon's view of Greek was similar in spirit to Pugin's defence of Gothic: Stell, 'Nonconformist Architecture', p. 321.

Fig. 12.17 Morley, Fountain Street, Primitive Methodist (T.A. Buttery, 1885–6).

rebuilt in Gothic in 1875 (Fig. 12.10), in the same town they erected the traditionally conceived Wesleyan Chapel (James Simpson, 1860–61) (Fig. 12.16) and Fountain Street Primitive Methodist Chapel (1885–6) (Fig. 12.17), the latter being ostentatiously classical, with a three-bay pediment supported by huge Corinthian pilasters. In Huddersfield the earliest major Methodist chapels built in Gothic were for the New Connexion (High Street) and the Wesleyans (Lindley) (Fig. 12.18), both in 1867. The latter chapel also received a chancel in 1896 (by Edgar Wood), but a local historian has estimated that even after 1880 a quarter of new Methodist chapels in the Kirklees area were still not in the Gothic style, including one of their new major suburban chapels (Gledholt, 1890), which externally looked more like a town hall or suite of offices than a place of worship (Fig. 12.19). Even when the exterior was Gothic, as with Longwood Wesleyan

Fig. 12.18. Huddersfield, Lindley Wesleyan (G. Woodhouse, 1867–8).

(1904) (Fig. 12.20), more often than not the interior (Fig. 12.21) remained a conventional preaching chapel.[24]

For if some Nonconformists were in two minds about the outward appearance of their chapels they were certain about their interior purpose. The significance of the phrase Nonconformist or Free Church Gothic is that it emphasises the contradiction between the exterior and the interior of the building. Although the use of Gothic exteriors was widespread by the third quarter of the nineteenth century the internal layout of a majority of such buildings was still that of the conventional chapel. The ambition of Established Church reformers in the

24. Stell, *North of England*, pp. 293–5 (Morley), p. 281 (Longwood); Haigh, *Huddersfield*, p. 123; A.R. Bielby, *Churches and chapels of Kirklees* (Huddersfield, 1978), pp. 90–4.

Fig. 12.19 Huddersfield, Gledholt Wesleyan (J. Kirk, 1890).

ecclesiological tradition was to build not only true Christian architecture on the best idealised medieval model but to provide a suitable theatre for the drama of the Eucharist, approached down a central processional aisle. The ambition of Nonconformists was to proclaim their equality with the Established Church, which meant keeping up with the latest fashions in church architecture, but at the same time their services continued to require Protestant preaching boxes with good acoustics and good sightlines between the pews and the pulpit. Many of their buildings combined the ideal of a family gathered around the pulpit in pews arranged on three sides of what, by the later nineteenth century, was becoming a rostrum with what has been called the 'oratorio' style, with provision for the organ and a large choir across the end of the chapel, facing their audience and ready to deliver Handel's *Messiah* or Mendelssohn's *Elijah* over the head of the preacher. This could not easily be done from

Fig. 12.20 Huddersfield, Longwood Wesleyan (J. Berry, 1904).

the secluded, sideways-facing chancel choir pews of a truly Gothic church.

The challenge of not only asserting that Protestant congregational worship could find a happy home in a Gothic building but of achieving this in practice was successfully met by the architect James Cubitt. In 1870 he published *Church design for congregations: its development and possibilities*, where he sought to combine a Gothic structure with his admiration for Christopher Wren's use of open space. The first practical implementation of the theory came with Emmanuel Congregational Church, Cambridge (1872–4), a Gothic nave and apse church with a central aisle and a gallery in the west tower, but with the clerestory carried on each side by only two arches and a single pillar, so as to maximise views of the pulpit. Then, to create a much larger auditorium for the congregation of Union Chapel, Islington (1874–7), Cubitt turned to an octagon to provide pews for 1650 worshippers gathered around the pulpit, which stood in front of the organ gallery but was almost surrounded by angled pews in the body of the church, with seven galleries looking down on the focal and spiritual centre of the church. The style has been described as 'Romanesque … an eclectic mixture: French Early Gothic detail combined with round-headed arches' (Fig.

Fig. 12.21 Huddersfield, Longwood Wesleyan, interior (J. Berry, 1904).

12.22). The same approach to creating a central open space, this time within a cruciform building with large transepts, was repeated by Cubitt for Westgate Baptist Church, Newcastle upon Tyne (1886), and in the same city by T. Lewis Banks at St James's Congregational Church (1882–4) (Fig. 12.23), a fine structure in Early English Gothic under a central lantern and spire.[25]

Nonconformist Gothic was caught facing two ways, as chapel stewards, deacons and elders proved less resistant to the attractions of the Gothic revival than they did to the liturgical revival and the spread of ritualism associated with it in the Established Church. The dilemma was felt by Priory Street Baptist chapel in York, designed by William Peachey in 1868 (Fig. 12.24), which, with its Gothic nave, transept and tower, had every outward appearance of a church. Indeed, at a Church Meeting in 1891 it was 'proposed that the name of the chapel be painted on the Lamp so that strangers might know that it was not a

---

25. Binfield, *Contexting of a chapel architect*, pp. 41–4; A. Richardson, 'The building of Union Chapel', in B. Cherry (ed.), *Dissent and the Gothic revival. Papers from a study day at Union Chapel Islington*, The Chapels Society Occasional Publications, 3 (London, 2007), pp. 5–18, p. 7; Wakeling, 'Rolling in the aisles', pp. 39–40; J.C.G. Binfield, 'The building of a town centre church: St James's Congregational Church, Newcastle upon Tyne', *Northern History*, 18 (1982), pp. 155–81, and, more generally, 'The Prime of T. Lewis Banks', in *Miscellany 2. Chapels and chapel people*, The Chapels Society Occasional Publications, 5 (London, 2010), pp. 73–108.

Fig. 12.22 Islington, Union Chapel, Congregational (J. Cubitt, 1874–7), from Herman Muthesius, Die Neuere Kirchliche Baukunst in England (Berlin, 1901).

church but a Baptist Chapel'. Any stranger who cared to enter would not have been misled for long. The interior was a conventional chapel, with a central pulpit and horseshoe-shaped gallery supported on delicate cast iron columns slender enough not to obscure the view, creating a fit place for church members and general congregation to gather around the pulpit to see and hear their pastor (Fig. 12.25). The interior could as well have been housed in a classical or Italianate chapel as in a building which the unwary might mistake for a Gothic church.[26]

26. Baptist Church Records, Priory Street, York, Minute Book (1862–1903), 29 December 1891; B. Seymour, *York's other churches and chapels* (Beverley, 1992), front cover, lower right corner, and pp. 61–2.

Fig. 12.23 Newcastle upon Tyne, St James, Congregational (T.L. Banks, 1882–4).

Much of the above has been written with town or suburban chapels in mind. Country chapels shared in some of these influences for change but in different ways. The small country chapel, seating perhaps a hundred or so worshippers, had no problems with acoustics, sightlines, pillars or arches; the organ, if there were one, was likely to be a harmonium, parked at the side of the central pulpit, and the choir likewise. In addition, style books were likely to have more influence on trustees in the villages since the job might well be entrusted to a local builder or perhaps a very local and minor architect. John Wills of Derby listed well over 100 chapels 'erected or remodelled from my Designs'. With the help of Jobson, Bidlake, Fowler and others, Gothic exteriors, or exteriors with Gothic features,

Fig. 12.24 York, Priory Street Baptist (W. Peachey, 1868), architect's drawing, from C.E. Shipley (ed.), The Baptists of Yorkshire (London, 1912).

spread across the countryside with more, or less, conviction, although for the most part the buildings remained at heart simple chapels.[27]

By the end of the nineteenth century most new Nonconformist chapels were being built in what passed for Gothic, but the mixture of styles thus labelled is both rich and confusing. At the one extreme lie Todmorden Unitarian and Albion Congregational, with their soaring spires, pointed arches, central aisles, side pulpits and chancels with side-facing choir stalls. At the other extreme are York Baptist and Longwood Wesleyan, Gothic on the outside but with oratorio choir pews, central pulpits and full galleries on the inside, no different from the

27. Stell cites Fordham, Cambridgeshire (1849), as an early example of a village chapel according to one of Jobson's designs: Stell, 'Nonconformist architecture', p. 326, and Stell, Eastern England, p. 33. A later example is Acaster Malbis, near York (1880).

Fig. 12.25 York, Priory Street Baptist, interior (W. Peachey, 1868).

interiors of buildings with classical exteriors. In between there are the hybrids, such as Lindley Wesleyan in its final form, with chancel, side-facing choir stalls and side pulpit, but no central aisle; and, the most original compromise of all, that style best represented by the great arched and galleried octagon of James Cubitt's Union Chapel, a chapel in purpose but thoroughly Gothic in spirit.[28]

The sources for this chapter have been as much visual as textual, and the references will in many cases lead the reader to drawings and photographs of the buildings discussed. These buildings were once neglected, being regarded as

28. Wakeling, 'Rolling in the aisles', pp. 40–1.

uninteresting and of little architectural merit. The original Pevsner series of Penguin guides to *The Buildings of England*, county by county, usually homed in on the parish church and forgot the humble, and not-so-humble, chapel. The later, revised volumes make some amends for this former neglect, but the best guide for the local historian is provided in Christopher Stell's monumental four-volume *Inventory of chapels and meeting houses*, covering the whole of England, although its emphasis is mainly on the period before 1850. But there is no substitute in local history for the eye of the informed observer. Although many Nonconformist chapels have been demolished or altered out of all recognition (especially their interiors), sufficient still survive to provide the local historian with a record of those changing aspirations and tastes of earlier generations, which remain such an important part of the social and cultural history of our local communities.[29]

---

29. The opportunity to share enthusiasms and field trips with like-minded people is created by membership of The Chapels Society: <http://www.britarch.ac.uk/chapelsoc/>. Some of the more important redundant chapels are now cared for by The Historic Chapels Trust: <http://www.hct.org.uk/>.

13. Evangelicals in a 'Catholic' suburb: the founding of St Andrew's, North Oxford, 1899–1907

Mark Smith

The foundation of St Andrew's, North Oxford, provoked a considerable bout of fluttering in Oxford's ecclesiastical dovecotes at the start of the twentieth century. This controversy, arising from the promotion of a scheme for a new church, is worth examining in some detail, both as an example of the complexities involved in the clash of ecclesiastical cultures in early twentieth-century England and for what it reveals about the consequences of such clashes for the parochial system which was intended to provide the backbone of the Church's pastoral work.[1]

The origins of both St Andrew's and its associated dispute can be found in the development of North Oxford as a residential suburb over the preceding 80 years and in the particular ecclesiastical character to which this gave rise. The process began in the 1820s with speculative building in the settlement which became known as Summertown on the northern edge of the ancient parish of St Giles, just beyond the city boundary.[2] The fields between Oxford and Summertown did not experience much in the way of development in the first half of the century. There was some piecemeal construction of small cottages and a handful of prestigious villas, but otherwise the area retained its predominantly rural character.[3] This began to change, however, in the 1850s: first with the building of the Park Town

---

1. For some parallels see R.W. Ambler, 'Evangelicals and the establishment: evangelical identity in a nineteenth-century market town', in M. Smith (ed.), *British evangelical identities* (Milton Keynes, 2008), pp. 74–84.

2. R. Fasnacht, *Summertown since 1820* (Oxford, 1977), p. 13–22. Summertown was incorporated within the municipal borough of Oxford in 1889; *Victoria County History Oxfordshire* (hereafter *VCH Oxon*) 4 (Oxford, 1979), p. 263.

3. T. Hinchcliffe, *North Oxford* (London, 1992), pp. 25, 31.

estate on the eastern side of North Oxford and then, in the following decade, with the beginning of controlled development of the land owned by St John's College into an archetypal Victorian middle-class suburb. The first large-scale developments were in Norham Manor, to the east of the Banbury Road, which was divided into generous plots for the construction of large villa-style properties, and in Walton Manor, to the west, which included some plots of a similar size as well as smaller ones aimed at a more modest market. Although in a number of cases building took considerable time to get going, by the late 1890s it had spread north as far as Linton Road and most of the remaining space between North Oxford and Summertown was earmarked for new residential development. In general, the largest houses were to be found on the eastern side of the suburb and plot sizes gradually declined to the west, culminating in artisans' cottages built between the middle-class suburb and the canal.[4]

Ecclesiastically, the whole of this new suburb lay originally within the parish of St Giles. As the population began to grow so the need for additional Anglican church accommodation became apparent and demand for a response by the Establishment began to emerge. Summertown was the first to benefit, gaining a chapel of ease in 1831, which became a full parish church in 1864.[5] This was followed by St Paul's Walton Street in the south-western part of the parish, whose district was carved partly out of St Giles and partly from the neighbouring parish of St Thomas in 1837.[6] Both of these new churches helped to relieve the pressure on accommodation in the parish, but by the early 1850s the need for a building which would relate more directly to the new suburb was obvious. In 1854 the churchwardens of St Giles wrote to St John's, drawing attention both to the restricted accommodation in the parish church, which, even 'with the greatest economy of space', could hold a maximum of 420 people, and to the growth in population (enumerated at the 1851 census as 2588 exclusive of the chapelries of Summertown and St Paul's). There was a particular problem, they pointed out, for the poorer residents because the bulk of the seats were appropriated to the larger houses. They supported their appeal for an additional church with a petition signed by 107 inhabitants of the parish.[7] Some eight years of negotiation and fund-raising later, the new church was finally opened, with a dedication to

---

4. *Ibid.*, pp. 38–89.

5. C. Hicks (ed.), J. Badcock, *The making of a Regency village: origin, history and description of Summertown in 1832* (Oxford, 1983).

6. *VCH Oxon* 4, p. 411.

7. Bodleian Library, Oxford (hereafter Bodl.), MS Top. Oxon. A.28 fos 2–4, Memorial from the inhabitants of St Giles.

St Philip and St James and a district taking in most of the Norham and Walton Manor developments, together with the remainder of North Oxford south of Summertown. The continuing growth of the suburb in the 1880s prompted the construction of a further church to the west of the Woodstock Road as chapel of ease to St Philip and St James, which was dedicated to St Margaret. When this church too was assigned an independent ecclesiastical district in 1896, taken from the south-western portion of Summertown parish and the north-western portion of St Philip and St James, the parochial development of the area appeared to be complete (Plate 9).[8] That, however, would be to reckon without the competing cultures of late nineteenth- and early twentieth-century Anglicanism.

Although North Oxford was amply supplied with parish churches there was a remarkable unanimity about the variety of Anglicanism on offer to its residents. St Paul's Walton Street had been a Tractarian stronghold since the mid-1840s, espousing forms of High Church doctrine and practice that attracted comment from the very beginning.[9] Its daughter church, St Barnabas (opened in 1869), which also accommodated some of the inhabitants of North Oxford, operated in a similar vein.[10] During the incumbency of W.B. Duggan, between 1871 and 1904, St Paul's moved in an increasingly ritualist direction, losing at least three curates to Rome along the way.[11] St Philip and St James, designed by G.E. Street with advanced High Churchmanship in mind, rapidly became a further centre of Anglo-Catholicism and the Romish style of its services attracted criticism as early as 1866.[12] Under E.C. Dermer, the vicar from 1872, this continued further and something of the character of his muscular Anglo-Catholicism can be gathered from his discussion in his parish magazine about a hearing by the two archbishops of an appeal by two parish priests against a decision that the use of incense was forbidden by the prayer book. In June 1899, Dermer noted that the hearing was full and fair and that it 'will be fair too that the Clergy who make this appeal shall accept the Archbishop's decision, whatever it is.'[13] In September, however, the archbishops having ruled against both incense and processional lights, Dermer's attitude was rather different:

8. Hinchcliffe, *North Oxford*, pp. 137–41; *VCH Oxon* 4, pp. 410–12.

9. R.K. Pugh (ed.), *The letter-books of Samuel Wilberforce 1843–68*, Oxfordshire Record Society, 47 (Oxford, 1969), pp. 134–5; *VCH Oxon* 4, p. 411. For the background to the spread of ritualism and Anglo-Catholicism from the 1840s see N. Yates, *Anglican ritualism in Victorian Britain* (Oxford, 1999).

10. G. Hargrave, *St Denys school Oxford 1857–1957* (Oxford, 1957); *VCH Oxon* 4, p. 411.

11. G. Lewis, *An Oxford parish priest being an account of the life and work of the Rev. W.B. Duggan MA* (Oxford, 1905), pp. 108–9.

12. W. Acworth, *The Acts of Uniformity set at nought in the diocese of Oxford* (Oxford, 1866), pp. 5–7.

13. *SS. Philip and James, Oxford, Parish Magazine* (hereafter *P&J*), June 1899.

In the 16th and 17th centuries it was generally believed that everyone could, and should, worship God in exactly the same way. No one believes that now: and it is not satisfactory to be told that the only and absolute rule for our worship in these days is an Act of Parliament 340 years old … At present the decision of the archbishops is not formally published, and is not binding on any parish priest until he is required by his own bishop to observe it.[14]

Some aspects of the ritual at St Philip and St James were altered after 1900 by its next incumbent, Charles Davey Biggs, who discontinued the placing of flowers on the altar and introduced new vestments as part of a move to 'give greater emphasis alike to the catholic and national character of our Book of Common Prayer'.[15] In 1906 it was one of the few churches in the city to use incense and to observe all the feasts of the Virgin Mary.[16] St Margaret's was similarly advanced at the outset under the leadership of its first incumbent Robert Hartley, who had been presented by Dermer, and it probably maintained the style of ceremonial originally established in the mother church. However, developments occurred here too: daily Eucharistic celebrations were introduced before the First World War and reservation of the sacrament in 1920.[17]

The identity of its churches was not the only marker of the ecclesiastical culture of North Oxford, as it also provided a home for a multitude of other High Church and Anglo-Catholic institutions. The suburb was the location of a number of new university colleges, including Keble[18] and Lady Margaret Hall. The latter was founded for the education of Anglican women without distinction of party; but its High Church reputation was reinforced by the initiative taken in its foundation by the Warden of Keble and also by the appointment of Elizabeth Wordsworth as its first Principal.[19] Anglo-Catholic education for the younger residents of the suburb was offered by St Edward's, a school for boarders and day boys which had originated as an initiative by the Tractarian vicar of St Thomas to ensure 'definite and careful training in the catholic principles of the Church of

14. *Ibid.*, September 1899.

15. *Ibid.*, September 1900, April 1901; *Oxford Times*, 1 December 1900.

16. *VCH Oxon* 4, p. 412.

17. *Ibid.*, p. 410.

18. G. Rowell, '"Training in simple and religious habits": Keble and its first warden', in M.G. Brock and M.C. Curthoys (eds), *The history of the University of Oxford*, 7 (Oxford, 2000), pp. 171–91.

19. B.J. Johnson, 'First Beginnings, 1873–90', in G. Bailey (ed.), *Lady Margaret Hall: a short history* (Oxford, 1923), p. 32; J. Howarth, 'The women's colleges', in M.G. Brock and M.C. Curthoys (eds), *The history of the University of Oxford*, 7 (Oxford, 2000), p. 250.

England'. Originally located in the centre of Oxford, the school migrated to the Woodstock Road in 1873 and entered, like the suburb in which it was located, on a period of expansion (despite some public unease about its encouragement of boys in the use of auricular confession).[20] Education for younger children was provided by the infant and primary schools of St Philip and St James, the former for both sexes and the latter for boys.[21] Education for older girls from the parish and further afield was available from upper, middle and elementary schools run by the Anglo-Catholic sisterhood of the 'Holy and Undivided Trinity', whose imposing convent, surrounded by a stone wall six feet high, was built on the Woodstock Road adjacent to St Philip and St James church.[22] When to this is added the presence of an outpost of a second Anglo-Catholic sisterhood, Priscilla Lydia Sellon's 'Society of the Most Holy Trinity', at 52 Banbury Road (renamed Holy Rood) between 1870 and 1883,[23] it seems not unreasonable to characterise North Oxford as a 'Catholic' suburb.[24]

At first sight, then, North Oxford appears to be not only an archetype of Victorian middle-class suburban development but also an archetype of the Victorian Church of England – the story of the heroic march of Anglo-Catholicism to a hegemonic position within the ecclesiastical culture of the nation. In this story other varieties of Anglicanism are all too easily marginalised or featured only as the representatives of an unconstructive and antediluvian opposition.[25] Inevitably, this was not the whole story, however, for Evangelicalism in particular remained a significant force in Oxford. It had parochial strongholds in the city centre and a capacity to generate new initiatives, including the Oxford Pastorate, founded in 1894 to minister to undergraduates in the University, and Wycliffe Hall, a training college for ordinands, which, when it established itself at 54 Banbury Road (next door to the Anglo-Catholic sisters at 'Holy Rood') in the 1870s, represented the only unambiguously Anglican evangelical institution in North Oxford.[26]

---

20. H.A. Dalton, *St Edwards School Oxford* (Oxford, 1882).

21. *A book of the parish of S. Philip and S. James, Oxford,* 2nd edn (Oxford, 1905), p. 13.

22. *Ibid.,* p. 3; Hargrave, *St Denys;* A. Saint and M. Kaser, *St Anthony's College Oxford: a history of its buildings and site* (Oxford, 1973), pp. 8–15.

23. T.J. Williams, *Priscilla Lydia Sellon* (London, 1950), p. 253; Hinchcliffe, *North Oxford,* p. 151.

24. Hinchcliffe, *North Oxford,* pp. 141–2.

25. This is a common feature of the historiography of Evangelicalism in this period. See, for example, K. Hylson Smith, *Evangelicals in the Church of England 1734–1984* (Edinburgh, 1989), pp. 227–9.

26. M. Smith, 'A foundation of influence: the Oxford Pastorate and elite recruitment in early twentieth-century Anglican evangelicalism', in D.W. Lovegrove, *The rise of the laity in evangelical Protestantism* (London, 2002), pp. 202–13; autobiographical memoir of William Talbot Rice (typescript copy in the possession of Mr Nigel Talbot Rice, Oxford), p. 18.

The choices available to the residents of the suburb whose spiritual inclinations lay towards Evangelicalism[27] or even to more traditional forms of High Churchmanship were severely restricted. St Giles, the ancient parish church, did offer plain services on traditional prayer book lines and a much more Protestant outlook than any of the new parishes to the north.[28] This was, however, little comfort to the residents, because the church was already overcrowded and thus unavailable to additional worshippers. The more consciously Protestant of the residents of the new suburb were thus faced with an unenviable choice of attending services which they found offensive or of trekking into the city centre to attend one of the Evangelical churches there. This latter option was difficult for the aged or infirm or for those with domestic responsibilities and thus a demand for another Anglican church at which plainer services might be guaranteed was quick to surface.[29] Proposals for such a church were put forward in 1874, 1879 and 1881 but each of these failed in the face of opposition, initially from St John's College and later from the pugnacious Anglo-Catholic vicar of St Philip and St James, E.C. Dermer, and from successive bishops of Oxford who objected to the vesting of the patronage of the parish in a private Evangelical trust.[30] By the turn of the century, however, with the need for a new church becoming ever more apparent, the disgruntled residents decided to try again, beginning with a memorial to the President of St John's which met with an encouraging response; and, although they were again rebuffed by Bishop Stubbs, circumstances soon appeared rather more propitious.[31] In 1900 Dermer moved on from St Philip and St James to be replaced by the distinctly more eirenic Charles Davey Biggs, and the following year a new bishop, Francis Paget, was appointed to the see of Oxford.[32]

On this occasion the promoters of the new church had a fully fledged and well-thought-out scheme with significant support. Financially the proposal was backed

---

27. Evangelicals at this period shared with traditional High Churchmen a commitment to the protestant basis of the Church of England and a preference for plain services according to the Book of Common Prayer. They retained, however, their distinctive theological emphasis on justification by grace through faith alone. For an excellent general account of late nineteenth- and early twentieth-century evangelicalism see D.W. Bebbington, *Evangelicalism in modern Britain* (London, 1989), pp. 151–228.

28. *Oxford Times*, 25 April 1903, 2 May 1903.

29. *Oxford Chronicle*, 27 June 1902.

30. St John's College, Oxford Archives (hereafter JCO): Estates Committee, 12 February 1874, 27 June 1879, 12 May 1882. Hinchcliffe, *North Oxford*, p. 142.

31. JCO, MUN V D 11, 128; J.S. Reynolds, *The evangelicals at Oxford 1735–1871: a record of an unchronicled movement with the record extended to 1905* (Appleford, 1975), p. 67; Church of England Record Centre (hereafter CERC), London, Church commissioners file 81,178, Part 1, Paget to Commissioners, 29 December 1904.

32. *P&J*, February 1900; E.H. Pearce and J.F.A. Mason, 'Francis Paget (1851–1911), bishop of Oxford', *ODNB*.

by William Talbot Rice, the vicar of St Peter-le-Bailey (one of the city-centre evangelical strongholds), who had agreed to raise £10,000 towards the establishment of a new church provided that its patronage was vested in the firmly evangelical, but eminently respectable, hands of the Council of Wycliffe Hall. This was a straightforward proposal under the provisions of the church-building acts that allowed the providers of significant endowment to hold or assign the patronage of new churches. The promoters also secured the support of the chief landowner and ecclesiastical patron in the area, St John's College, which had identified a plot on Linton Road that it would be prepared to donate as the site for a new church. They had even gained the consent of the new vicar of St Philip and St James to the division of his parish to allow the assignment of a district for the new church, between Bardwell and Linton Roads, which might be supplemented with land taken from the parish of Summertown, to the north (Plate 10).[33] In these circumstances – with the offer of a site and a substantial endowment and the consent of both the patron and the incumbent of the parish which was to be divided – the foundation of a new church should have been plain sailing.

Only when the bishop was approached did problems begin to emerge. The proposal was put to him in the form of a memorial signed by 134 householders whose residences were scattered all over North Oxford from St Giles to Summertown and also in a correspondence, opened in October 1901, by their chief spokesman, Colonel Le Mesurier. Le Mesurier, a barrister, City Councillor and former army chief engineer in Ireland, was a resident of St Margaret's Road – just a few yards from St Margaret's church – but a member of the congregation of St Peter-le-Bailey and a friend of Talbot Rice.[34] He was to prove a tenacious campaigner for the new church. The bishop took considerable time to make up his mind and it was not until 15 May 1902 that he provided a response. He appeared to welcome the proposal for an additional church, but refused to consent to the project unless the patronage be given to him, although he explained that, against his better judgement, he would consider a body of Trustees comprising himself, his archdeacon, the President of St John's and two evangelical representatives as an alternative.[35] Given the recent track record of the bishop of presenting ritualist clergymen to prominent benefices in his gift[36] such a proposal was unlikely to find favour with the memorialists, who, as Le Mesurier pointed out, considered themselves 'practically excommunicated from our

33. Memoir of Talbot Rice, pp. 41–2; Oxford Chronicle, 21 June 1902; Oxford Times, 14 March 1903.

34. Memoir of Talbot Rice, p. 40; J.S. Reynolds, Evangelicals, p. 67.

35. Oxford Chronicle, 27 June 1902; Oxford Times, 14 March 1903.

36. Oxford Times, 25 April 1903.

parish churches' by the ritual and doctrinal innovations they encountered. Indeed, security of patronage was the entire point, for the intention of the new church was to provide an ongoing ministry *not* for an ordinary town congregation but for what the Colonel described as 'a segregation of like elements from several adjacent parishes'. In addition to a desire for a greater share of patronage in the city,[37] the bishop may have been perturbed by the prospect of what the memorialists might do once gathered into a congregation under a ministry over which he could exert little control. One correspondent of the *Oxford Times* suggested that the bishop's real fear was of an 'opposition church', and that 'a militant vicar with a freehold in the north of Oxford might seriously disturb the peace of the neighbourhood'.[38] The bishop appeared immovable and, in search of a way around the roadblock, Le Mesurier wrote unsuccessfully to the Ecclesiastical Commissioners to enquire whether they might be able to constitute a new district without the bishop's consent. Davey Biggs, meanwhile, in an attempt to assist his aggrieved parishioners, pursued an alternative scheme for a chapel of ease to provide more traditional prayer book services – a scheme that would have proved acceptable to the bishop but offered insufficient security to the memorialists.[39]

The Colonel, however, had already deployed his heavy artillery. A supplementary memorial signed by 15 of the more prominent supporters of the scheme was sent to the bishop and subsequently published in the local press. Faced with a list of signatories that included prominent local lawyers, businessmen and city councillors, a three times Mayor of Oxford, the professors of Arabic, Chemistry and Classical Archaeology and the Grinfield Lecturer in Biblical Greek, not to mention the Sub-librarian of the Bodleian and the Secretary of the Curators of University Chest, it was not so easy to write off the scheme as unreasonable or fanatically militant.[40] Although the bishop initially stood firm, faced with opposition of this calibre and a scheme that was attracting increasing support from elsewhere[41] he ultimately took refuge in that traditional ploy of ecclesiastical bureaucracy, the appointment of a commission. In this case,

---

37. *Oxford Chronicle*, 27 June 1902.

38. *Oxford Times*, 21 March 1903.

39. CERC, Church commissioners file 81,178, Part 1, Le Mesurier to the Ecclesiastical Commissioners, 7 April 1903; JCO, MUN V D 11, C. Davey Biggs to the President, 15 June 1903; *P&J*, January 1903; *Oxford Times*, 14 March 1903.

40. CERC, Church commissioners file 81,178, Part 1, Ms Notes. *Oxford Times*, 14 March 1903. Some opponents of the scheme nevertheless continued to attempt to portray it in that way. *Church Times*, 20 March 1903.

41. For example, from the vicar of St Giles and E.H. Gifford, the former archdeacon of London. *Oxford Times*, 18 April 1903, 3 December 1904.

however, Paget took care that it should be under the safe chairmanship of the bishop of Reading.[42] The commissioners' report, when it appeared in December of 1903, must therefore have come as something of a bombshell. It was unanimous on the need for improved provision in North Oxford and the desirability of achieving this both by expanding the district previously assigned to St Margaret's and by establishing a new church. This latter proposal was greeted unenthusiastically by the bishop, but even less palatable was the Commissioners' conclusion on the matter of patronage, where they voted by a majority of one to accept the proposal that it be assigned, as the promoters had wished, to Evangelical patrons. Finally cornered, the bishop had little choice but to accede, although his disappointment was apparent in his response to the report:

> my anxiety to abide, so far as I rightly can, by the outcome of the
> Commission which I appointed, leads me to say that I shall not refuse
> assent to the constitution of the new parish, even with the condition
> attached to the contribution of £10,000. Further than this I cannot go.
> Much more than £10,000 will be needed for the building of the Church
> and the constitution and endowment of the parish: and I could not
> support or commend an appeal ...[43]

Rarely can a bishop have greeted the offer of a new church less warmly. However, Le Mesurier and his committee, noting that the bishop had agreed both to the construction of a new church on Linton Road and to their patronage arrangements, immediately sought to put the scheme agreed with the vicar of St Philip and St James into effect. Talbot Rice began his fundraising and by October 1904 had gathered enough to deposit £5,000 as the endowment for the parish. This enabled a formal application for the establishment of the new district, provisionally named St Andrew's (which included land taken from both St Philips and St James and Summertown), to be lodged with the Ecclesiastical Commissioners.[44] On 1 December Le Mesurier and his committee convened a public meeting at Wycliffe Hall with Davey Biggs in the chair to report on progress and encourage additional support. They were able to report a donation of £250 for the immediate construction of a temporary building so that services

---

42. JCO, MUN V D 11, Copy of Bishop's commission.

43. *Report of the commissioners together with the reply of the Lord Bishop* (Copy in Bodl., G.A. Oxon 4° 394ᵃ; hereafter Madan scrapbook).

44. Madan scrapbook, Le Mesurier to Madan, 16 April 1904; CERC, Church commissioners file 81,178, Part 1, Le Mesurier to Ecclesiastical Commissioners, 10 October 1904.

Fig. 13.1 St Andrew's, North Oxford (Henry W. Taunt, 1908). © Oxfordshire County Council Photographic Archive.

could begin as soon as possible, and that the bishop had relented so far as to donate £20 towards the cost of the church.[45]

Finally the establishment of St Andrew's appeared to be plain sailing; but just at this point Robert Hartley took a hand. Hartley had been appointed by E.C. Dermer as a curate to work in the district that eventually became the parish of St Margaret's, and when that church was founded he became its first incumbent. His motive was straightforwardly financial. His parish was poorly endowed, with

45. *Oxford Times*, 3 December 1904.

an income of only £90 a year, and he wanted to secure its future by extending it in the way most likely to increase its value – by taking in a substantial number of larger properties to the east of the Banbury Road. He thus applied, with the support of his vestry (backed by petitions signed by 202 parishioners and 134 non-resident members of his congregation), to the bishop, St John's and the Ecclesiastical Commissioners for such an extension to be granted (Plate 11). This proposal would effectively pre-empt the assignment of a district to St Andrew's.[46] Noting the incompatibility of the two schemes, the Commissioners approached Paget in February 1905 for guidance as to an acceptable solution. The bishop explained that one of the possible configurations favoured by his own Commission had been to extend St Margaret's eastward so that its northern boundary would run along the middle of Linton Road, and he recommended this third configuration as a means of conciliating Hartley while still leaving enough space to squeeze in a district for the new church (Plate 12).[47]

Le Mesurier and his committee were aghast. After apparently agreeing to the creation of their new parish with a church on Linton Road, the bishop had now suggested to the Comissioners that the district in which several of them lived, including the site offered by St John's College for their new church building, should be assigned to the parish of St Margaret's. Indeed, from their point of view, while a viable district was desirable even more crucial was the location of the church itself. Intended to cater for those alienated by Anglo-Catholicism in the whole area from Walton Manor to Summertown, it was essential that it be located as centrally as possible and if the Linton Road site were denied them they would be pushed to the next available location on the newly developed Lathbury Road – much too far north to achieve their purpose.[48]

In the event the effect of these developments was to widen the controversy from a simple contest between the North Oxford Protestants and their bishop by adding a further conflict between different varieties of Anglo-Catholicism. For, as their correspondence with the Ecclesiastical Commission makes clear, Hartley and his colleague Davey Biggs were far from seeing eye to eye. The changes made by Davey Biggs shortly after his arrival seem to have troubled some of the congregation of St Philip and St James and a number left to attend St Margaret's. Davey Biggs noted this process in his return to the bishop's visitation of 1902, commenting on 'the

46. JCO, MUN V D 11, Hartley to the President, 24 September 1904, Vestry Resolutions and Petitions, 15 November 1904.

47. CERC, Church commissioners file 81,178, Part 1, Commissioners to Paget, 24 November 1904, Paget to Commissioners, 29 December 1904.

48. CERC, Church commissioners file 81,178, Part 1, Le Mesurier to Commissioners, 22 February 1905.

attachment of former worshippers less to God and his Church than to details of ministry and ritual'.[49] In this context, it is significant that almost all of the 134 non-resident members of the St Margaret's congregation who signed the memorial of 1904 lived in the parish of St Philip and St James. Moreover, while the endowment of his parish was poor, Hartley himself was extremely wealthy. He chose to live not in one of the substantial residential properties on St Margaret's Road itself but in the largest single property in the whole of North Oxford – 'The Mount' on Banbury Road, set in extensive grounds almost twice as big as those of its nearest competitor and with its own entrance lodge. Hartley seems to have used this asset to extend both his own social consequence in the neighbourhood and the influence of his parish. In 1900, for example, Hartley secured the presidency of the prestigious St Philip and St James and St Margaret's Horticultural Society, whose patrons were the duke and duchess of Marlborough and whose president had previously been the vicar of the mother church. His grounds at The Mount became the invariable location of the society's great annual show and the parish magazine and local newspapers regularly printed glowing reports of the ever more elaborate entertainments laid on by Mr and Mrs Hartley.[50] Davey Biggs certainly seems to have been concerned about this aspect of his colleague's ministry and commented somewhat acidly on the 'generous hospitality' that 'has attached to Mr Hartley so many of his adherents'.[51] The vicar of St Philip and St James was, moreover, clearly taken aback by both the force and the substance of Hartley's intervention, of which he had no inkling until after the applications had been made to the commissioners, the patrons and the bishop. As he explained to the *Oxford Times*:

> I have never had any communication on the subject with Mr Hartley, and am therefore unaware of his feelings about it. It is impossible for me to suppose that had he desired the extension of his parish at the expense of mine, he would never have alluded to the subject to me either in conversation or by correspondence. This however is the case.[52]

Davey Biggs might have consented to Paget's compromise if it had proved acceptable to all parties, but he clearly considered himself to be under a prior

---

49. JCO, MUN V D 11, Dermer to the President, 31 March 1905; Oxfordshire Record Office (hereafter ORO), Oxford, Ms Dioc Oxf C368.

50. *P&J*, September 1896, February 1900, September 1902, September 1903; *Oxford Times*, 8 December 1900, 17 August 1901.

51. CERC Church commissioners file 81,178 Part 1, Davey Biggs to Commissioners, n.d.

52. *Oxford Times*, 1 April 1905.

obligation to the promoters of St Andrew's; and his preferred solution to the problem of St Margaret's had been to extend it northwards and also to attach to it an area of smaller houses to the south-west of St Margaret's parish which was located rather closer to Hartley's church (see Plate 10). In consideration of this he had also offered to increase the income of St Margaret's by £15 a year at the expense of his own. [53] This scheme had been refused by Hartley (despite the fact that over a third of the signatures from his non-resident congregational petition came from the area to the south-west proposed by Davey Biggs), who clearly preferred the more congenial prospect of ministering to the inhabitants of the larger properties to the east of the Banbury Road. Hartley did suggest, however, that he might be willing to extend his parish northward to take in the substantial houses to be built there in the near future, if the eastward extension was granted according to his original specification. This proposal would have made it virtually impossible to find space for a new district anywhere in North Oxford. [54] In the event, after consultation with the bishop, the Commissioners tried a compromise of their own: a combination of Paget's version of the extension to the east with the exclusion of the site of the new church and Davey Biggs' extension to the south-west. [55] Predictably, this proved acceptable to no one. By March 1905 Hartley (despite an attempt at mediation by Dermer, who was moved to describe his own protégé as 'an obstinate Yorkshireman') was threatening to resign if he did not get his own way. [56] The bishop nevertheless persisted and could be found as late as May 1905 attempting to salvage some version of his scheme for the enlargement of St Margaret's to the east. [57]

He was halted, in the end, not by the increasingly frustrated evangelicals but by the equally impatient Anglo-Catholic Davey Biggs, who reckoned, as he informed the Ecclesiastical Commissioners, that as soon as the new church in its original district 'becomes an actual fact, the better will it be for the peace, as I believe, and spiritual development of the Church in North Oxford'. Biggs pointed out that a northward extension of Hartley's parish should meet the real needs of the district since 'The class of houses being built in the new streets to the north of the present boundary of St Margaret's are of so good a class that the residents in them would presumably be able to contribute handsomely to the funds of whatever parish they were assigned to', although he could not resist adding 'they could not of course be compelled to attend St Margaret's'. He also

53. CERC, Church commissioners file 81,178, Part 1, Davey Biggs to Commissioners, n.d.; *P&J*, July 1905.

54. CERC, Church commissioners file 81,178, Part 1, Paget to Commissioners, 29 December 1904.

55. *Oxford Times*, 8 April 1905.

56. JCO, MUN V D 11, Hartley to the President, 19 March 1905, Dermer to the President, 31 March 1905.

57. CERC, Church commissioners file 81,178 Part 1, Paget to Commissioners, 27 May 1905.

noted that 'My parishioners who desire the erection of St Andrew's will not like being transferred from me to St Margaret's – in fact I may safely say they would prefer being under my charge.'[58] He effectively called a halt to this round of the dispute by refusing consent to the division of his parish if the disputed portion were to be handed over to St Margaret's. The Ecclesiastical Commissioners consequently granted a district to St Andrew's incorporating the area between Bardwell and Linton Roads.[59] The promoters pressed on with building their new church, which was finally opened in 1907 (the temporary building having been converted, perhaps appropriately, into a rifle range) (Fig. 13.1).[60] In 1906 Hartley, having failed to achieve the kind of district he wanted for St Margaret's, finally resigned as its incumbent.[61]

At one level this intricate dispute about patronage in the Church of England and the minutiae of parish boundaries can be read as a small controversy of only local interest. Read with close attention, however, it draws attention to three features often overlooked in more general accounts of the early twentieth-century Church of England. One is the variety of religious cultures accommodated under the umbrella of the Established Church and their capacity to combine in unexpected and complex ways. The promoters of St Andrew's were a coalition of convinced Evangelicals and more traditional High Churchmen who saw in an evangelical patronage trust a way of ensuring the provision of Anglican services free from ritualist innovations in doctrine and practice. The potential and outcomes of this sort of alliance in the early twentieth-century Church deserves more reflection from historians – especially as the longevity of Protestantism as a source of identity, through the crisis over Prayer Book revision and beyond, comes under new scrutiny.[62] The creation of St Andrew's was facilitated by the intervention of an eirenic Anglo-Catholic incumbent with serious pastoral intentions and a scepticism about what he may have regarded as the champagne and garden party Anglo-Catholicism of his North Oxford colleague. This contrast is suggestive of more complex and nuanced taxonomies of the Anglican clergy than those yielded by the application of the simple party labels to which historians remain addicted.

Perhaps most revealing of all is the light shed by this episode on the functioning of the parish system. Loyalty to any given parish church had long

---

58. CERC Church commissioners file 81,178 Part 1, Davey Biggs to Commissioners, n.d.; 6 October 1905.

59. CERC, Church commissioners file 81,178 Part 1, Davey Biggs to Commissioners, n.d., 25 April 1905; Paget to Commissioners, 27 July 1905.

60. *Oxford Times*, 6 June 1908.

61. *St Margaret's Oxford Parish Magazine*, April 1906.

62. J. Maiden, *National religion and the prayer book controversy, 1927–1928* (Woodbridge, 2009).

been negotiable in urban environments; but this phenomenon is depicted with unusual clarity within the suburb of North Oxford where Hartley, for example, could cite his success in attracting members of his congregation from another parish as grounds for extending his parish boundaries to cover their place of residence. Indeed, so established was this phenomenon in the area that Davey Biggs assured his vestry in 1906:

> That it would be impossible to secure by any rearrangement of boundaries that all people resident within a particular district would attend or support the parish Church of that district; and that the frank acceptance of the congregational principle was in present circumstances the wisest and happiest course.[63]

The solution found in this case, however (an innovation whose legitimacy none of the parties in the dispute seem to have questioned), was a step further – the creation of a parish church which was never intended to act as a *parish* church. A church designed to draw in the disaffected from all the surrounding parishes – Le Mesurier's 'segregation of like elements' – explicitly promoted in such terms and approved for that purpose by the Church authorities would have been unthinkable only two or three decades earlier. The founding of St Andrew's as a church with a mission to the whole of North Oxford demonstrates the capacity of the clash of Anglican cultures in the early twentieth century, perhaps especially when promoted by influential laymen, to disrupt not just individual parishes but the whole notion of parochial Anglicanism itself. This kind of official endorsement of consumer choice as a way of negotiating religious difference was to have incalculable consequences for the Church in the second half of the century and beyond.

---

63. ORO, PAR 216/2/A1/1, St Philip and St James Vestry Minutes, 24 April 1905.

14. The kings bench (crown side) in the long eighteenth century

Ruth Paley

Prosecuting misdemeanour

On 22 June 1772 John Day broke a window while riding in a hackney coach from Oxford Street to Temple Bar. When Day refused to pay for the damage he and the coachman, Richard Watson, began an argument that developed into a scuffle. Afterwards Watson, accompanied by a sympathetic crowd, followed Day to his chambers in the Temple, still demanding payment. Day invited him in, locked the door and threatened him before kicking him down the stairs. Day (a barrister and undoubtedly a gentleman) was so angry with this upstart coachman that he complained about him to the hackney coach commissioners, thus ensuring that Watson lost his licence – and with it, his livelihood. Watson retaliated by prosecuting Day for assault at the Middlesex sessions. Day was convicted and fined £5. The jury directed the two men to talk, meaning that they wanted the two men to settle their differences. Watson agreed to reduce the fine to a shilling if Day would help him get his licence reinstated, but even when this was done he could not afford to set himself up in business again and continued to harbour a grudge. Realising that the assault had occurred on both sides of Temple Bar (the border between the City of London and Middlesex), he began another prosecution at the City of London sessions, which he then transferred to the court of kings bench by a writ of *certiorari*. This second case ended only when the two men entered another mediation process. We know about it in such detail because that process was conducted by means of written affidavits that still survive.

As this case demonstrates, information about minor crimes can be extremely illuminating about the everyday activities and preoccupations of ordinary people and their communities. What seems surprising is that it ended up in the kings bench, the highest court of common law in England and Wales, rather than at quarter or even petty sessions. This chapter concentrates on the criminal jurisdiction or 'crown side' of the court, and falls into two parts: an introductory overview of the court and its processes followed by a guide to the major series of records in the National Archives which the researcher needs to tackle in order to build a picture of particular cases or localities.

Process in the kings bench was expensive, which, in an age when starting and sustaining a prosecution was more often a matter for private individuals than for the state, made it a particularly useful weapon for individuals determined to harass their enemies.[1] Cases heard in kings bench also attracted a disproportionate amount of public and press attention, which was sometimes attractive in itself. Some cases addressed tricky points of law, and some resulted from serious misdemeanours such as libel, fraud and perjury, but many, especially in the City of London and its urban overspill, were, like John Day's, remarkably trivial. And, again like John Day's, many were settled by a mediation process which involved the submission of written statements in mitigation and aggravation.

The kinds of case that could be taken to the kings bench were governed by complex procedural rules. For the researcher anxious to get at the 'meat' of a case, these may at first seem both daunting and irrelevant, but it is necessary to understand something about them in order to understand the intricacies of the records they created. Unlike other criminal courts, the kings bench had multiple jurisdictions and the way in which it interpreted its jurisdictional rules was subject to far-reaching but piecemeal alterations over time.

Supervisory jurisdiction

Supervisory jurisdiction enabled the kings bench to review the actions of the lower courts by means of a series of writs. The most commonly used of these writs was *certiorari*, which transferred proceedings from inferior courts into kings bench. *Certiorari* was used to remove indictments and, less frequently, summary convictions (that is, convictions that did not involve a jury). It was also used to remove and review orders made by the lower courts, most often those that related to decisions made by lay magistrates about the settlement and removal of paupers.

The potential abuses of *certiorari* led to proposals for statutory reforms that were discussed in parliament as early as 1667; a bill passed the Commons but failed in the Lords, apparently because of the opposition of the judges (not unrelated to the prospect of a diminution in fee income).[2] Piecemeal restrictions

---

1. For the remainder of this essay all references to the kings bench are to be construed as references to crown side.

2. Parl. Archives, Committee book 2, 15 and 18 February, 22 April 1668.

were made after the Revolution of 1688, sometimes by statute and sometimes by decisions of the judges. The first major restriction came in 1694, when a statute required defendants seeking *certiorari* to enter into recognisances to pay costs to the prosecutor. Later it came to be said that granting or refusing a *certiorari* to a defendant had always been within the discretion of the court and that it was necessary for defendants to show good reason for the application. In reality, 'good reason' was a somewhat elastic concept. In the absence of other factors, a defendant's desire for a special jury (one chosen from higher-ranking individuals than normal) did not constitute good reason; his rank and consequence, which amounted to much the same thing, did.[3] From the mid-1730s (and probably earlier) the court decided that it would no longer permit *certiorari* to be used to transfer cases from courts where one or more of the royal judges presided – i.e. the assizes and the Old Bailey – without evidence of good cause or the consent of the prosecutor. As a result *certiorari* came to be concentrated on those courts where justices of the peace officiated.[4] By the second half of the nineteenth century *certiorari* on an indictment was only available in cases that raised difficult questions of law, and where *certiorari* was used to remove indictments from assizes it was usually as a preliminary to outlawry. Such cases were rare. Between 1740 and 1800, 24 Staffordshire indictments were removed to kings bench; only one was specifically intended to result in outlawry.[5] To date extensive sampling of cases arising in London and Middlesex for six sample years chosen at roughly 40-year intervals between 1700 and the abolition of the court in 1875 has not revealed a similar case (total sample: 290 writs of *certiorari* on indictment).

The writ of *habeas corpus* has an iconic status in the popular history of British liberties. In practice, after the Revolution of 1688 the well-established procedures of the English courts meant that most persons imprisoned and awaiting trial for ordinary, non-political crimes had little need of the writ.[6] More commonly, the illegal imprisonment was a domestic matter. Through their responses to applications for *habeas corpus*, wives and daughters give us first-hand testimony of their experiences at the hands of husbands and fathers whose patterns of behaviour ranged from the merely unsympathetic to out-and-out brutality. In 1766 Ann Gregory, not yet 20 years old, described how at the age of 14 she had eloped with

---

3. R. Gude, *The practice of the crown side of the court of kings bench*, 2 vols (London, 1828), 1, pp. 136–7.

4. *The English Reports*, 177 vols (Edinburgh, 1900–1932), 94, p. 611, 93, pp. 693, 804, 911, 1127.

5. Another ended in outlawry but that had not been the primary purpose of the *certiorari*. D. Hay, *Criminal cases on the crown side of kings bench 1740–1800*, Staffordshire Record Society, 4th series (Stafford, 2010), forthcoming.

6. Note, too, that there were several forms of the writ, including one that was used to move prisoners from the jurisdiction in which they had been arrested and imprisoned to the jurisdiction in which they were to face trial.

Abraham Gregory and married him. Within a few months her mother, driven by her fear of the shame of illegitimacy, consented to a second (and unquestionably legal) ceremony. Ann Gregory soon lost her romantic illusions. Her husband was a drunkard who did not work (even when set up in his own business by his new mother-in-law) and who repeatedly threatened and assaulted her. When she became pregnant, he resorted to that age-old abortifacient, the kick in the belly. He also gave her venereal disease. After two years, she fled to France with her mother's help. We know of her plight because Abraham Gregory was determined to regain control of his wife (and the few hundred pounds she stood to inherit) and chose to do so via an application for *habeas corpus* in which he accused his mother-in-law of 'seducing' his wife away and concealing her whereabouts. Because the case raised interesting legal issues about the rights of husbands over their wives a brief account is included in the formal law reports, but it is only by reading the affidavits preserved in the archive of the kings bench that the fuller story is revealed.[7]

Another use of *habeas corpus* was to settle child custody disputes. Lord and Lady Valentia took just such a case to the court in 1796. Newspapers had no hesitation in reporting that Lady Valentia was living in adultery; her husband's sexual reputation was a rather different matter. The press reported that Lady Valentia's affidavits, making 'foul imputations' about her husband, had shocked all who heard them. Valentia's barrister, Thomas Erskine, remarked that, if the allegations were true, Valentia was not only unfit to have custody of a child but unfit to live in society. The inference of homosexuality is obvious but the newspapers' self-imposed censorship meant that until the publication of Hay's *Criminal cases*, some 200 years later, details about Valentia's alleged relationship with his valet (and his repudiation of them) were available only in the kings bench archive.[8]

Habeas corpus applications also throw light on the plight of the mentally disordered. In 1759 Margaret Hicks protested that her feeble-minded brother had been virtually kidnapped by a woman pretending to be his wife whose sole motive was to take 'some unjust advantage of his person and property'.[9] Other cases provide disturbing evidence about the activities of private mad-houses, revealing just how easy it was to dispose of a difficult or unwanted relative in such a place. Often, but not invariably, the unwanted relative was a female whose incarceration left her husband or other male guardian in undisputed possession of her money and property.[10]

---

7. The National Archives (hereafter TNA), KB 1/16, Mich. 7 Geo. III, affdts. Ann Gregory, 28 November 1766 and of Abraham Gregory, 6 November 1766; *English Reports*, 98, p. 38.

8. *Star*, 28 April 1796; *Sun*, 5 May 1796; *Gazetteer and New Daily Advertiser*, 6 and 10 May 1796; Hay, *Criminal cases*.

9. TNA, KB 1/14/4, Trin. 33&34 Geo. II, Re Thomas Hicks Esq, affdt. Margaret Hickes and another, 16 June 1759.

10. See, for example, the case of D. D'Vebre, cited in B. Hill (ed.), *Eighteenth century women: an anthology* (London, 1984), pp. 146–7. The original affidavits are at TNA, KB 1/14/3.

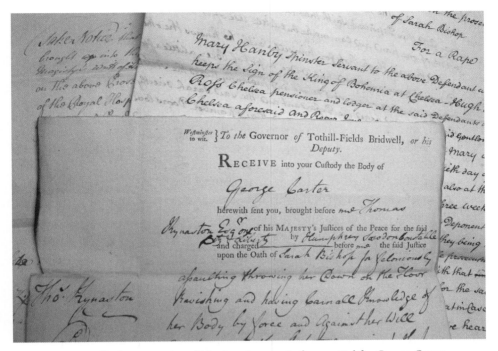

Fig. 14.1 Notice of bail, prosecution affidavit and warrant of committal for George Carter, charged with the rape of Sarah Bishop. TNA, KB 1/19/2, Mich. 1772.

During the law terms there was, until 1785, a specific jurisdictional issue in Middlesex which meant that prisoners requesting bail had to use *habeas corpus* to bring the matter before a judge. Their applications often reveal full details of the proposed defence. In 1772 George Carter and Thomas Denby, accused in two separate cases of raping their female servants, did just this. Both used the same solicitor; both ran virtually identical defences. They marshalled an array of witnesses (all of whom were financially dependent on them) to paint a picture of an innocent man falsely accused by a vindictive and mendacious woman. So successful was the defence strategy that only one, George Carter, was actually tried – and he was speedily acquitted. There is a printed account of his trial but the affidavits in the kings bench archive are much fuller and provide a chilling picture of the vulnerability of very young girls hired as maids by predatory males.[11] They

---

11. In both cases the *habeas corpus* is filed at TNA, KB 16/17/3 with affidavits in KB 1/19/2. Process entries for Denby are in KB 21/40, Mich 13 Geo. III, Fri. after the morrow of St Martin; for Carter in KB 21/40, Mich. 13 Geo. III, Wed. on the octave of St Martin, Mon. after the octave of St Martin, Hil. 13 Geo. III, Fri. after the octave of the purification of the blessed Virgin Mary; details of Carter's trial in December 1772 are available via <http://www.oldbaileyonline.org/> accessed 9 December 2010.

also provide information that is otherwise rarely available, such as the names, addresses and occupations of the men prepared to offer bail for Carter and of the magistrate and constable responsible for his arrest and committal (Fig. 14.1).

Mandamus provided a method of compelling inferior courts, magistrates and other offending parties to take particular courses of action in cases where justice had allegedly been obstructed. It was occasionally used by alliances of discontented rate payers and other action groups to order the production, inspection or copying of books and papers in an attempt to uncover evidence of wrongdoing by local government officials, and was often used to compel the admission or restoration of persons to office (whether spiritual or temporal). Even more commonly, it was used to compel the election of mayors of boroughs or to challenge the composition of corporations and thus to influence electoral outcomes.[12]

Lesser-used processes included writs of error, which permitted a form of (very limited) appeal, of prohibition, which ordered an inferior court to cease any action over the case in question, and *excommunicato capiendo* (issued by Chancery but returned to kings bench in order to authorise the sheriff of the relevant jurisdiction to arrest the excommunicant). A further writ, that of *quo warranto*, had been used extensively and notoriously in the reigns of Charles II and James II to alter the chartered rights of corporations and thus to secure their political compliance.[13] During the reign of Queen Anne it was largely superseded by a new form of process, the information in the form of a *quo warranto* which is discussed below.

Original jurisdiction

Following the abolition of Star Chamber in the mid-seventeenth century the kings bench was said to have acquired 'all that was good and salutary' of its jurisdiction.[14] This gave it immediate ('original') jurisdiction over any action that could be construed as criminal throughout England and Wales 'as the *custos morum* [guardian of the morals] of all the subjects of the realm'.[15] By the eighteenth century it had restricted its jurisdiction to crimes classified as misdemeanours. As with supervisory jurisdiction, there were several ways in which cases could be initiated.

---

12. R. Sedgwick (ed.), *The House of Commons 1715–1754*, 2 vols (London, 1970), 1, p. 506, 2, pp. 189, 390; L. Namier and J. Brooke (eds), *The House of Commons, 1754–1790*, 3 vols (London, 1985), 2, p. 132; R.G. Thorne (ed.), *The House of Commons 1790–1820*, 5 vols (London, 1986), 2, pp. 42, 82, 459, 493. Newspaper evidence indicates that the use of *mandamus* for political purposes was far more widespread than these references suggest.

13. For a detailed study of the local impact of the Stuart brothers' *quo warranto* campaign, see P. Halliday, *Dismembering the body politic: partisan politics in England's towns, 1650–1730* (Cambridge, 1998).

14. W. Blackstone, *Commentaries on the laws of England*, 4 vols (Oxford, 1765–9), 4, p. 263.

15. Gude, *The practice of the crown side of the court of kings bench*, 1, p. 5.

Informations *ex officio* were those exhibited by the attorney (sometimes the solicitor) general for offences that 'peculiarly tend to disturb or endanger the kings government ... [and are] ... so high and dangerous, in the punishment or prevention of which a moment's delay would be fatal'.[16] At times of political unrest they were used in cases of seditious libel; at other times they were employed to prosecute offences such as assaults on customs officers. The process bypassed the grand jury and there was no opportunity for the defendant to discover the strengths and weaknesses of the prosecution case until the actual trial. Not surprisingly, informations *ex officio* were regarded as a particularly contentious abuse of executive power. Concerted criticism of the process meant that it had largely fallen into disuse by the 1830s, although it was not abolished until the second half of the twentieth century.

Criminal informations were exhibited by the master of the court on the complaint of a private individual. Like informations *ex officio*, the procedure bypassed a grand jury but from 1692 it was necessary for the prosecutor to establish, to the satisfaction of the master of the court, that there was a case to be answered. Written affidavits were supplemented by oral arguments from barristers. Criminal informations were used to prosecute a range of offences including libel, forgery, perjury and riot. The use of affidavits means that even unsuccessful attempts to prosecute an information can be extremely revealing.

Informations *qui tam* were prosecutions initiated by informers for specific offences created by statute. The informer was rewarded by receiving a share of the fine. A variety of offences could be prosecuted in this way but the largest category was offences against the game laws, which could be prosecuted either in the local courts or, from 1721, in the central courts at Westminster, including kings bench.[17] Almost by definition such offences were characteristic of rural or fringe urban areas. The evidence from Staffordshire suggests that in such areas informations *qui tam* may have been the most commonly used kings bench process. The proceedings required an initial affidavit of the facts but these were filed separately from the main series of affidavits and only specimens survive, so it is necessary to trace cases through the procedural records.[18]

As noted above, writs of *quo warranto* were superseded by informations in the nature of *quo warranto*. These were brought under the Municipal Offices Act[19] and tested whether an office (mayor, bailiff, burgess, alderman, freeman), was

---

16. Blackstone, *Commentaries*, 4, p. 304.

17. 8 Geo. I c.19.

18. TNA, KB 32/23.

19. 9 Anne c.25.

legitimately held by an individual. Like the writ, such informations were associated with attempts to influence, or overturn, the results of parliamentary elections. Unlike the writ, they took the form of a criminal prosecution and aimed to punish the defendant with a fine as well as to remove him from office. The preliminary procedure mimicked that of a criminal information in that it required the leave of the court and thus generated written submissions which are very revealing about the composition and nature of the ruling elites in local corporations (including the City of London).

Articles of the peace were exhibited by persons who claimed to be in physical danger from an opponent. It was up to court to decide whether the danger justified intervention; if it did the defendant would be required to enter recognisances to keep the peace for a year. Failure to do so would lead to imprisonment – as Anthony Robinson discovered when his wife swore the peace against him in June 1771. He was in gaol for nearly two years before obtaining a discharge.[20] The defendant could not dispute the allegations, except by prosecuting for perjury. Very few original articles of the peace survive, so it can be difficult to reconstruct the details except in cases where exhibiting articles of the peace was a preliminary to a parallel indictment for assault.

Local jurisdiction

The presence of the kings bench within any county extinguished all other jurisdictions. As it had been settled in Westminster Hall since the later Middle Ages this gave it jurisdiction of first instance in Middlesex and Westminster. The nature of this local jurisdiction makes the kings bench an exceptionally important source for the history of the various local communities that made up the metropolis, especially as the survival of records of the Middlesex sessions is extremely poor. In effect, during term time the kings bench substituted for the sessions, calling its own grand juries and even summoning the Middlesex and Westminster constables to make presentments of wrongdoing in their parishes.

The caseload and its geographical distribution

The caseload that resulted from this multiplicity of jurisdictions and processes was hugely varied: accusations of nuisance (disorderly houses, ruined pavements) and assault jostled for attention alongside charges of seditious libel and treason. In between these extremes lay cases of criminal libel, pornography, corruption, extortion, fraud, forgery, perjury, riot, illegal imprisonment and politically motivated attacks on the electorate of corporations. Furthermore, the

20. TNA, KB 21/40, Fri. after 15 days of Easter, 13 Geo. III.

surviving affidavits regularly alert the researcher to otherwise opaque underlying local issues. Thus an attempt to overthrow the conviction of an alleged hawker by the mayor of Carlisle in 1772 reveals the underhand methods by which the town's shopkeepers conspired to remove competitors.[21] Similarly, an apparently straightforward dispute over licensing an alehouse in Montgomeryshire (modern Powis) provides an insight into the local power struggle that resulted from the decline of the once dominant Pryce family of Newtown Hall.[22]

Although the court was resident in Westminster Hall most trials were remitted back to be heard locally under a writ of *nisi prius*. Removing a trial from local jurisdiction to the kings bench and then allowing it to be returned may seem, superficially, to have been a pointless exercise, but the objective was either to harass one's opponent or to obtain a special jury – which, as noted above, consisted of individuals subject to a higher property qualification than normal.

The kings bench heard appeals from Ireland until 1782. It was also empowered to hear cases against colonial officials, as when Thomas Picton, governor of Trinidad, was tried in 1806 for allowing the judicial torture of a young girl.[23] Its main business, however, was in England and Wales. Metropolitan business far outweighed that of any other county. Between 1740 and 1800 it has been calculated that Staffordshire produced a total of 119 cases (excluding *habeas corpus*);[24] the comparable metropolitan caseload ran at between 150 and 250 cases every year. Even in the provinces it seems that the inhabitants of some counties resorted to kings bench more readily than others. The explanation for the high case load in the London area probably lies in the social structure of the metropolis, coupled with the ready availability of legal advice. Elsewhere in the country the variations are more difficult to explain. One hypothesis is that the presence of one or more parliamentary boroughs – with their propensity to electoral disputes – enabled local attorneys to develop procedural knowledge and useful contacts with London lawyers. Another hypothesis is that the social and economic structure of some counties might have stimulated a larger number of appeals resulting from poor law cases. Like electoral disputes, poor law appeals would create a pool of local expertise about the availability of redress from kings bench. An initial survey of provincial cases in Easter and Trinity terms of 1740 and 1773 merely confirms how much work remains to be done on these largely

---

21. TNA, KB 1/19/1/2, William Hunter and others, 3 July 1772.

22. TNA, KB 1/18/1/2, Bridget Vaughan, Bell Lloyd, 6 February 1770, KB 1/18/1/4, Sir John Powell Pryce, 12 May 1770.

23. *State Trials*, 30. cols 676–960, 1345–6.

24. Hay, *Criminal cases*.

unexploited records. The two samples confirm a wide geographical spread of cases, from Cumberland in the north to Sussex in the south and Cornwall in the west, but provide no obvious clues to explain the pattern of distribution. Perhaps in the end we might be left with the most difficult of all hypotheses to prove, the creation of local knowledge through the activities of a single determinedly litigious individual or group.

Searching for cases

The records are organised in complex, overlapping series with no single point of entry, and in order to trace the progress and outcome of a case it is necessary to track it across several series of records. To make matters even more difficult, there is no adequate guide to help or encourage users and the records are poorly listed. Local historians are fortunate in that the original organisation of the records almost always includes an indication of the county or corporation in which the case arose. *Habeas corpus* applications and articles of the peace are exceptions to this because they were technically in a country-wide jurisdiction; even here, however, the clerks often added a note of the county.

Informations, together with indictments and convictions removed by *certiorari*, are numbered and arranged by term: those for London and Middlesex defendants 1675 to 1845 are in record series KB 10; provincial or 'out county' defendants 1676 to 1845 are in KB 11. Informations can be distinguished from indictments by their opening rubric: an information begins 'Be it remembered that' (*Memorandum quod*) followed by a reference either to the attorney general by name (in the case of an information *ex officio*) or to the master (coroner and attorney) of the court, also by name (in the case of an ordinary criminal information), while an indictment begins 'The jurors for our lord the king [or our lady the queen] on their oath present that' (*Juratores pro domini regis* [or *domina regina*] *super sacramentum suum presentant*). Indictments removed by *certiorari* are readily identifiable as they are attached to the writ of *certiorari* itself and to a caption which states when and where the indictment was originally filed.

Researchers need to bear in mind all the normal caveats of using legal records. Formal procedural entries (but not the text of affidavits) are written in Latin (often heavily abbreviated) and in archaic scripts until 1733. Some of the scripts and Latin abbreviations persisted in annotations even after that date. The most common ones are 'po.se.' (an abbreviated form of *ponit se super patriam*, literally 'puts him/herself on the country' and meaning pleads not guilty) and 'li. lo.' (*licentia loquendi*, literally liberty to speak or declare, meaning time given by the court to the defendant to enter a plea). The clerks' annotations are usually written above rather than below the item to which they refer. Annotations about process on indictments

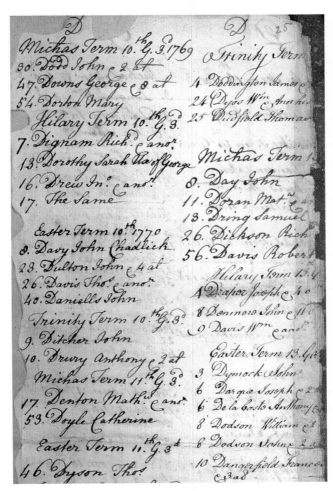

Fig. 14.2 Extract from the pye book showing London and Middlesex defendants with surnames beginning with D, 1769–72. TNA, IND 1/6674.

removed by *certiorari* are those that had been made in the lower courts, not in the kings bench. Indictments removed by *certiorari* are untrustworthy sources of information as they use conventional legal fictions, such as listing the place of the crime as the defendant's place of residence. Conversely, informations can provide useful detail, especially in cases of libel (whether seditious or criminal), as the information sets out exactly which words and phrases were alleged to be libellous.

Where the name of the defendant and a rough idea of the date of the case is known, the first step is to check whether there is a surviving pye book. These list informations and indictments alphabetically by first letter of the defendant's

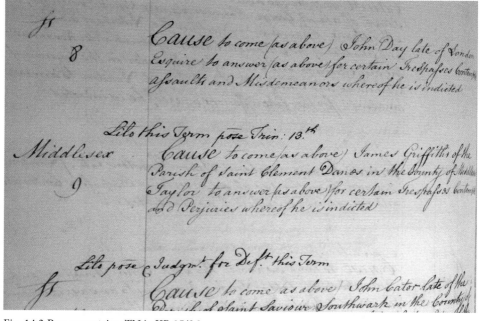

Fig. 14.3 Process entries. TNA, KB 15/26.

surname and then by year and term. The pye books for London and Middlesex defendants for the period from 1673 to 1843 are in IND 1/6669–6677; for provincial defendants 1638 to 1704 and 1765 to 1843 they are in IND 1/6680–6684. There are also two volumes listing London and Middlesex defendants and some defendants in northern counties 1682 to 1699 in IND 1/6678–6679. The number noted by the side of the defendant's name is a direct reference to the position of the information/indictment within the rolled file (Fig. 14.2).

If no pye book survives or the researcher is making a speculative search for criminal cases arising in a particular county or corporation then the most obvious course of action is to search the indictment files – each item on the file is clearly marked with its jurisdiction. There is, however, a useful shortcut. The first section of the controlment rolls (KB 29), known as the bag roll, lists all the cases begun each term with an entry in the left-hand margin indicating the county or corporation from which it originated and a numerical reference that links it directly to the informations and indictments in KB 10 or 11.

Having located an indictment or information the researcher then needs to go back to KB 29, or, if researching a case in London and Middlesex between 1737 and 1820, to the process books in KB 15 in order to track the case further. For London and Middlesex cases the preferred option would normally be to use one of the process books in KB 15. They are physically easy to handle and the entries are arranged chronologically in a clear and uncomplicated lay out. They are often annotated with the outcome of the case. In John Day's case the relevant process book is KB 15/26 (Fig. 14.3). Unfortunately this is one of the cases that is not annotated, so it is necessary to go back to the controlment rolls in KB 29, starting at the roll that includes Michaelmas 1772 (KB 29/432), instead. As already noted, the first section of KB 29 lists all the cases commenced by information or indictment in that term. The second section, the roll of entries, lists those cases in which some action has been taken. It is necessary to continue searching the second section of each successive term until an entry is found. In Day's case the entry is just one term later; in other cases it may be necessary to search further. The entry for Day shows that he allowed judgement to go by default (in effect threw himself on the mercy of the court) and was convicted in Hilary 1773. If there had been more steps in process the entry would look more like that for William Smith, on the same membrane. The entry and annotation taken together show that Smith entered a demurrer (a formal legal challenge) to the indictment and was acquitted. The words 'without day' below the entry mean that proceedings against him were terminated. The date of the judgement can be used to find the formal record of the case on the plea roll; the plea roll for Hilary 1773 is KB 28/283.

Further information about the progress of a case can be found in the rule books (KB 21) and draft rule books (KB 36). These are particularly useful for identifying the terms in which affidavits were filed and for discovering more about costs and sentencing. The rule book reveals that John Day was fined 6s 8d. Discovering that a defendant was fined 1s or 6s 8d, that judgement went by default or that the case was referred to the master all indicate that there was some sort of settlement between the parties. In such cases affidavits were used by both parties to tell their own versions of the story and usually include additional statements by witnesses. The affidavits can be extensive; even in a relatively straightforward case like that of John Day they run to some 5000 words. Entering the mediation process required defendants to allow themselves to be convicted, but they regularly used their affidavits to deny guilt. John Day was convicted but he still argued that his earlier conviction at the Middlesex sessions barred a second prosecution; he also justified his conduct, presenting himself as a respectable gentleman driven to extreme measures by an impertinent and ruffianly member of the lower classes.

Where the researcher is seeking information about a failed attempt to exhibit a criminal information, the key documents will again be in the affidavits (KB 1), with associated entries in the rule books (KB 21). The earliest affidavit in KB 1 dates from 1682 but the survival is generally poor until the later 1720s. They are not listed except by term and year, so finding relevant material is not an easy task, especially as the various affidavits relating to a case may be scattered in several different bundles. From 1738 some help is provided by the records in KB 39, which record, term by term, affidavits filed. However, they are listed by case rather than by deponent and the entries are known to be incomplete, probably because the volumes were meant as fee books rather than as genuine indexes. There is also a gap in the series between 1755 and 1760. To be absolutely sure of tracing all surviving affidavits it will almost always be necessary to reconstruct the procedural outlines of a case; this is in any event desirable because it will help identify the motivation behind the case as well as the final outcome.

A search for the removal of orders by *certiorari* will be rather more time-consuming. These documents are filed with the *recorda* in KB 16 in bulky files with no obvious filing order; each document has to be read carefully in order to identify it. The *recorda* files also include original writs of *habeas corpus* endorsed with the 'return' – the reasons that allegedly justified the detention of the individual in question. Copies of writs issued, with the returns, are also found in KB 29, in the third or special writ section of each term's entries. Returned writs are also enrolled on the crown roll (KB 28). Supporting affidavits are in KB 1 (but only if made in term time),[25] while details of process can be reconstructed from the rule books in KB 21 in just the same way as for criminal cases.

Other sources

So far this essay has concentrated on the records of the court itself, but it is perhaps worth pointing out that the determined researcher might be able to find out even more about the cases that interest him/her by being prepared to explore other sources. The private papers of litigants, lawyers and even judges may survive in local and specialist repositories and provide significant insights into the strategies and motivations of the various participants. Transcripts of trials in the kings bench rarely survive,[26] and it is therefore difficult to discover what was said by the parties and their witnesses or counsel in court, but some of these deficiencies can be supplied by the formal law reports and newspaper accounts. As noted above, George Carter's trial at the Old Bailey was published; earlier proceedings before the magistrates at Bow Street were covered by the press. Even

---

25. Affidavits not made in term time do not survive.

26. A notable and rare exception is the transcript of the trial of the transvestites Ernest Boulton and Frederick Park in 1870: TNA, DPP 4/6. For a fuller account of the case see R. Paley, 'Dragging the law into disrepute', in A.D.E. Lewis, P. Brand and P. Mitchell (eds), *Law in the city: proceedings of the seventeenth British Legal History Conference, London, 2005* (Dublin, 2007), pp. 283–304.

those brief accounts add to our contextual knowledge of the case, demonstrating just how little sympathy was available to rape victims. According to the *Morning Chronicle*, it was impossible to believe that a girl could have been raped twice in one evening by the same man; she must have consented.[27] In the case of Ann Gregory the law report adds no further detail about her sufferings but it does tell us what interested the lawyers: the right of a husband to demand that his wife cohabit with him and the grounds on which a wife could refuse to do so. The law report tells us what the affidavits do not, that the court ruled against compelling her to return to her husband because she took advantage of her enforced appearance in court to formalise her allegations of ill usage and to swear articles of the peace against him. The law report also reveals that Ann Gregory requested, and received, the services of the court's tipstaff so that she could make her way home without fear of molestation by her estranged husband.

Conclusion

Over the course of the century those who appeared as victims or prosecutors certainly included the rich and titled (several earls and a duke) as well as the famous (the writer Daniel Defoe and the actor Theophilus Cibber), but opening up even a single small bundle of affidavits, plucked at random, soon demonstrates that the overwhelming majority were ordinary people going about their ordinary business. The bundle in question (Michaelmas 1739, KB 1/6/2) contains statements from a Cornish yeoman and a London clock-maker who both figure as prosecutors; other litigants included victuallers, butchers, plumbers, cordwainers, watermen, lightermen and a 'small coal man'. The subject matter includes several cases of assault, a dispute over the administration of a will, riot, criminal libel, a contest over the guardianship of a minor and a husband trying to recover his runaway wife. The affidavits are all the more valuable because, rather like bills and answers in chancery suits, they tell two sides of the same story, agreeing on central issues but differing over the way those issues should be interpreted. They often incorporate details of pre-existing disputes and provide a mass of valuable incidental detail. KB 1 also includes a variety of other documents, such as the 'evidence copy' of alleged libels (this particular bundle contains two newspapers and a pamphlet), as well as formal documents marking steps in procedure, such as notices of bail or the service of rules of court, applications to respite recognizances or dispense with personal appearance and general releases (a formal agreement to discontinue a case, usually on payment of compensation). Even these are not without interest – they

---

27. *Morning Chronicle and London Advertiser*, 5 November 1772.

supply the names, occupations and addresses of persons offering bail and help to build an account of the conduct of a case and how much it cost. These records open a window onto the daily life of eighteenth-century men, women and children, providing unexpected and vivid insights into the structures – economic, legal, cultural, political and social – that bounded their lives.

Compared to the records generated by assizes or quarter sessions the archive of the kings bench, consisting as it does of several interlocking series that have no single point of entry, is difficult to use. Matters are made no easier by listings that are best described as skeletal.[28] As a result it remains largely unknown and unexploited. I hope the foregoing has demonstrated just how richly informative it can be and just why it ought to command greater attention from historians, especially those interested in exploring the nature of local communities.

28. A more detailed discussion is provided in Hay, *Criminal cases*.

15. Local history in the twenty-first century: information communication technology, e-resources, grid computing, Web 2.0 and a new paradigm

Paul S. Ell

It is appropriate that, in this volume, just as W.G. Hoskins might have argued more than 60 years ago, local history stands on the cusp of a revolution. This revolution is not simply methodological. It is not simply concerned with more resources becoming available for the local historian than Hoskins could ever have foreseen. It is not simply about publishing the work of local historians in different ways. Rather, it represents a step change in the discipline, and one that will have far-reaching implications for the subject.

So, what is the revolution? Put simply, it is the widespread use of information communications technology (ICT). Sceptics might dismiss ICT as the Internet rebranded, and nothing new. This is far from the case. This chapter will examine the proliferation of electronic scholarly resources (or e-resources) of utility to the local historian. With more than half of Arts and Humanities Research Council (AHRC) awarded grants resulting in some form of electronic resource it might be suspected that many local historians have more resources available for their studies than has been the case at any previous point in history.

Many scholars in the discipline may disagree with this assertion, arguing the paucity of e-resources for their subject and locale of interest. This leads on to the chapter's second area of concern. While we are already suffering from a 'data deluge', the fundamental problem is the discovery of e-resources that exist. Several approaches to addressing this problem will be discussed, including the development of e-Science in the arts and humanities generally and the specific role of the Data Grid. It is of interest that there is an increasing emphasis on organising information by location, a key concern, of course, to local history.

The next section of this chapter moves on to social networking and how research findings can be validated by the use of local historians, both professional and amateur. There are few larger expert community groupings than the vast body of local historians. Through the use of social networking, ranging from the exploitation of Facebook to specific discussion lists, we can build knowledge. Local historians understand their local environments and the history of these environments. There are also developing techniques which go further. Approaches encompassed by Web 2.0 change the way the Internet works, from a top-down approach of information provided *for* the consumption of users to the provision of data *from* those users. This might range from information about local field names to using crowd sourcing to suggest the location of a deserted village. A combination of Web 2.0 approaches and Grid Computing provide new avenues for local historians to publish and share their work. Small datasets relating to specific locales can be made available by their compilers. This data can be compared either to other sources for the same location, or the same source for other places. The potential to share and extend knowledge is endless. Some may perceive the Internet to be completely unregulated and may be concerned that, as a result, chaotic and misleading information might appear; but there are many ways to ensure accurate information is provided, through, for example, community-led control to direct moderation of a website or discussion list.

The purpose of this chapter is to paint a compelling picture of how ICT can change local history. This change will not be painless, however, and the chapter will review some of the challenges we face. These include the reluctance of some to adopt new technologies and issues concerning the computerisation of vast paper-based collections, although digitisation is becoming ever more cost-effective. Both physical objects and e-resources need to be preserved, although the costs are usually far less for the latter. Such change may also perhaps result in significant restructuring of record offices through investment in digital infrastructure. In libraries, particularly in the US, an increasing reliance is being placed on electronic materials. While digitisation costs may be high (but falling), the reduction in the need for buildings and larger numbers of staff to provide access to analogue resources can result in long-term savings. Equally, remaining staff can devote their time to assisting users in the use of the electronic material rather than physically moving books, preserving existing collections or monitoring overdue library returns. The analogy for the record offices would be high initial costs to create digital content, but a reduction in long-term plant and staff costs, with remaining subject-expert staff better able to serve users through enhanced electronic access to collections and far more time to spend working with the materials. We should not forget that the e-resource has far more utility and flexibility than the analogue record. These are the challenges, but they are the inevitable results of a step-change in scholarship.

Electronic resources and the local historian

From the early and ground-breaking work of the Cambridge Group for the History of Population and Social Structure in 1964, the Economic and Social Research Council Data Archive and the History Data Service and its successor the Arts and Humanities Data Service: History, to the specific scholarship of individual academics such as Professor Sir E.A. Wrigley, Professor Michael Anderson, Dr Peter Laslett and Professor K.D.M. Snell, there has been much time and effort invested in what might be termed today 'digital local history'. Indeed, years and sometimes decades have now elapsed from their ground-breaking work and only now is the term 'digital humanities' being adopted widely and recognised as a discipline in its own right.

Initially, pure scholarship resulted in e-resources almost as a by-product in research. In the pre-Internet world these resources were not available online, existing rather on disk or other formats. As the outputs of much of such scholarship were books and journal articles, the research materials upon which these works were based were typically considered to be both the property of, and for the exclusive use of, the scholars involved. Even when data was shared it was frequently not designed for this purpose: information tended to be poorly documented, methods of collection were not explained, caveats in the use of the data were not detailed, raw data itself might have been lost, with just the researchers' derived data available, and the method of derivation was often unclear. The typical model of scholarly research in local history, in fact, reflected the *lone scholar* model common in the humanities. This involved the scholars gathering their own data, publishing from it and either not making the data available or, worse still, not retaining it at all. As a result scholars were often repetitively covering the same material in isolation.

However, before the advent of the Internet the by-product of research (i.e. the data on which it was based) did come to be seen as of possible value. As a result bodies began to be set up with the aim of preserving and making available such data: for example, the Social Science Research Council (SSRC) Data Bank was established in 1967. Of greatest significance to local history is the UK Data Archive (in effect the SSRC Data Bank after numerous name changes), which hosted the History Data Service from 1992. Increasingly, grant awarding bodies also recognised the importance of electronic outputs from the projects they funded. In due course both the Economic and Social Research Council (ESRC) and AHRC required projects to make their data available to relevant data archives. And the importance of such archives themselves increased: in 1996, with joint funding from AHRC and the Joint Information Systems Committee (JISC), the Arts and Humanities Data Service (AHDS) was formed with a federated structure supporting many arts and humanities subjects.[1] Of greatest relevance to local historians were AHDS History (in essence the History Data Service) and AHDS Archaeology. These centres were tasked with offering advice to the creators of digital materials but also acted as long-term repositories for the data.

As the value of digital resources in their own right became clearer, scholars increasingly ensured that their data could be reused by others more easily. Initially this desire was expressed in the development of supporting documentation describing the resource, the methodology adopted in its collection and any caveats in its use. Data standards that formalised previously informal documentation began to develop. Thus, metadata augmented the data itself. Metadata is simply data about data, but in using common structured languages such as Dublin Core it provided a basic minimum amount of information for e-resources to be used by scholars and, through the common language, allowed interdisciplinary resources to be more easily used.

All of these developments have resulted in a plethora of e-resources of value to the local historian. Perhaps of greater worth still are resources which were created as bespoke datasets for scholars independent of a specific research agenda. During the early years of the twenty-first century, in what might be regarded as the golden age – which has now passed, as will be discussed in the final section of this chapter – of digital resource development, a great deal of funding was made available to populate the Internet with scholarly content. Arguably these developments built on the work of individual scholars, or groups of scholars, to create what they regarded as 'strategic electronic resources'. These included a small but significant number of large resources, of which there is only space here to mention two exemplars. The Database of Irish Historical Statistics was one of the earliest, if not the earliest, large-scale data capture project, gathering census statistics from the published Irish Census volumes, from the first census in 1821 to the last completed in an analogue form in 1971 (after 1971 censuses were computerised as the data were collected). It focused on collecting recurrent series of census statistics for spatial units larger than the parish. The

---

1. The AHDS Executive was based at King's College, London. There were five federated subject centres: AHDS Archaeology based at the University of York, AHDS History based at the University of Essex, AHDS Literature, Languages and Linguistics based at the University of Oxford, AHDS Performing Arts at Glasgow University, and AHDS Visual Arts based at the University for the Creative Arts at Farnham.

Irish Censuses from 1821 contain rich seams of demographic, social and economic data, information simply not gathered by the British Census. For example, information on religion is available consistently from 1861, with some data relating to the 1831 census, whereas for Britain it is only available in 1851 and 2001. The census also included early data on literacy, on the prevalence of the Irish language and, uniquely, on housing quality. The project directly addressed a perceived need for better access to historical census data at a time when much quantitative historical work was being conducted on Ireland. Following its completion in 1996 it was the largest corpus of historical quantitative data in the world, containing more than 32 million data values, and remains available through the History Data Service.[2]

Of more interest to English local historians will be the Great Britain Historical Geographical Information System (GBHGIS) developed by the Universities of Portsmouth, Leeds and Queen's Belfast, with the project entering its full developmental stage in 1998.[3] Like the Database of Irish Historical Statistics, the GBHGIS holds large amounts of digitised census data. In this instance, however, earlier data is available, as the first British Census took place in 1801, and information at a greater spatial resolution is provided, with statistics at parish level. Further, information on changing census administrative boundaries has been gathered and alterations of these boundaries over time noted. Thus, the GBHGIS allows skilled users to map census geographies for Britain.

The key element of both of these exemplar projects is that they provide well-documented large-scale resources of interest to large numbers of scholars. They are broad in their area of concern, both in terms of subject area and spatial coverage. Put simply, both provide some information for everywhere in Britain and Ireland.

Following the trend of making resources of widespread interest available, British History Online (BHO) brings both primary and secondary sources to the local historian. Whereas the Database of Irish Historical Statistics and the GBHGIS focus on specific primary sources, BHO holds a plethora of sources ranging through parliamentary records, taxation sources, ecclesiastical information, chronicles, diaries and more. Extensive secondary sources are available, not least more than 160 volumes of the *Victoria County History* (*VCH*). While the BHO content is extensive, advanced functionality is more limited, as is noted below in the *VCH* discussion.

---

2. See <http://hds.essex.ac.uk/history/data/census-statistics.asp>. This web page and others cited here were accessed 9 December 2010.

3. For more information on the history of the Great Britain Historical GIS see <http://www.port.ac.uk/research/gbhgis/abouttheproject/history/>. The project home page can be found at <http://www.port.ac.uk/research/gbhgis/>.

From these was born the concept of creating digital content of value. This drive to bring more e-resources to the Internet was most strongly expressed in three national programmes – the New Opportunities Fund Digitisation Programme, the AHRC Resource Enhancement Scheme and the JISC Digitisation Programme. Using National Lottery funds in 1999 the New Opportunities Fund made available £50 million to create quality Internet-based content. It funded more than 150 projects and of particular relevance to local historians will be the outputs from the *Sense of Place* consortiums, which cover all of the English regions.[4] The AHRC Resource Enhancement Scheme was concerned with providing easier and extended access to research materials. It offered funding of up to £300,000 and made around 300 awards during its existence, and, while it covers all of the arts and humanities, many of its e-resources will be of value to local historians. The programme was discontinued in 2005, as discussed in the final section of this chapter. JISC invested and continues to invest heavily in digitisation projects which, although open to all disciplinary areas, tend to have a focus on the arts and humanities and, again, outputs are of value to local historians. In their Digitisation and e-Content Programme, running from April 2003 to March 2011, they aim to expose under-utilised collections to scholars, develop a critical mass of material, establish business models for sustaining digital content and build communities using new technologies. All of these objectives relate to local history, and key funded work includes Nineteenth-Century British Newspapers, Archival Sound Recordings, Newsfilm Online and Historic Boundaries of Britain.[5]

We see an exponential trend, therefore, in the development of digital resources of value to local history from the early innovators, to the creation of strategic resources, to many scholars producing digital content through their normal research. There has also been a fundamental change in the way scholars regard their data and the data of others. Largely gone are the days of the lone scholar spending decades in archives creating bespoke research materials for their own use and jealously guarding that investment in time and expertise from colleagues with similar research interests. It has become increasingly apparent that research can be enhanced by sharing data and working in a more collaborative environment. Examples of this are many, but worth special mention is the work of Professor B.M.S. Campbell, who has spent many years working on that most elusive and difficult source, medieval manorial accounts. Professor Campbell secured access to the work of the late Professor David

---

4. See <http://www.nof-digitise.org/>.

5. See <http://www.jisc.ac.uk/whatwedo/programmes/digitisation> for more information on JISC activities.

Farmer and the agreement of Professor Jan Titow and other scholars to share their work on extracting crop yield data; this work represents many decades of scholarship but it is all now freely available to scholars via the Internet.[6] Making this data available will result in enhanced research in this field, as Professor Campbell's work increasingly demonstrates. It will also allow scholars to build on existing knowledge to understand the past more clearly.

Local historians have also benefited from more generic large-scale, mass digitisation. The digitisation of print publications initially was highly focused on specific works reflecting the exceptional holdings of a library, the rarity of printed volumes, or particular interest among scholars. The Google Books programme changed this through its 2004 agreement with five international reference libraries to 'make it easier for people to find relevant books' through, in effect, mass digitisation of out-of-copyright and, it became apparent, in-copyright books. Google's aspirations later still extended to magazines and newspapers. While these aims have been, for the present at least, significantly impacted by various legal cases relating to copyright on in-copyright work, Google will, nonetheless, make available a vast catalogue of books of value to scholars even if most recent work is excluded.

It might appear, therefore, that we have attained a nirvana-like state with e-resources concerning almost every conceivable aspect of interest to the local historian easily available and accessible. Regrettably, however, there are matters still to be resolved before we reach that situation.

E-science, grid technologies and local history

Many professional and amateur local historians, if asked if e-Science and the Grid were of relevance to their research, would either have no idea of the existence of these concepts and tools or would dismiss them as being relevant only to the sciences and certainly not the arts and humanities. Perceptions are beginning to change, however. They might be surprised to learn that AHRC, JISC and the Engineering and Physical Sciences Research Council in 2006 collectively funded the Arts and Humanities e-Science Support Centre to promote the adoption of these technologies.[7]

The Research Council e-Science Core Programme has the following definition of e-Science:

---

6. See <http://www.cropyields.ac.uk/> for Professor Campbell's medieval crop yield site complete with the yield data itself.

7. See <http://www.ahessc.ac.uk/>.

What is meant by e-Science? In the future, e-Science will refer to the large scale science that will increasingly be carried out through distributed global collaborations enabled by the Internet. Typically, a feature of such collaborative scientific enterprises is that they will require access to very large data collections, very large scale computing resources and high performance visualisation back to the individual user scientists.

The Grid is an architecture proposed to bring all these issues together and make a reality of such a vision for e-Science. Ian Foster and Carl Kesselman, inventors of the Globus approach to the Grid, define the Grid as an enabler for Virtual Organisations: 'An infrastructure that enables flexible, secure, coordinated resource sharing among dynamic collections of individuals, institutions and resources.' It is important to recognise that resource in this context includes computational systems and data storage and specialised experimental facilities.[8] However, the AHRC provides a rather more relevant explanation of how e-Science and associated grid technologies relate to the arts and humanities and local history:

> Digital resources in the A&H have grown at an astonishing rate in the last ten or twenty years; out of over £100m spent by the AHRC since 1999 on research project awards, half has been given to projects with some kind of digital output. The problem is that researchers do not yet have the technology to make the fullest use of these resources, because they are generally not connected together. e-Science provides a set of solutions for this problem, and for the related development of facilities for research collaboration using the Internet. e-Science thus stands for a specific set of advanced technologies for Internet resource-sharing and collaboration: so-called grid technologies, and technologies integrated with them, for instance for authentication, data-mining and visualisation. This has allowed more powerful and innovative research designs in many areas of scientific research, and is capable of transforming the A&H as well.[9]

As noted in the introduction to this chapter, the challenge local history faces is not the paucity of e-resources but difficulties in finding and using them. Here e-Science, as noted by AHRC, is key.

The current problem is that there is a vast array of e-resources ranging from

8. See <http://www.nesc.ac.uk/nesc/define.html>.

9. See <http://www.ahrcict.rdg.ac.uk/activities/e-science/background.htm>.

national or international strategic datasets to a small database on a university website. In other words, there are large numbers of data silos which are not interlinked. Moreover, while, as noted in the previous section, data standards have started to be implemented through metadata, this is far from uniform. It is unlikely, therefore, that even if the local historian could discover relevant resources from different sites they would be able to use them with ease. There is a further problem in that each resource is likely to have a bespoke interface which the potential user must master. All of these factors have been a major brake to scholarship.

There are three main components of Grid technologies: the Access Grid, which is largely concerned with online collaboration between scholars; the Computational Grid, which offers access to significant computer processing power; and the Data Grid. The Computational Grid is likely to be of little value to local historians. The Access Grid may have more utility and this will be addressed in the next section. The key technology is the Data Grid. As the AHRC argue:

> Most importantly, the tools for large-scale data management and sharing provided by data grid technology will be a vital means of meeting the present grand challenge to A&H e-science: how to locate, access and integrate the content of resources that embrace text, still and moving images and sound, are highly distributed, of variable quality, encoded and described using different standards, and often incomplete, fuzzy, and complex.[10]

Through the application of the Data Grid, the vast range of resources described above and the overabundance of new resources which are being developed on an almost daily basis would become available to the local historian. Not only would they be available, but they would have far greater utility than existing paper, or even electronic, resources. Primarily this is because not only would more information be available but it would be possible to interrogate it in different ways. Looking at secondary sources first, at present the typical approach to using analogue material is to read them in a linear fashion. A journal article, for example, will normally be read by the scholar from the first page to the last. That journal article would have been discovered by the scholar either through a reference to it in another work or through a survey by subject area of journals likely to contain articles of interest. Much the same can be said about the use of monographs. It is possible now to search for relevant monographs by their title with the hope that the title would indicate that the work would be of relevance to the researcher. Alternatively, the monograph might be well known and referred to by other authors, or a library

---

10. See <http://www.ahrcict.rdg.ac.uk/activities/e-science/background.htm>.

catalogue subject search might be relied upon. Using current practice, as a final resort the scholar might physically visit a library and browse the shelves, aware, in the case of the discipline of history, that the books would probably be organised by subject, or country, and roughly in chronological order. For primary sources in analogue form a similar resource discovery exercise would take place – browsing through a record office catalogue or shelves, follow-up of references to the source by other researchers, and literally searching the archives. To a degree, even for e-resources, the scholar's interrogation of the material will be dictated by the framework into which the resource has been placed by its developer and the utilities tool kits they may, or may not, have provided.

The Data Grid affords an opportunity to change all of this. Conceptually it will allow searches of almost any existing e-resource. It will facilitate not only the discovery of e-resources (and currently there are far too many pre-Grid manual attempts by local historians to provide static listings of electronic resources which simply take the scholar to a website, without deep-linking to the content of these websites) but also the ability to harvest those resources. So, for example, with regard to Professor Campbell's work on crop yields, e-Science would not simply result in a scholar finding out that there was a website which contained crop yield data but would allow linkage to the specific information required, perhaps a particular manor and yield data for a specific chronological period. E-Science completely removes the linear analogue approach. It becomes possible to search resources by subject, chronology, location and person, pinpointing not only the website which contains this information but retrieving the precise data the scholar is interested in.

To some readers this may seem fanciful, but exemplars of e-Science and the Data Grid are already in place; they will be reviewed briefly here.[11] One of the most basic tools for a researcher are journals, but in the analogue world their use is severely restricted. As described above, there is a well-established but fundamentally flawed approach to using journals in research. In short, it is difficult to find relevant articles, particularly in less popular journals, older volumes or journals which are no longer current. Where articles are found they tend to be read in their entirety in a linear fashion. It is generally impossible to find articles by location, key to the local historian, unless they appear in a geographically based journal, such as, for example, the *Transactions of the Leicestershire Archaeological and Historical Society*. Under JISC funding, and in collaboration with Journal Storage (JSTOR), the Centre for Data Digitisation and

11. The three exemplar projects have all either been based at, or have involved significantly, the Centre for Data Digitisation and Analysis.

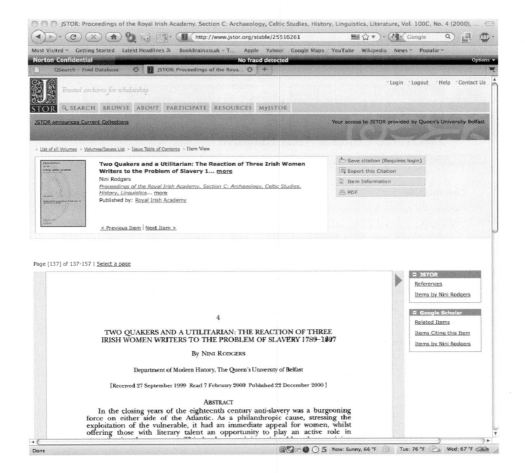

Fig. 15.1 The JSTOR Ireland Collection created by the Centre for Data Digitisation and Analysis.

Analysis (CDDA) has established a largely journal-based e-resource, *The Ireland Collection*. This includes around eighty key Irish Studies Journals, including many that are out of print and not widely available (Fig. 15.1). They are all available at no cost in Britain and Ireland through JSTOR. The collection itself, representing more than 600,000 pages, is far more comprehensive than the analogue holdings of any one institutional library, but it is not this that makes this project stand out, it is the functionality available to users.

The collection can be used in the traditional linear way but, vitally, it is possible to search the whole collection, or indeed selected journals or volumes, by place-name, person name and more. It is also possible to link instantly to other journals referenced in an article if they exist in electronic form anywhere in

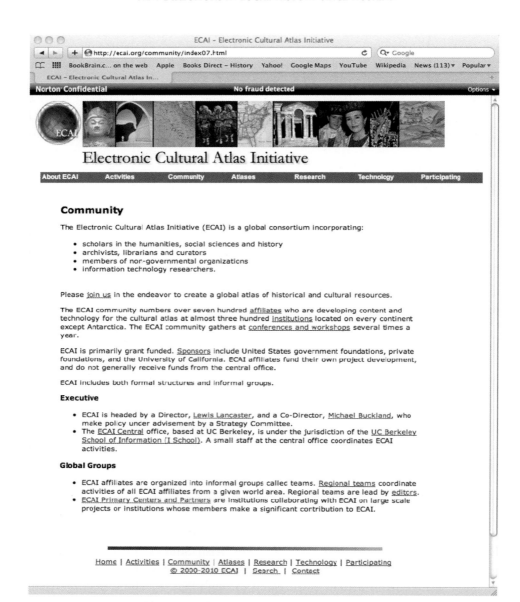

Fig. 15.2 The Electronic Cultural Atlas Initiative's community web page.

the world, as long as they are available on the Internet. Moreover, users searching for information on, say, a specific place are not simply directed to the article, they will be sent to the specific place-name entry. This work is already resulting in a significant increase in the citation of lesser-known Irish Studies Journals, and an increased range of citations in new journal articles. Further, local historians will be familiar with using JSTOR and there is no learning curve, no new software to master, no new skills required, to use this resource. It is indicative of how the application of the Data Grid as envisaged by the AHRC can result in dramatic advances in scholarship.

A second exemplar project relates to the work of the Electronic Cultural Atlas Initiative (ECAI) based at the University of California at Berkeley (Fig. 15.2).[12] ECAI has more than 700 affiliates in the form of scholars from around the world but with a particular emphasis on participants from the British Isles, the US and eastern and south-eastern Asia. Almost all of the affiliates hold some electronic data. In some instances, such as the holdings offered by the CDDA, these datasets are extensive. In other cases they are small. What is clear is that these disparate resources are worth far more collectively than they are in their individual parts. ECAI has developed a detailed metadata system that allows affiliate datasets to be retrieved instantly by location, subject, time-period or person with the specific data being delivered to the user's computer. In the pre-Grid age comprehensive access to such varied and geographically distributed resources would not have been possible.

Finally, in the context of exemplars, reference must be made to *The Vision of Britain through Time Project* which has built on the GBHGIS, described earlier (Fig. 15.3). The project website, www.visionofbritain.org.uk, is not a Data Grid application in the true sense, as it is a closed system, and information has to be placed within the database which drives the website. However, it does demonstrate the potential that the Data Grid offers to draw together multimedia materials by location. There is a danger for local historians in examining specific locales in isolation or, indeed, examining specific sources for specific locales in isolation. In the past this was unavoidable. Local knowledge is precious and cannot easily be acquired by a local historian for different regions. Often sources were complex to gather and analyse, affording little opportunity to become quickly apprised of other sources. The Vision of Britain, bringing together the census data and administrative boundaries of a traditional Historical Geographical Information System, along with descriptions from historical gazetteers, travel writing from past centuries, historical maps and more,

---

12. See <http://ecai.org/>.

Fig. 15.3 The Vision of Britain through Time website, indicating the rich range of materials that are available by place.

illustrates the power of information integration. Through this integration of local information the Vision of Britain has attracted a large user base which has allowed the site to attract advertising revenue via 'Ads by Google', resulting in a modest income stream to support the preservation and development of the resource. Moreover, plans are in place to extend the Vision of Britain concept to Ireland and potentially to other areas in Europe, something made possible, at least in part, by the structure of the underlying architecture of the resources which makes it extensible at relatively low cost.

The future for Data Grid developments appears promising, bearing in mind its clear potential impact on the practice of local history. Some of the steps necessary to realise this potential are discussed in the final section of this chapter.

Web 2.0, social networks and crowd sourcing

In its first iteration the Internet was very much about information being provided for users. University websites typically described the courses and facilities they offered; learned societies would detail their membership and the criteria for membership, or election, for the worthy. By the new millennium some changes were already apparent to this top-down implementation. It became possible for students to post questions online to a university enquiring about a specific course. Some learned societies allowed applications for membership to be made online, or at least for paper-based forms to be requested. Today the Internet is dramatically different. No longer is it the case that it is used to supply information: now much of its content is provided by users.

This new trend is known as Web 2.0, the second 'version' of the Internet following from Web 1.0.[13] It does not represent a fundamental change in the technology of the World Wide Web, but rather in the way that it is used. Web 2.0 is expressed in the form of social networks such as Facebook, blogs, Wikis, folksonomes, discussion groups and crowd sourcing. All represent the supply of information from users, which is then made available online either to a select community or anyone using the Internet.

Already local historians use some of these techniques. Many will be familiar with e-mail discussion groups such as the JISCMAIL Local-History list.[14] This offers a forum to discuss local history generally but it is more often used to ask specific questions relating to sources or particular localities. As most members of the discussion list are knowledgeable local historians, whether academics or interested members of the public, fast and well-informed responses to questions are usually forthcoming. Members of the list often contest ill-informed or contentious queries and lists can have a Moderator to prevent misinformation being posted. Importantly, as JISCMAIL provides archiving facilities to queries, the discussion list itself becomes a centre of knowledge, and one developed solely through input from the user community. Perusal of these archived discussions makes clear that others quickly question fallacious postings. Many other lists for local historians exist.

Wikis are becoming increasingly common. A Wiki is a collection of web pages in which each page contains information on a specific topic. Users can create new

13. See <http://oreilly.com/web2/archive/what-is-web-20.html> for a much fuller definition.
14. See <https://www.jiscmail.ac.uk/cgi-bin/webadmin?A0=LOCAL-HISTORY>.

topic pages and other users can edit them. The best-known Wiki is Wikipedia, which contains more than three million pages or articles and has a vast user community.[15] As a Wiki is often completely user-driven there is a danger that incorrect information will be posted; however, almost all Wiki software (which is freely and readily available) keeps a record of previous iterations of articles which allow another user to remove amendments they feel are incorrect. Equally, they may replace text with their own observations. Local historians represent a large expert user group which tends to provide high-quality information to Wikis, and a number of Wikis relating specifically to local history already exist. For example, Leeds Library and Information Service provide a Wiki on the local history of the Leeds area.[16] Here, some articles are written by Leeds Library staff and cannot be edited directly by other users, whereas other pages can be edited and, indeed, new articles created (Fig. 15.4). This is an excellent way for local historians to bring their expertise on a particular location or source to a wider audience. In sharing this information they are likely to receive additional data from other contributors, improving their knowledge-base and developing better articles for other readers. In essence, a virtuous circle of knowledge-sharing comes about. Similar Wikis that exist for a variety of local history interest groups include the *Lewisham War Memorial Wiki*, *Faces of Dover* and the *Alfreton History Wiki*.[17] National organisations with Wiki services include the *VCH*, where registration is required to access the articles, and British Local History.[18]

English local history already has a presence on the social networking facility Facebook, membership as of mid-2010 exceeding 4000.[19] It is likely that more focused groups will develop over time concerning the local history of individual places, or indeed specific sources. In contrast to most Wikis, but reflecting the general model of discussion groups, registration is normally required to join a Facebook group. In common with discussion groups and some Wikis, the contributions are normally exclusively from the user group. But, unlike the iterative Wiki process, where the aim is to create a near-definitive article or statement, discussion groups are less focused.

---

15. See <http://wikipedia.org>.

16. See <http://addyourlocalhistory.wetpaint.com/>.

17. For the *Borough of Lewisham War Memorial Wiki* see <http://lewishamwarmemorials.wikidot.com/>; for the *Faces of Dover* see <http://www.facesofdover.org/faces/Main_Page>, and for the *Alfreton History Wiki* see <http://alfretonwiki.co.uk/alfretonwiki/index.php?title=Main_Page>.

18. For the *Victoria County History* Wiki see <http://www.victoriacountyhistory.ac.uk/wiki/Login.jsp?redirect=Main>, and for British Local History see <http://www.balh.co.uk/> accessed 9 December 2010.

19. See <http://www.facebook.com/pages/Local-history/106440756058879?v=wiki>.

Fig. 15.4 A wiki for the local history of the Leeds area.

There is little doubt that these technologies will become more widespread in the future and will help local historians to network more effectively. An element of e-Science has potential impact here. In the previous section the importance of the Data Grid (methodologies for linking disparate information) was discussed and brief mention was made of the Access Grid. This allows participants to collaborate more effectively by working in real time with complex communication software using high-bandwidth data connections provided, in the UK, to universities through the JANET network. The specialised network requirements mean that, in the short term, Access Grid facilities are likely to be available only to students and faculty in the academic sector. The technology can come close to creating an immersive environment and, at the very least, facilitates, via multiple high-definition large monitors, virtual meetings. Of more significance is the ability to review and annotate information in real time. Scholars working on, for example, a medieval poll tax could examine a very high-quality scan of the document and annotate and interpret it collectively. The technology is of particular value in bringing together scholars in different parts of the world with highly developed and specific research skills. It makes feasible intercontinental collaborations requiring frequent interaction between busy academics in specialised fields, whereas in the past this would not have been possible. In the UK the Access Grid Support Centre acts as advocate for the technology.[20]

There is one further area where the expert group of local historians can contribute to our understanding of the subject and specific debates within it, which is through contributions to sources posted online. The digitisation of large and complex resources will inevitably result in some errors in the final product, and there is considerable potential to use local historians and Web 2.0 technology to advise resource creators of errors and even offer alternatives to the current content. They can also enhance existing content. A current project under development at the CDDA and the English Place-Names Society (EPNS) at the University of Nottingham would make older EPNS volumes available online and ask for commentaries from users. Local historians would, we feel, be able to enhance these volumes significantly, contributing highly local information such as field names and even correcting the original EPNS text.[21] In another project, *Context and Relationships: Ireland and Irish Studies*, CDDA is working with the School of Information at the University of California Berkeley to allow an expert user group to highlight place-names and person names in Irish Studies texts in order to aid in information retrieval. The texts already exist in digital form but place-names and person names have not been identified. While natural language processing software can do some of this work, such a corpus of more than 600,000 pages of text could be enhanced only by a large expert user body and not a small group of academics.[22]

Finally, crowd sourcing has interesting possibilities. This allows individuals to post information they regard as being correct and arrive at a consensus together with many other contributors. Crowd sourcing might be used to try to identify a deserted village, the boundaries of an ancient parish or the location of a battle site. More practically, in the short term it might be used by a library or archive to find out more about their collections. An example is the identification of historical photographs, when the time and place of the image captured is in doubt. Photographs are exposed to the public and, hopefully, useful information is gathered by crowd sourcing

---

20. See <http://www.ja.net/services/video/agsc/AGSCHome/>.

21. The Institute for Name-Studies at the University of Nottingham hosts EPNS. See <http://www.nottingham.ac.uk/~aezins//index.php>.

22. See <http://ecai.org/neh2007/> for a description of the project.

community memories.[23] Another project, 'Were You There', seeks to use crowd sourcing to construct collective memories of more recent events, from the Japanese attack on Pearl Harbour to the performances of Elvis Presley![24]

Overall, therefore, by using social networking and Web 2.0 we will in the future be able to make far greater use of community knowledge and expertise that will greatly enrich electronic resources and resulting scholarship.

Conclusion

The aim of this chapter has been to portray technological advances which can harness both sources and community expertise, resulting in a great advance in the discipline. It is possible to foresee an environment where all key strategic resources of value to local history are available online; a world in which the expert local knowledge of local historians is harnessed nationally and internationally; a time when we can trust e-resources because they are informed by expert user groups. All of these will result in a better understanding of the subject and advanced research. The development of the online world should be acknowledged by the largely exclusive references to online resources in this chapter, reflecting the speed of developments online (and the slow pace of paper-based publications) and the changing nature of scholarship.

Three potential difficulties may delay, but not stop, this revolution. First, there is access to electronic resources. Until recently the arts and humanities in the UK were well served by the Arts and Humanities Data Service which, through its Executive and Subject Centres, archived and made available electronic research data. Funding was withdrawn from the AHDS in 2008 and there is now a real danger that vital content of importance to local history will be lost. Partly in place of the AHDS, a Humanities ICT Expert Network of Centres has been established.[25] In addition, libraries are beginning to take responsibility for maintaining e-resources. Sustaining complex websites is expensive, however, and business models to guarantee their continued existence are few. Second, too many resources are still being created without sufficient reference to standards or consideration of how they might form part of the Data Grid infrastructure of materials. A clear example of this is the emerging online version of the *VCH*.[26] All English local historians will be aware of the value of this meticulously researched

---

23. See <http://www.dclab.com/crowdsourcinghistory.asp>.

24. See <http://www.wereyouthere.com/>.

25. See <http://www.arts-humanities.net/noc> for more on the Humanities ICT Expert Network of Centres.

26. See <http://www.victoriacountyhistory.ac.uk/NationalSite/Publications>.

series of county works which started in 1899, and there can be no doubt that in terms of strategic resources for local historians the *VCH* is vital. However, in its developing electronic form it makes no use of Grid technologies or of Web 2.0 approaches, and appears to be a work in isolation. It should form a key part of Data Grid infrastructure – a framework around which other resources can be linked. When, for example, mention of a Domesday entry is made in a *VCH* volume there should be functionality to link to Domesday itself. It could link to many other sources as well, such as the Campbell crop yield data and other manorial accounts, the 1279–80 Hundred Rolls, the 1290, 1327/1332, 1334 and 1524–5 Lay Subsidies, the 1291 *Taxatio*, the 1340–42 *Nonae*, the *c.*1360 Gough Map, the 1377 Poll Tax and more. While a number of these sources are not currently available online, many are fully or partially in print and could be easily digitised. Currently the online version of *VCH* is largely a copy of the paper editions. This is merely one of the higher-profile e-resource undertakings based on less than firm foundations. Finally, and associated with the comments concerning the *VCH*, there is a need for investment in the development of strategic resources which provide that framework in which local historians can place a single manorial account, for example, and link it to the wider world. *VCH* provides part of that infrastructure, or could do. The *Vision of Britain* provides another. The digitisation of the EPNS volumes would offer a third. However, there is less appetite from the funders today to invest in e-resources independently of a specific research project just at the time when we are able to use these resources effectively. There is some hope there, however, as JISC continues to invest in e-resources in the arts and humanities.

It could be argued that this chapter has been especially challenging. The aim has been not to reflect on the changes in local history over the last sixty years, but to look to the development of the discipline in *future* decades. As a result some may regard it as speculative, and to a degree they may be correct. Nonetheless, local history is on the cusp of a revolution, even though its precise form may be debated. With such widening access and participation, there can have been few more exciting times to practise local history. Fifty years after the publication of *Local history in England*, and eighteen years after his death, if W.G. Hoskins were with us now there can be little doubt that he would agree.

Index